Dr. Abraham Rudolph Gonce
Missouri Pioneer
3 May 1833 – 4 December 1912
(A Short Biography)

Covering extant documentation of his career and civic positions, his four wives and seventeen children, multiple arrests, two terms in the State Penitentiary, and other published anecdotes.

Also included are extensive transcripts of "Doc" Gonce's trials for bigamy and murder.

For whatever reasons, there is a higher than expected number of criminals and/or suicides among the first few generations of "Doc" Gonce's descendants – short histories of several of these colorful folks, including the "Baby Bandits" of Colorado and the "Senior Citizen Burglars" of Nevada are therefore included as well.

Frank Oberle

Doctor Abraham Rudolph Gonce, Missouri Pioneer

Copyright © 2010, 2011, 2013 by Frank Oberle

Revised October 2011, October 2013

Cover Photograph by the Author

ISBN-13: 9-780615-912448
ISBN-10: 0615912443

Rev III

PREFACE

My mother is a Gonce, and while researching her branch of my family history, I naturally took an interest not only in data related to her direct ancestors, but in any information I encountered relating to the many other descendants of Justice Gonce [ID 2577][1], my sixth great-grandfather, no matter how peripherally related these other Gonces may have been.

Justice and his wife Magdalen first settled in Cecil County, Maryland with their three sons in the second half of the eighteenth century[2]. By the beginning of the nineteenth century, their oldest son Rudolph's children and their families had migrated to the frontier in Tennessee, and this branch subsequently spread south to Alabama, west to Missouri and eventually to Texas and other states. My own Gonce ancestors, however, were part of the family that remained in Maryland through the twentieth century. Early on, therefore, I didn't spend much time researching the "southern" Gonces, intending to assess information related to that branch at some later date.

Along the way, however, I kept encountering rumors of a very interesting character known as "Doc Gonce," who turned out to be Abraham Rudolph Gonce [ID 2883], and who is my third cousin four times removed. Our only common ancestors are the aforementioned Justice and Magdalen Gonce, whose youngest son Daniel was my fifth great-grandfather. Such a tenuous relationship would not normally merit much in the way of genealogical investigation but for the many seemingly outlandish stories, most undocumented, that I encountered about Doc during my research. Once I began investigating some of these rumors, though, it was difficult to stop. To exorcise these distractions to the pursuit of my own line therefore, I gave in to my curiosity – leading directly to the writing of this manuscript.

"Doc," as it turns out, was indeed a practicing physician[3]. He was also a Missouri pioneer, exhibited signs of personal bravery, served as a Justice of the Peace, and for many years provided the only medical care to many communities across an eight hundred square mile area of southern Missouri. What makes his story more interesting is that he also served two terms in the Missouri State Penitentiary – first for bigamy, and later for murder. Along the way, he managed to marry at least four women and father at least seventeen children. This is Doc's story.

---

1   The ID numbers are from my genealogy database and are provided to permit correlation with various different reference material and other publications and documents I have created.
2   The history of the Gonce line from Justice to my mother is covered in detail in another book titled "Our Gonce Ancestors" ISBN 978-1-61600-253-4.
3   To be precise, I have found no evidence that he was a "licensed" physician, but potential patients were generally not as particular about such niceties in those days.

Ancestors of Abraham Rudolph Gonce

The diagram below shows the known ancestors of "Doc" Gonce. Justice, Magdalen, and their children arrived in America in about 1759.

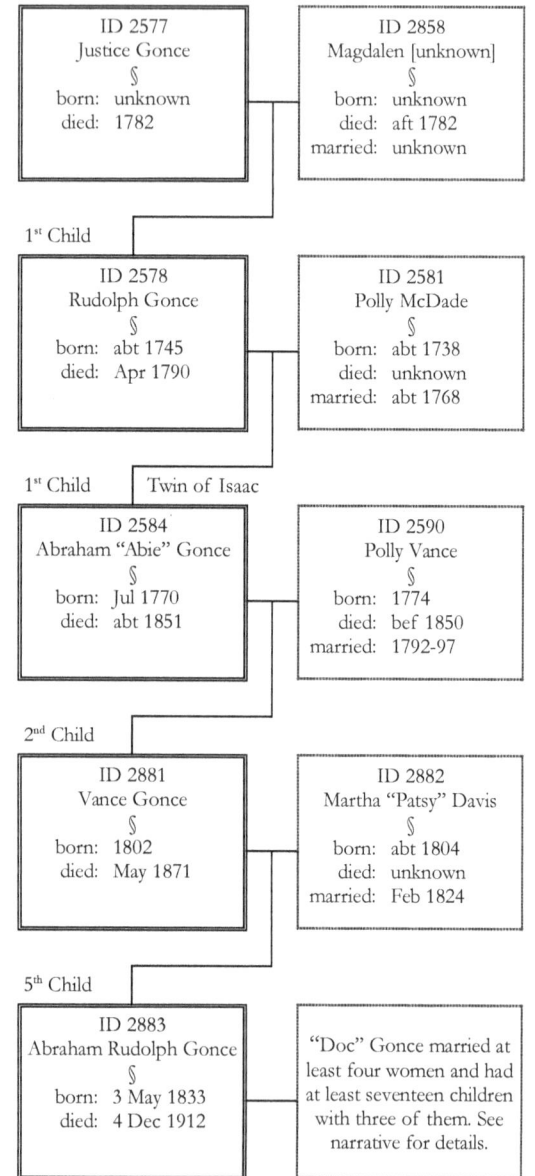

Justice and Magdalen had three sons: Rudolph, Abraham, and Daniel, all of whom arrived in America in about 1759 – most likely at the port of New Castle in the Delaware province of Pennsylvania.

In addition to the twin boys, Rudolph and Polly had three younger daughters.

In about 1797, after both parents had passed away, "Abie" and all his siblings migrated to Tennessee with their families.

Vance and Patsy had thirteen known children, although not all survived childhood.

Table of Contents

PREFACE III
ANCESTORS OF ABRAHAM RUDOLPH GONCE IV

Section I: A Short Biography 1
Doc's Early Life in Tennessee 3
6th Census of the United States – 1840 4
7th Census of the United States – 1850 5
8th Census of the United States – 1860 6
Doc First Appears in Missouri 8
Anecdote about the Union Soldier Samuel Marion Davis 8
Doc and his Family Reunite in Indiana 9
Doc and his Family Settle in Missouri 9
Doc Gonce's Medical Practice Locations 9
Evidence of Doc Gonce as a Missouri Justice of the Peace 10
Evidence of Doc Gonce as an Estate Curator 10
9th Census of the United States – 1870 11
Residents of Ozark and Vicinity in the Nineteenth Century 12
Christian County Missouri Land Tax Payments 13
1876 Census of the State of Missouri; page 16 – Doc and his Family 14
1876 Census of the State of Missouri; pages 16 and 17 – Doc's Adult Children 15
Bigamy Charges 16
Marriage Records, Stone County, Missouri 1851 – 1900 17
Land Sale 17
Missed Trial Date 19
Subpoena 19
Divorce Proceedings 20
New Felony Charges (Assault and Display of Deadly Weapon) 21
Motion to Quash 23
The Bigamy Trial 24
Reward for Doc Gonce's Capture 25
10th Census of the United States – 1880 – Doc's ex-wife Mary and children 26
10th Census of the United States – 1880 – Doc in the Penitentiary 27
Doc's Parole 28
Penitentiary Record for Abraham Rudolph Gonce (First Visit) 28
Doc returns to Freedom 28
The Murder of Charlie Keyser 29
Physician's Letter to Governor regarding Pardon 40
Board of Inspector's Endorsement to Governor regarding Pardon 41
12 July 1893 Pardon by Governor 42
Penitentiary Record for Abraham Rudolph Gonce (Second Visit) 43
Dr. A. R. Gonce Pardoned out of the Penitentiary to Die 44
Doc's Resurrection and New Marriage 45
Third Divorce 45

12th Census of the United States – 1900..46
Thirteenth Census of the United States – 1910..47
Death Certificate of Doc Gonce..49
POSTSCRIPTS **51**
Obituary of Mrs. Sarah E. Keysser..51
Rolyn and Myrtle Gonce..51
MISCELLANY **52**
Aunt Charity's Visit...52
Pioneer Doctor: The True Story of Pioneer, Dr. Abraham R. Gonce...............52
Dr. Heck regarding Abraham Rudolph Gonce...55
Doctor John D. Collins regarding Abraham Rudolph Gonce..........................55
Malpractice ?..56
Doc's Year of Birth..57
Hezekiah Gonce's Year of Birth (Doc's Older Brother)....................................58
Known Children of Abraham Rudolph "Doc" Gonce.......................................59
Doc's Children with Mary A. Frazier as reported in Various Documents.....60
State of Missouri – Counties of Interest in Doc Gonce's Life..........................63
Southern Missouri – Important Towns and Locations in Doc Gonce's Life.......64
Chronology of Events in the Life of Abraham Rudolph Gonce......................65

Section II: Bigamy Trial Transcriptions...71
BIGAMY TRIAL TRANSCRIPTIONS **73**
Preface..73
The Indictment for Bigamy: 5 April 1877...75
Mary A. Gonce's Petition for Divorce: 26 September 1878..............................84
Divorce granted to Mary A. Gonce: 26 September 1878..................................85
Felonious Assault & Display of Weapon: 26 February 1879...........................89
Abraham Rudolph Gonce's Trial for Bigamy: beginning 26 August 1879.....93
The Jury's Verdict... 108
Denial of Appeal and Doc's Escape... 108
Reward for Doc Gonce's Capture.. 109

Section III: Murder Trial Transcriptions..111
MURDER TRIAL TRANSCRIPTIONS **113**
Preface... 113
COURT PROCEEDINGS – 21st Judicial Court Of Christian County............. 115
Grand Jury Indictment, Plea, and Continuance: beginning 25 August 1884...... 116
Change of Venue requested and granted: 23 February 1885........................ 127
COURT PROCEEDINGS – Circuit Court Of Greene County........................ 131
Defendant's Motion for Continuance: 1 June 1885.. 131
State of Missouri vs A. R. Gonce: Case for the Prosecution:......................... 135
Oath Sheets in Greene County Archives for Gonce Murder Trial................ 141
State of Missouri vs A. R. Gonce: Case for the Defense:................................ 156
State of Missouri vs A. R. Gonce: Prosecution Rebuttals:.............................. 173
State of Missouri vs A. R. Gonce: Defendant's Requested Instructions to the Jury:......... 183
State of Missouri vs A. R. Gonce: Verdict of the Jury:.................................... 189
State of Missouri vs A. R. Gonce: Defendant's Motion for a New Trial: 13 June 1885....191
State of Missouri vs A. R. Gonce: Index to Testimony and Affidavits.......... 203
State of Missouri vs A. R. Gonce: Greene County Summons Issued for Appearance..... 204

Section IV: The Legacy of Doc Gonce 207
DOC GONCE'S OUTLAW DESCENDANTS: PREFACE — 209
- Lester Olonzo Gonce 209
- Sarah Jane Bright 210
- Mysteries And Questions: 213
- Marriage of Lester Olonzo Gonce and Sarah Jane Bright 213

THE BABY BANDITS OF COLORADO — 215
- The Boys Escape 217
- Lester Olonzo Gonce kills the Deputy Sheriff 226
- Lester "Chet" Gonce, Jr. Paroled and Married 227
- Vollie Vernon "Sam" Gonce Serves Time 228
- Thelma Irene Gonce Dies 229
- Forrest "Bud" Gonce Released from Prison 229
- Lester "Chet" Gonce, Jr. Pardoned 229
- Forrest "Bud" Gonce Joins the Military 230
- Sarah Jane (Bright) Gonce Dies 230
- Lester "Chet" Gonce, Jr. Begins a New Career 230
- Vollie Vernon "Sam" Gonce 231
- Denoument 233
- The "Baby Bandits" Tale Comes to an End 234

THE SENIOR CITIZEN BURGLARS OF NEVADA — 236
- The Target 236
- The Heist 237
- New Investigation 237
- The Arrests and Recovery of the Loot 238
- The Indictments 238
- The Sentencing 239
- Aftermath 240
- Summary: The Legacy of "Doc" Gonce 240

Appendix I: Bright Murders Press Coverage 241
PRESS COVERAGE OF THE BRIGHT MURDERS — 243

Dr. Abraham Rudolph Gonce (1833 – 1912) in his prime

SECTION I:
A SHORT
BIOGRAPHY

3 May 1833 – 4 December 1912

Doc's Early Life in Tennessee

Abraham Rudolph "Doc" Gonce was born on 3 May 1833[4] in Clinch Valley, near Rogersville, in northeastern Tennessee, to Vance Gonce [ID 2881] and Martha "Patsy" Davis [ID 2882]. Doc's direct ancestors are shown in the diagram on page 4. Doc's paternal grandfather Abraham [ID 2584] was part of the 1797 migration from Maryland to Tennessee that formed the beginning of the "southern branch" of the Gonce family. I believe his great-great-grandparents Justice [ID 2577] and Magdalen [ID 2858] to have been the oldest generation of the Gonce family to settle in the new world, originally in northeastern Maryland and nearby Delaware[5].

There is no known documentation of Rudolph's[6] childhood; in the Sixth U.S. Census for 1840[7], he is presumed to be the "White Male aged 5 to 9"; his older brothers William and Hezekiah Davis are the "2 White Males; age 10-14." Vance Gonce was, of course, the head-of-household and the only person actually listed by name.

Also living in Hawkins County at the time were two of the town's physicians. The older was Dr. Hugh Walker, age 49, who lived in Rogersville[8] with his wife Frances (Fanny) and their four children. Fanny, born in 1795, was the daughter of Joseph Rogers, founder of the town of Rogersville[9]. Dr. Walker, then age 58, his wife Fannie, and their four children were still living in the same location at the time of the 1860 Census[10].

The younger Rogersville area doctor at the time was a Dr. A. Carmichael, whose first name I have been unable to ascertain. The 1850 U.S. Census[11] shows Dr. Carmichael, age 32, his wife Rachel, and their three children also living in Rogersville (District 10).

---

4   In spite of many reports that he was born in 1829, I don't believe that is possible. See the discussion of Doc's year of birth and the accompanying chart on page 57.
5   See the book "Our Gonce Ancestors" for a history of my direct ancestral line, including Justice, Magdalen, and their children.
6   Doc was referred to by his middle name during childhood, possibly to distinguish him from his Grandfather.
7   National Archives Microfilm Series m704, Roll 526, Page 236. (1840 Census) See illustration on page 4.
8   National Archives Microfilm Series m432 Roll 832 Page 384. (1850 Census) Dr. Walker lived in District 10.
9   Joseph Rogers lived from 21 August 1764 to November 1838. From Tennessee Cousins – A History of Tennessee People; Worth Stickley Ray; Genealogical Publishing Company; Baltimore, MD, 1980 (originally published in Austin, Texas in 1950), page 86
10 National Archives Microfilm Series m653 Roll 1255 Page 100 (1860 Census)
11 National Archives Microfilm Series m432 Roll 832 Page 385 (1850 Census)

Based on his later claims[12], Rudolph eventually apprenticed for several years with both Dr. Walker and Dr. Carmichael, although exactly when he did so isn't clear.

6th Census of the United States – 1840
National Archives Microfilm Series m704 Roll 526 Page 236

Residence is Hawkins County, Tennessee   Transcription below

Family member names were not listed in 1840; the only name specified is Vance Gonce, the head-of-household. The other names listed are my inferences based on information derived from other sources. Sequence indicates the children's order of birth in the family.

In the 1840 census, I assume Abraham Rudolph Gonce is the "1" in the second column, indicating the number of males aged between "5 & under 10." The Gonces' oldest daughter Elizabeth, born about 1822, had already married McLellan "Clem" Pearson, and doesn't appear with Vance's household. Vance and Patsy later had two more daughters named Melinda and Lucinda.

My ID	Surname	Inferred Name	Description and Count given on Census	Sequence
3025	Gonce	Jefferson	1 White Male; age < 5 (born 1836-1840)	11
2883	Gonce	**Abraham Rudolph**	**1 White Male; age 5-9 (born 1831-1835)**	6
3020	Gonce	William D.	1 of 2 White Males; age 10-14 (born 1826-1830)	2
3021	Gonce	Hezekiah Davis	2 of 2 White Males; age 10-14 (born 1826-1830)	4
2881	Gonce	Vance *(stated on form)*	1 White Male; age 30-39 (born 1801-1810)	Head
3023	Gonce	Martha	1 of 3 White Females; age < 5 (born 1836-1840)	8
3024	Gonce	Nancy A.	2 of 3 White Females; age < 5 (born 1836-1840)	10
	Gonce	Unidentified	3 of 3 White Females; age < 5 (born 1836-1840)	9
3022	Gonce	Louisa Jane	1 of 2 White Females; age 5-9 (born 1831-1835)	7
4029	Gonce	Unidentified	2 of 2 White Females; age 5-9 (born 1831-1835)	5
3131	Gonce	Margaret	1 White Female; age 10-14 (born 1826-1830)	3
2882	Gonce	Patsy	1 White Female; age 30-39 (born 1801-1810)	Wife

---

12 See Dr. Heck's quotations from his correspondence from Doc Gonce on page 55.

On 28 March 1850, before the 1850 Census[13] was taken, Abraham Gonce married a girl named Mary; some have identified her as Mary Ann Frazier, but I have been unable to confirm that surname. Some have also said that Doc had earlier married a girl named Sarah Nancy Fraizer (note the different spellings), but I find this improbable given the ages shown for Doc and Mary on the 1850 Census. Whether "Mary Ann" and "Sarah Nancy" are different names for a single person is difficult to guess with no further information.

7th Census of the United States – 1850	
National Archives Microfilm Series m432 Roll 882 Page 313	
Residence is District 2, Hawkins County, Tennessee	Transcription below

Section of the 1850 Census form showing "Doc" Gonce, still a farmer, and his wife Mary, age 19. I suspect that this 1850 Census may be the source of the incorrect 1829 year of birth some have stated.

My ID	Surname	Proper Name	Age	Implied Year of Birth
2883	Gonce	Abram	21	about 1829 (this age is certainly incorrect; it should be 17)
3320	Gonce	Mary	19	about 1831

Although "Abram" is listed as a farmer in the 1850 census above, he would evidently begin studying medicine within a few years under the aforementioned Drs. Walker and Carmichael. On page 32 of his history of the Davis family, Dr. Arch Heck quotes from a letter written by "Doc" Gonce on 21 June 1891 from Jefferson City, Missouri[14]:

> "My father was Vance Gonce. - - my mother was a Davis, a sister of Hezekiah and all the six brothers. ... I read medicine for three years in Rogersville under Doctors Walker and Carmichael."

---

13 National Archives Microfilm Series m432 Roll 882 Page 313 (1850 Census); see illustration above.
14 "Descendants of Hezekiah Davis I" by Arch O. Heck, Copyright 1965 by Arch O. Heck, Columbus, Ohio; Abraham Rudolph's mother Martha "Patsy" Davis [ID 2882] was part of this family. Although Dr. Heck doesn't state (and may not have known) where in Jefferson City the letter was written from, Doc was in the State Penitentiary at the time serving a sentence for second-degree murder. See the entire context of this quotation on page 55.

Dr. Abraham Rudolph Gonce

"Doc" and his wife Mary had their first two sons William McClellan [ID 3480], known as "Mac," and Arthur Davis [ID 3318] in August 1851 and May 1854 respectively. In about 1856, "Doc" and Mary had twin daughters Nancy [ID 3848] and Martha E. [ID 3532], followed by another daughter Mary Ellen (Ella) [ID 3533] in about 1859.

8th Census of the United States – 1860
National Archives Microfilm Series m653 Roll 1255 Page 14

Residence is Lee Valley; Hawkins County, Tennessee   Transcription below

Section of the 1860 Census (bottom of page 14 and top of page 15) showing "Doc" Gonce's wife Mary and two of their children living near his older brother Hezekiah and family..

My ID	Surname	Proper Name	Age	Implied Year of Birth	Comments
3320	Gaunce	Mary A.	28	about 1832	Doc's Wife Mary, listed as a "Widow"
3480	Gaunce	William M.	9	about 1851	Son of Doc and Mary
3848	Gaunce	Nancy	4	about 1856	Twin Daughter of Doc and Mary
	Willis	Indell	19	about 1841	Unidentified neighbor
	Willis	Susan	20	about 1840	Unidentified neighbor
3532	Gaunce	Martha	4	about 1856	Twin Daughter of Doc and Mary
3533	Gaunce	Mary	0.5	about 1859	Daughter of Doc and Mary

Note that Mary A. Gaunce (sic) was still living in Hawkins County, Tennessee with two of her children next door to Doc's older brother Hezekiah, and is listed as a "Widow." Martha (one of the twins) and the new baby Ella (Mary Ellen) are living with the neighbors Indell and Susan Willis, and her husband Abraham's parents Vance and Martha are living in the next sequential household. Intriguingly, neither Abraham nor his son Arthur Davis, then about six years old, seems to be living anywhere in the area[15].

It seems apparent, therefore, that "Doc" must have left the family around or shortly after his daughter Ella's birth, taking the younger of his two sons (the second of his five children) with him. The fact that his wife Mary listed herself as a "widow" suggests the possibility that she may have thought he left her, or considered her marriage at an end, but there is not enough evidence to state this conclusively.

I have not been able to further identify Indell Willis and his wife Susan. Lara Athens Gonce [ID 3091], a granddaughter of Abraham Rudolph Gonce's oldest brother William D. Gonce [ID 3020] by his second wife, married a man named Charles Mack (Charlie) Willis [ID 3292] fifty-seven years later in 1917, but I don't know if there is an earlier connection between the Willis and Gonce families or they were simply neighbors. Willis was a very common surname in Hawkins County. I haven't been able to locate a Susan Gonce born in the 1840 time frame, suggesting that Susan Willis probably wasn't a Gonce.

In his book, Dr. Heck also says "Abraham was an M.D.; he went to Kentucky to practice medicine; he was also in Maryland[16]". This suggests the possibility that Doc may have gone to Kentucky (or even Maryland) to try establishing a medical practice before moving his whole family but, if so, I have found no record of him in any of those places. If establishing a medical practice was his goal in leaving, I can't come up with any reason why Doc would have taken Arthur with him.

Doc's later escapades make it difficult to ignore the possibility that another woman[17] may have played a part in his 1860 absence, and might even provide an explanation for Arthur's absence as well, but unless and until some other evidence surfaces, this can only be considered speculation.

---

15 I have been unable to locate any reference to either of them in any other state in the 1860 census.
16 This is a very intriguing reference – I have uncovered no evidence at all to suggest that he spent any time in Maryland, but Doc's Missouri death certificate reports that he came from Kentucky, which, although incorrect, could be construed as supporting Dr. Heck's statement that Doc Gonce had spent time in Kentucky.
17 Perhaps the elusive Sarah Nancy Fraizer mentioned on page 5.

Doc first appears in Missouri

Slightly more than a year after the 1860 Census, however, there is evidence that Doc was practicing medicine in Missouri, as described in the article below.

Background: Samuel Marion Davis of Galena in Stone County Missouri and his father were apparently both Union soldiers – unusual in this heavily Confederate area. On the 28th of August in 1861, Sam's father was killed and Sam was severely wounded by Missouri State Guard (Confederate) soldiers supposedly retreating from the Battle of Wilson's Creek, which had taken place eighteen days earlier. In fact, and likely more to the point, they all happened to be in debt to the elder Davis.

Anecdote about the Union Soldier Samuel Marion Davis	
History of Stone County, Missouri, Volume 1, page 394	
Repeated almost verbatim in **White River Valley Historical Quarterly (WRVQ)** Volume 6, Number 12, Summer 1979 Copyright 1979 by Donna Davis Ricchiuti	28 AUG 1861
"After the men departed, Sam began crawling and dragging himself down the hillside. Hours passed before he stumbled into the cabin of his Uncle John. No home was safe to a Unionist and a weary, wounded and grief-stricken Sam was forced to keep moving until he was safely hidden in a cave. His wife and Doc Gonce were summoned and were cautiously led to the cave by Uncle John. It has been told that Abraham Gonce was not a bona fide physician but practiced the profession nonetheless. Doc probed for the bullet lodged in Sam's side with a long, rusted hat pin. The bullet remained with Sam during his lifetime giving him chronic pain and serving as a constant reminder of his ordeal. Vina continued to return to the cave by herself. She was in constant fear of being followed and refused to carry a pine torch or even a candle to light her way through the dark forest. Vina was then sixteen years of age."	 Samuel Marion and Nancy (Manning) Davis. *Tetanus wasn't identified yet, but "Doc" was apparently trying…*

I have found no evidence that Samuel Marion Davis or his uncle John was related to Doc's Mother's family[18]. Even if that were the case, Doc's actions still seem to indicate a certain level of fearlessness or courage.

---

18 Doc's letter to Dr. Arch Heck on page 55 indicates that at least some of his mother's relatives were living in Missouri, and censuses show Fielding Gonce and some other relatives in western Missouri.

Doc and his family reunite in Indiana

Abraham eventually reunited with his family, and he and Mary settled in Indiana[19], where they had two more children (the couples' sixth and seventh): Olive Alice [ID 3534], born in about 1864 and Thomas Jefferson [ID 3535], born on 8 January 1866.

Since the earlier incident, where Doc treated Samuel Marion Davis, indicates that he must have been in Missouri in August 1861, we can assume that Doc likely arrived in Indiana between then and 1863, and that he likely practiced medicine in Indiana as well.

Unfortunately, I have been unable to locate any trace of Doc or his family in extant Indiana records.

Doc and his family settle in Missouri

Some time in about 1867, the family had moved again to Finley Township in Christian County Missouri, just outside Ozark, where Doc and Mary had their eighth child Laura Alice [ID 3536] in about 1869. Doc quickly established a thriving practice in this mountainous are of southern Missouri and, at least for several years, seems to be one of only two doctors serving the area.

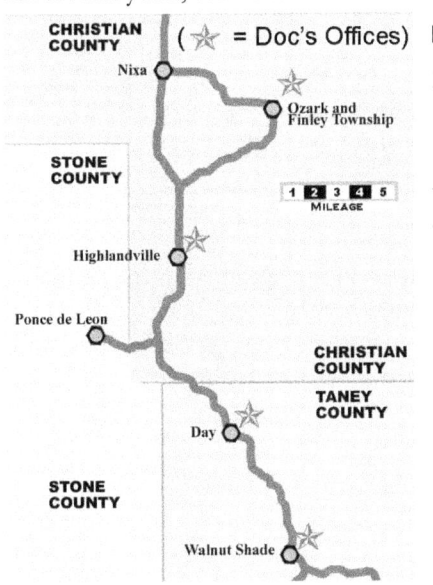

Doc Gonce's Medical Practice Locations[20]

Doc Gonce had medical offices in:

Ozark, Christian County
Highlandville, Christian County
Day, Taney County
Walnut Shade, Taney County

These are shown by stars on the map to the left.

His home in Finley Township was just outside Ozark; the town has long since been subsumed into Ozark proper.

He also had a "drug store" in Walnut Shade, where he mixed his custom (and alcohol-based) tonics.

Later in life, he had another "drug store"/saloon in Kirbyville that he acquired in 1895, and a hardware store in Day that he bought in 1900.

---

19 This can be inferred from the 1870 US Census, National Archives Series m593 Roll 769 Page 388, which lists the place of birth for Doc, Mary, and all of their children, including Arthur, who was missing in 1860. See page 11.
20 See a larger version of this map with more information on page 64.

Various extant records indicate that, in addition to practicing medicine, Doc had taken on some other roles in nearby Stone County, Missouri, where he had one of his four medical offices[21]. The following references are both from Stone County archives from the year 1868.

Evidence of Doc Gonce as a Missouri Justice of the Peace	
Excerpted from Marriage Records Stone County, Missouri 1851 – 1900 in **White River Valley Historical Quarterly (WVRQ)** Volume 7, Number 4, Summer 1980	JAN 1868
BENHAM, John and DENNIS, Julia on 23 Jan. 1868; by A. R. Gonce, J. P.	

Evidence of Doc Gonce as an Estate Curator	
Excerpted from **Stone County Missouri Abstracts of Wills and Administrations**	OCT 1868

From page 15: GONCE, A. R.
 	
    Curator of estates of Rebecca S., George M., Nancy E. E. and Jesse R. M. Harris, minor heirs of Calib Harris. Sec. William Kendall and James W. Butler, bond filed 20 Oct. 1868; page 88
 	
From page 17: BERRY, FRANCIS P.
 	
    Guardian and curator of Rebecca S., George M., Nancy E. E. and R. M. Harris, minor heirs of Caleb Harris, deceased. Sec. James Baker and James H. Cox, bond filed 20 July 1869; page 107	

As far as I can determine, Doc Gonce had no relationship to the people named in these records, likely indicating these actions resulted from his official duties. Francis P. Berry, whose name appears two pages after the reference to Doc in the October 1868 records, provided testimony in Doc's later trial for murder in 1885.

---

21 See the story "Pioneer Doctor: The True Story of Pioneer, Dr. Abraham R. Gonce" on page 52. This story isn't, as they say, "the whole truth and nothing but the truth," but gives an indication of Doc's status in the community.

9th Census of the United States – 1870

National Archives Microfilm Series m593 Roll 769 Page 388

Residence is Finley Township; Christian County, Missouri   Transcription below

By the time of the 1870 Census, "Doc" and his family were living in Finley Twp, just outside of Ozark, in Christian County, Missouri. Note birth places listed in column 10.

My ID	Surname	Proper Name	Age	Implied Year of Birth	Comments
2883	Gonce	Abraham	38	about 1832	
3320	Gonce	Mary A.	39	about 1831	Doc's Wife Mary
3318	Gonce	Arthur	17	about 1853	Son of Doc and Mary
3532	Gonce	Martha E.	14	about 1856	Twin Daughter of Doc and Mary
3533	Gonce	Mary E.	10	about 1860	Daughter of Doc and Mary
3534	Gonce	Alice	6	about 1864	Daughter of Doc and Mary
3535	Gonce	Thomas	4	about 1866	Son of Doc and Mary
3536	Gonce	Laura A.	1	about 1869	Daughter of Doc and Mary

William McClellan "Mac" Gonce, aged 18 by this time, had already married and was living with his wife in Howell Township, Howell County. Nancy, one of the twins, who would have been 14 at the time of the 1870 census, is not listed, and is presumed to have died between the 1860 and 1870 censuses.

Doc and Mary A. had the last of their nine children together, Benjamin Franklin Gonce [ID 3688], in about 1872.

> **Flashback**: A thirty-four year old Taney County farmer named Alexander Logan ID 4108 and his wife Eliza ID 4109 had a daughter Sarah Elizabeth Logan ID 4110 on 29 October 1846. After his wife's death, Alexander Logan married Charity Elizabeth Wiggins ID 3473 in the late 1860s. At the time this happened, therefore, Sarah Elizabeth, who was by then in her late teens, became Charity's stepdaughter – even though Charity was at least two years younger than Sarah. On 16 March 1871, Sarah, then 24 years old, married Charles G. Keyser ID 4111 in Christian County, Missouri.
>
> Charity Wiggins Logan, her stepdaughter Sarah Elizabeth Logan, and Sarah's husband Charles Keyser were to play significant roles in Doc Gonce's saga in the coming years.

Barbara Logan[22] believes that Charles Keyser is the same Keysser mentioned in the book "The Kentlings of Highlandville" by Gene Geer. In the book, Geer states "Keysser was a runaway from a German noble family who had acquired much cheap land in Christian County, in the hills below the village of Nixa"[23].

Frank Kentling, who appears as a witness in Doc's later murder trial, determined that there would be a good business opportunity in providing a stopover and trading post on the Old Wilderness Road that went from Springfield, Missouri, south to Harrison, Arkansas[24]. He purchased some land at what he calculated was an appropriate location from Charles Keyser and established what eventually became the town of Highlandville. Frank Kentling became the first Postmaster of the area, and was then succeeded in that post by Charles Keyser.

Residents of Ozark and Vicinity in the Nineteenth Century	
White River Valley Historical Quarterly (WRVQ) Volume 2, Number 10, Winter 1966 by William Neville Collier	1872
In 1872 among the citizens of Ozark were the following: Mrs. Christman, who ran the Finley House, the Pettyjohns, Doctor Gonce, Mr. Ramey, a Baptist preacher; G. W. Logan, John A. Richardson; A. C. Cram; Henry Clark; A. H. Cravens; S. M. Caudle; William Weber; Morgan Bell; E. L. Shepard; Captain Dorland; Doctor Bedford Brown; Essau Smith; James R. Vaughan; A. T. Yoachum; Samuel Payne; Thomas McPettyjohn; Mr. Isenberg; Boyd; Pierpoint Edwards; John L. Tunnell; David William Wrightsman; Mrs. McGaugh; Joseph Kimberling; Doctor Robinson; John Whitlock; J. D. Caudle; T. J. McCord; Milo Weaver.	*Abraham Rudolph Gonce appears at the end of the second line – he had an office here as well as in Highlandville, Day, and Walnut Shade.*

---

22 Barbara's husband Don Logan is a descendant of Alexander and Charity Logan.
23 See Nixa at the top of the map on page 9.
24 There were, at the time, major shipments of Alabama cotton north to Springfield.

By the middle of the decade, it was apparent that Doc Gonce was doing well. He owned property both in his own name and in partnership with others.

In addition to his home and other properties in Taney County, the records of Christian County indicate that he was paying land taxes on at least eight lots there. It is interesting in light of later events that none of this property seemed to be jointly owned with his wife Mary, although at least six parcels were jointly owned with a man named J. L. Robberson, whose relationship to Doc I have been unable to ascertain.

The transcript below shows Doc's Christian County land tax payments for the year 1875:

Christian County Missouri Land Tax Payments		
Excerpted from **Christian County Missouri Tax Records**		1875
Gonce, A. R.	2 Lots $275 Ozark Block 7. Lot 2; Ozark Block 8. Part of Lot 2	*I have not yet identified J. L. Robberson.*
Gonce, A. R.	See J. L. Robberson	
Robberson, J. L.	6 Lots $875 Ozark Block 16. Lots 1-2; Ozark Old Town Block 6. Lot 18 – 21	

In 1876, when Doc was forty-three years old, the State of Missouri conducted its own census, and this gives us a picture of Doc's family and that of his grown children, some of which had now established their own families. Images and transcriptions of these censuses appear on the following two pages.

1876 Census of the State of Missouri; page 16 – Doc and his Family	
Residence is Finley Township; Christian County, Missouri	Transcription below

At the time of the 1876 Census of Finley County Missouri, Doc was still living with Mary A. Frazier. L. J. Chrisman was Lafayette James Chrisman, who married Doc and Mary's daughter Mary Ellen Gonce, shown here as "Ollie." Mr. Chrisman will play an important role in Doc's life later, as we shall see.

My ID	Name on Census	Assumed to be	Age Range	Comments
4088	L. J. Chrisman	Lafayette James Chrisman	21-45	Doc's son-in-law
3533	Ollie Chrisman	Mary Ellen Gonce	10-18	Daughter of Doc and Mary
2883	**A. R. Gonce**	**Abraham Rudolph Gonce**	**21-45**	
3320	M. A. Gonce	Mary A. Frazier	21-45	Doc's Wife
3532	M. E. Gonce	Martha E. Gonce	18-21	Doc's daughter
3534	O. A. Gonce	Olive Alice Gonce	10-18	Doc's daughter
3535	T. B. Gonce	Thomas Jefferson Gonce	10-18	Doc's son (why T.B., not T.J.?)
3536	L. A. Gonce	Laura Alice Gonce	< 10	Doc's daughter
3688	B. F. Gonce	Benjamin Franklin Gonce	< 10	Doc's son

The initials T. B. on line 32 of the above census page, which must refer to Thomas Jefferson Gonce are, as far as I can tell, simply a mistake[25] and don't provide any new information.

---

25 It is possible that the initials on the form really are "T.J.," but it doesn't appear that way to me.

By 1876, three of Doc and Mary's children had married and established their own families. At this time, Doc had at least four grandchildren, as can be seen in the illustration of William and Arthur's families below:

1876 Census of the State of Missouri; pages 16 and 17 – Doc's Adult Children	
Residence is Finley Township; Christian County, Missouri	Transcription below

On these two pages of the 1876 Census of Finley Township in Missouri, the families of Doc's oldest two sons can be seen. The "M. M. Gonce" can't be anyone other than Minnie B. Gonce, who was born in January of 1876.

My ID	Name on Census	Assumed to be	Age Range	Comments
3318	Arthur Gonce	Arthur Davis Gonce	21-45	Doc's second child
4125	Susan Gonce	Susan (Pruitt) Gonce	21-45	First Wife of 3318
3565	M. M. Gonce	Minnie B. Gonce	< 10	Daughter of 3318 and 4125
3480	Mack Gonce	William McClellan Gonce	21-45	Doc's oldest son
3481	M. A. Gonce	Martha Ann (Sims) Gonce	21-45	Wife of 3480
3680	James Gonce	James McClellan Gonce	< 10	Son of 3480 and 3481
3682	Carroll Gonce	Carl Abraham Gonce	< 10	Son of 3480 and 3481
4140	C. Gonce	Clemmons Gonce	< 10	Daughter of 3480 and 3481

Although Doc was living with his first wife Mary in Finley Township at the time of the 1876 Missouri Census, he had apparently already met and begun a serious affair with a woman named Martha Ann Keithley [ID 4007]. Martha lived in nearby Ozark, one of several locations where Doc had an office in which he saw patients. According to A. F. (Derry) St. Clair, "Matt Keithley was ... a good woman and real nice looking." [26]

Whether Doc had earlier abandoned Mary when he first left Tennessee is unclear, but in mid-October of 1876[27], he abandoned Mary and moved in with Martha Keithley. Doc and Matt went south to Arkansas shortly there after, and were married there on the first of November[28]. Whether Martha knew of Doc's marital status at this time isn't recorded anywhere that I could find, but it seems unlikely that she could have been completely unaware that he had been married and had both young[29] as well as grown children.

Bigamy Charges

Accordingly, based on a complaint filed by Mary, Stone County, Missouri issued an Indictment for Bigamy[30] presented below:

Missouri Judicial Index Database	
Stone County Box 4, Folder 2, Case 3, Sheet 26[31]	
Creator	Record Group	Stone County Circuit Court, 1852-1899
Title	Series	Circuit Court Case Files
Contributor	Defendant	Gonce, A.R.
	Plaintiff	State of Missouri
Date	Date Filed	5 April 1877
Coverage	County	Stone
Description	Cause of Action	Bigamy
	Case Summary	Mary Gonce & Martha Ann Keithly, wives, 2nd marriage in AR
Location	Box	04
	Folder	02
Identifier	Case Number	3

---

26 A transcription of the full article from which this quote was taken is presented on page 52. A photograph of Martha appears on page 62, and another is shown on page 209 of Section III.
27 In her divorce filing, Mary claims he left her on October 17th. See Stone County Archive B4F17C44, sheet 32 on page 85.
28 This is reported in the indictment above (also see page 76). I have yet to find a record of this marriage.
29 His 9th and youngest child Benjamin was only about four years old at this time.
30 As far as I can tell, Mary was still living in Finley Township in Christian County at the time, and I haven't been able to determine why the charges were filed in Stone County.
31 The sheet number is my own, as explained on page 73.

Images and a transcription of the indictment for bigamy are presented in "Section II: Bigamy Trial Transcriptions" beginning on page 75.

Based on the Indictment for Bigamy, an Arrest Warrant was issued on the 6th of April by Stone County and sent to the Sheriff of Christian County for execution. A copy of the warrant is provided on page 78 of the Bigamy Trial Transcriptions section.

It isn't clear why he did so, but five days after the bigamy charges were filed, Doc and Matt had a second marriage ceremony performed on 10 April 1877 – this time in neighboring Stone County where the indictment was returned against him. It isn't clear if this was intended to be a legal maneuver by Doc's attorneys or, if it was, what the benefits were expected to be.

Below is a transcription from the Stone County archives showing this second marriage between Abraham R. Gance (sic) and Martha Ann Keithley. The presiding minister, Westley Henry (shown in the transcription as "Wesley") would later be called to testify at Doc's bigamy trial.

Marriage Records, Stone County, Missouri 1851 – 1900				
Copied/Transcribed from originals by Mrs. Loren Loden **From Volume 7, Number 7**				10 APR 1877
Groom	Bride	Date	Presiding	
GANCE, Abraham R.	KEITHLEY, Martha Ann	10 April 1877	Wesley Henry, Clergy	

Doc was arrested after this and placed in a Stone County jail cell to await trial, but posted a $500 recognizance bond five days later, cosigned with Amos S. Kelly, and was released. This document can be seen on page 80.

Land Sale

Doc now needed to raise cash, certainly for his defense, but possibly also to support his two wives while his income was being interrupted. As we have seen earlier, he seemed to have owned a significant amount of property, much of it in his own name. But – he chose instead to sell property that he and Mary owned jointly – a parcel of farmland on the White River.

On May 30, 1877, this property was sold for one thousand dollars to the former Charity A. Wiggins, now the second wife of Alexander Logan, and not, as would have been the usual practice at the time, to the Logans as a couple. Since Alexander, who was about thirty-seven years older than Charity, had adult children (and potential heirs) from his first wife Eliza, who had died some thirteen years earlier, it is possible that he was attempting to insure that Charity was able to retain the property without any difficulties in the event of his death[32] by placing it in her name alone. Charity would remain on this

---

32 I haven't determined his date of death, but Alexander was still alive at the time of the 1880 census.

farm until her death, but Doc would make an attempt to get her to deed the land back to him some years later, as we shall see.

I haven't located anything to suggest that Mary knew of Doc's other land holdings but even so, it still seems curious to me that Doc was able to convince his soon-to-be-divorced wife to agree to the sale. There is no evidence that she received any of the proceeds other than her expenses for the divorce as reported in her divorce decree[33]:

> *"the said Plaintiff have and retain the custody and control of the said children and that she have and recover of and from the Defendant her costs in the said cause laid out and expended"*

The circuit court judge was apparently curious about Mary's easy acquiescence to the sale as well. The court-appointed notary separated Mary from her husband and questioned her about the transaction in an effort to insure that she had not been coerced in some manner. The segment of the deed pictured below[34], from a somewhat unusual portion after the actual transfer of the land, says the following:

> *"...act and deed for the purposes therein mentioned and the said Mary A. Gonce being by me first made acquainted with the contents of said instrument <u>upon an examination separate and apart from her husband acknowledged that she executed the same and relinquishes her dower in the Real Estate therein transferred freely and without fear Compulsion or undue influence of her said husband.</u> I was qualified May 5, 1875. My term expires March 17 1879. In Witness Whereof I have hereto set my hand and affixed My Official Seal at my office in Ozark the day and year first above written."*

---

33 From Stone County B4F17C44; sheets 32 and 33, which are transcribed on page 85.
34 The Land Deed, transcribed fully on page 81, is located in Taney County Deed Book 3, pp 508 & 509, available from the Recorder of Deeds; P.O. Box 428; Forsyth, MO 65653. The underlining is mine.

Missed Trial Date

Shortly after the land sale, Doc seems to have fled the area. He must have done so with a minimum of fuss, since preparations for the trial, scheduled for the August 1877 session of the circuit court and including the issuance of subpoenas on 23 June 1877[35], proceeded normally. The trial was eventually rescheduled for the court session due to start the following February.

Subpoena

On 31 August 1877[36], an additional subpoena was issued – this time for Westley Henry, the clergyman who performed Doc and Martha's second wedding in Missouri. This is shown below.

Stone County Archives: Box 4, Folder 2, Case 3, Sheet 5

[106]

SUBPŒNA---~~COUNTY~~ Circuit COURT.

State of Missouri, } ss. ~~IN THE COUNTY COURT~~ Circuit,
County of Stone }

The STATE OF MISSOURI, to Wesley Henry

You are hereby Commanded, That, setting aside all manner of excuse and delay, you be and appear in proper person before the Judges of our ~~County~~ Circuit Court, at the Court House, in the town of Galena, within and for said County of Stone, on the fourth ~~, the~~ Monday of February 1878 then and there to testify and the truth to speak, in a certain matter of controversy now pending in our said Court, wherein the State of Missouri is Plaintiff, and A R Gonce is Defendant, on the part of said Plaintiff; and this you shall in no wise omit. And the person or officer serving this Writ is commanded to have the same at the time and place aforesaid, certifying thereon his return.

Witness my hand and the seal of our said Court. Done at office in Galena, in the County aforesaid, on this 31st day of Aug, A.D. 1877

W. W. Fike Clerk.
By Frank Fike D.C.

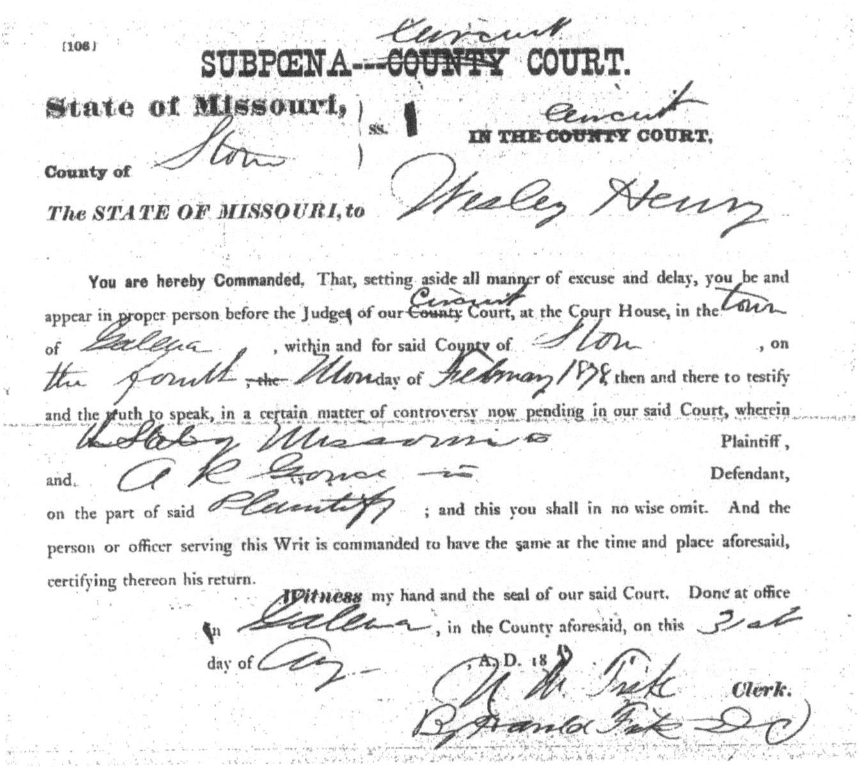

I have been unable to ascertain Doc's whereabouts for certain during this period[37] but, during this absence, on 23 September 1877, Martha Keithley gave birth to the first of her three children with Doc, their son Rolyn.

35 Stone County Archives: Box 4, Folder 2, Case 3, Sheets 2 and 3.
36 Stone County Archives: Box 4, Folder 2, Case 3, Sheets 4 and 5.
37 Mary's divorce petition suggests that Doc and Martha were living in Arkansas for some of this time.

Doc's absence continued until sometime in the fall of 1878, resulting in two further postponements[38] of the bigamy trial. Upon his return to Taney County, he was again arrested and placed in jail to await transfer to nearby Stone County for his bigamy trial.

Divorce Proceedings

No longer content to await the results of the now elusive Bigamy trial, Mary filed a petition for divorce on 26 September 1878[39], alleging that:

> "... in the State of Tennessee lawfully maried (sic) to Deft that she continued to live with Deft until about 17 day October 1876 that during that time she faithfully demeaned herself and discharged all her duties as wife of Deft ... Deft wholly degraded his duties as her husband ... did abandon Pltf and go away with one Martha A. Keithley into the State of ArKansas did subsequently in said state cohabit with said Keithley ..."

Doc's attorneys filed his denial of all the allegations contained in Mary's petition[40], and presented some very interesting defenses in this action. Doc began by denying that he and Mary had ever actually been married in the first place. When that failed, Doc then submitted what he purported to be a Kentucky divorce decree[41], but the State produced several witnesses (including Doc's own attorney) to say that the handwriting was remarkably similar to Doc's.

In spite of Doc's contradictory attempts at rebuttal, the judge granted the divorce[42] and gave Mary custody of all her minor children on the same day[43].

> "... after having the testimony in the cause doth find that the Plaintiff and Defendant were united in matrimony in the year 1850 in the State of Tennessee, ... that the Defendant now is the lawful husband of the Plaintiff that the facts stated in the petition are true; ... that about the 17th day of October 1876 the Defendant abandoned the Plaintiff and has since been living in adultry (sic) and unlawful criminal intercourse with Martha A. Keithley (sic) ...
>
> ... the bonds of Matrimony ... are hereby dissolved and that the said Plaintiff have ... custody and control of the said children and that she have and recover of and from the Defendant her costs in the said cause laid out and expended and that execution issues therefore..."

---

38 The February 1878 and August 1878 terms of the Circuit Court.
39 Stone County Court Records Box 4; Folder 17; Case 44, pg 35. See transcription on page 84.
40 Stone County Court Records Box 4; Folder 17; Case 44, pg 34. See transcription on page 84.
41 Kentucky being presumably the only State that issued Divorce Decrees to couples who went unmarried. One has to give Doc or his attorneys credit for at least trying to amuse the judge.
42 Stone County Court Records Box 4; Folder 17; Case 44, pp 32 & 33. See transcription on page 85.
43 Note that Doc and Mary's daughter Laura A. Gonce is not mentioned in the divorce decree, suggesting that she may have died sometime in 1876.

New Felony Charges (Assault and Display of Deadly Weapon)

On the first of February 1879, several days prior to his rescheduled Bigamy trial, a preliminary hearing was held near Bull Creek in preparation for the trial.

As A. F. St. Claire tells the story:

> "They were trying Doc Gonce at the old log cabin on Bull Creek[44]... They paneled the jury, got set for the trial. Mr. Cupp (Justice of the Peace) gave the court a coffee break for fifteen minutes before they started. The doctor and the constable (Babe Weatherman) had a few words. It ended with a shootout, though no one was injured."

Some of the particulars of Mr. St. Claire's account seem questionable, since Elmer L. "Babe" Weatherman wasn't born until 24 April 1877, and was therefore probably a little too young to have taken part in a gunfight. [45]

Nonetheless, there is certainly an element of truth in the story, although Doc's intended victim was actually Alexander Osborn. For reasons that are unclear, Doc wasn't arrested for this incident until the 24th of February. He posted yet another $500 Recognizance Bond the next day and was released. On 26 February, two new Indictments were issued. The first, for displaying a weapon[46], charged the following:

> "... did unlawfully and willfully exhibit and display in the presence of Alexander Osborn A fire arm to wit a pistol ... in a rude, angry and threating [sic] manner and not in the necessary defence of his person, family, or property..."

The second and more serious Indictment, for Felonious Assault[47], charged the following:

> "... on or about the 1st day of February 1879, at the County of Stone, State aforesaid, did then and there unlawfully, willfully and feloniously make an assault on the body of one Alexander Osborn and did then and there on purpose unlawfully willfully and feloniously with a deadly weapon to wit a pistol which pistol he the said A. R. Gonce, in his right hand had and held charged and loaded with gunpowder and leaden balls did then and there unlawfully willfully and feloniously on purpose make an assault with the intent him the said Alexander Osborn then and there to kill..."

---

44 This refers to the creek itself, and not the nearby town of Bull Creek, which is in Taney County.
45 See the reference and text of the full article from which this quote was taken on page 52. Babe died on Thursday, April 20, 1971 in Mercy Villa, Springfield, at age 94. Since his father William P. Weatherman was around at the time (but was not called Babe and was not a constable), Babe may have simply been the person who told St. Clair the tale.
46 Stone County Box 4, Folder 10, Case 26, Sheet 8. See a full transcription on page 89.
47 Stone County Box 4, Folder 10, Case 26, Sheet 16. See an image of this Indictment on the next page; a full transcription is given on page 90.

INDICTMENT.

State of Missouri, } ss. In the _____ Court of Stone
County of Stone   County _____ TERM, A. D. 1879

THE GRAND JURORS for the State of Missouri, summoned from the body of Stone County, empannelled, charged and sworn, upon their oaths, present that A. R. Gonce _____ late of the County aforesaid, on the _____ about 1st day of February 1879, at the _____, County of Stone, State aforesaid, did feloniously and unlawfully, willfully and feloniously, make an assault upon the body of one Alexander Osborn, and did then and there on purpose unlawfully, willfully and feloniously with a deadly weapon to wit a pistol which held he the said A. R. Gonce, in his right hand and by'd charged and loaded with gunpowder and leaden balls, did then and there unlawfully, willfully and feloniously, on purpose make an assault with the intent him the said Alexander Osborn then and there to kill.

Contrary to the form of the statutes in such case made and provided, against the peace and dignity of the State.

A TRUE BILL:

_____
Foreman of the Grand Jury.

Thomas J. Gideon
Prosecuting Attorney.
Pro Tem

Motion to Quash

Based on a Motion to Quash[48], Doc's attorneys were able to get the less-serious charge of displaying a deadly weapon dropped two days later because:

> "... it does not charge any crime against this defendant, and ...does not charge that deft made an assault upon Alexander Osborne ..."

For all of their other failings, Doc's attorneys seemed to be quite adept at nitpicking, and the indictment was quashed. On the same day (28 February 1879), Doc posted yet another $500 Recognizance Bond for the Felony Assault charges.[49]

---

48 Stone County Box 4, Folder 10, Case 26, Sheet 10.
49 Doc needed to post quite a few of these, including the one mentioned (Box 4; Folder 10; Case 26, Sheet 4), one on 15 March 1879 (Box 4; Folder 10; Case 26, Sheet 22), and another on 22 April 1879 ((Box 4; Folder 10; Case 26, Sheet 7). All were for amounts of $500.

> **Meanwhile**: In March of 1879, while Doc was still managing to put off his Bigamy Trial, William and Lucinda Hargrove had the last of their nine children, a daughter named Susan. Although Doc was close to fifty years old when Susan was born, they would later become romantically involved.

The Bigamy Trial

Finally, on the 26th of August 1879, the trial of Doctor Abraham Rudolph Gonce for the crime of Bigamy got underway. The trial was itself fairly anticlimactic, and covered much the same facts that were brought out in Mary's earlier divorce action. Interestingly, Doc presented much the same defenses that he had in that action which, unfortunately for him, were greeted with the same skepticism. The trial lasted for little more than a day. As it closed, and before the jury was permitted to deliberate, Doc and his attorneys filed a motion to exclude certain testimony, a motion in arrest of judgement, and a bill of exceptions[50]. They further objected to the proposed jury instructions and submitted their own[51] for the court's consideration. All of these motions and submissions were summarily denied.

Finally, on August 27, 1879, Doc was found guilty[52] of Bigamy and given a two-year sentence in the state penitentiary. The jury foreman's note to the judge is shown below.

> "we the jury find the Defendent guilty of the charges set forth in the indictment and assess his punishment at ~~imprisonment in the state penitentiary~~ two years in the ~~penitentiary~~
> Thomas H Peterson foreman"

Over the next few days, Doc and his attorneys filed an appeal, but this, like all their previous motions, was denied and Doc was ordered off to serve his term in the Jefferson City penitentiary.

Although there doesn't seem to be any extant information on how he accomplished it, Doc managed to escape before he could be taken to the penitentiary. Shortly, as was the usual practice in Missouri, the Governor authorized a reward for his capture and return.

---

50 Stone County Box 4, Folder 17, Case 44. All these items are transcribed beginning on page 104.
51 Stone County Box 4, Folder 17, Case 44, Sheets 39, 36, 37, 38, 21, and 40. See the transcriptions beginning on page 106.
52 Stone County Box 4, Folder 17, Case 44, Sheet 20.

> **Reward for Doc Gonce's Capture**
>
> **The Messages and Proclamations of the Governors of the State of Missouri**
> Compiled and Edited by Grace Gilmore Avery, A.B. and Floyd C. Shoemaker, A.M.; Volume VI; Published by the State Historical Society of Missouri, Columbia, Missouri, 1924. From Pages 222 and 223 (S151)
>
> ### OFFERING A REWARD
>
> SEPTEMBER 15, 1879
>
> *From the Register of Civil Proceedings 1879-1882, p. 89*
>
> STATE OF MISSOURI, EXECUTIVE DEPARTMENT
>
> WHEREAS, A. R. Gonce was convicted and sentenced by the circuit court of Stone county to two years in the penitentiary for the crime of bigamy; and afterwards broke jail, and has fled from justice and cannot be arrested by ordinary process of law,
>
> NOW THEREFORE, I John S. Phelps Governor of the State of Missouri, by virtue of authority in me vested and for good and sufficient reasons appearing, do hereby offer a reward of One hundred and fifty dollars for the arrest and delivery of said fugitive to the sheriff of said county of Stone, at the county seat thereof, at any time within one year from the date of these presents.
>
> John S. Phelps
>
> (Seal)   In Testimony Whereof I have hereunto set my hand and caused to be affixed the Great Seal of the State of Missouri. Done at the City of Jefferson, this fifteenth day of September Ad 1879.
>
> By the Governor
> MICH'L K. MCGRATH, Secretary of State.

Doc was captured in less than two months, although I've been unable to determine who, if anyone, received the reward. The escape and delayed entry didn't seem to affect the length of his sentence, however. Although he didn't begin serving his sentence until October 24, 1879, his eventual parole under Missouri's ¾ rule[53] was calculated from his original reporting date of August 27, 1879 – not from his actual reporting date in October.[54]

Doc's original family seemed to have all remained in the area during his incarceration. Of his eight surviving children with Mary, four were living with her in 1880 (see census extract on page 26). Her son Arthur's wife Susan, shown in the 1876 Missouri Census, had died in the interim; Arthur and his daughter Minnie moved back to his mother's household.

---

53 A well-behaved prisoner could be paroled once he had served three-quarters of his sentence.
54 See a synopsis of his prison record on page 28.

10th Census of the United States – 1880 – Doc's ex-wife Mary and children
Church of Latter Day Saints Microfilm Series 1254681 Page 52

Residence is Finley Township; Christian County, Missouri	Transcription below

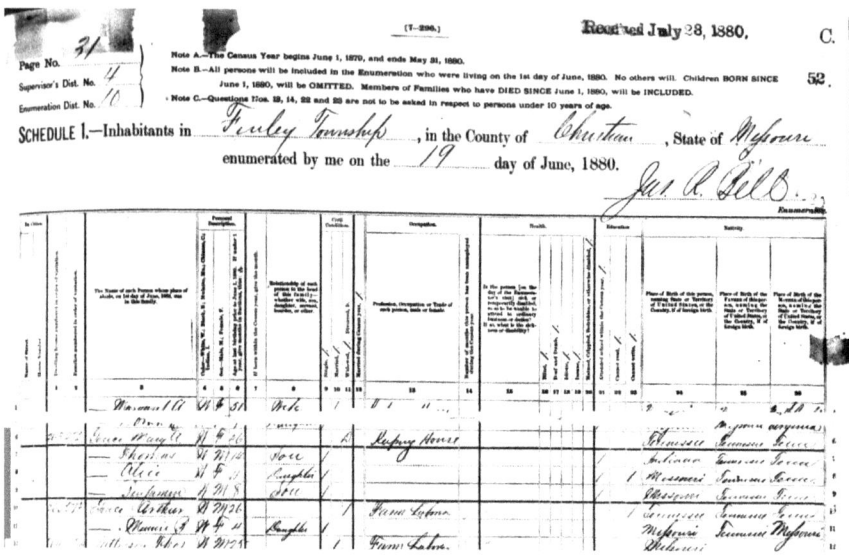

"Doc" Gonce's first wife Mary A. and three of her children were now living alone. As can be seen in the image above, Mary's son Arthur Davis Gonce and his daughter Minnie are living next door, suggesting that Arthur's wife Susan had died, likely in childbirth.

My ID	Surname	Name	Age	Implied Year of Birth	Comments	Seq
3320	Gonce	Mary A.	46	about 1834	Doc's recently divorced wife	Head
3535	Gonce	Thomas	14	about 1866	Doc's 7th child with Mary A.	7th
3536	Gonce	Alice	11	about 1869	Doc's 8th child with Mary A.	8th
3688	Gonce	Benjamin	8	about 1872	Doc's 9th child with Mary A.	9th
3318	Gonce	Arthur	26	about 1854	Doc's 2nd child with Mary A.	2nd
3565	Gonce	Minnie B.	4	about 1876	Arthur's daughter	

The apparent discrepancy in this census – Thomas is shown as being 14 years old, older than Alice who is listed as age 11[55] – is misleading. The Alice listed here is Laura Alice Gonce, not the Olive Alice Gonce (then also called Alice) listed in 1870. Olive Alice was 16 at the time of this census, and already married to her first husband. My reasons for these conclusions are detailed on page 60.

---

55 The 1870 census, for instance, shows an "Alice" as age 6 and Thomas as age 4; see the image on page 11.

Another daughter, Ella (Mary Ellen [ID 3533]), is living nearby[56] with her husband Lafayette James (Fayette) Chrisman [ID 4088] and their first two children. Fayette would later support Doc's parole from prison in 1893.

Doc and Mary's oldest son William "Mac" Gonce and his family had recently moved to Clear Creek Township in Cooper County[57], although they would move back to the Ozark area within a few years.

As yet, I haven't been able to locate Doc's new wife Martha Keithley in the 1880 census. She had one child with Doc by this time. (Martha died in Sterling, Rice County, Kansas on 8 April 1899, but since she testified at Doc's 1885 murder trial as his wife, she had probably not left Missouri in 1880 and was likely still living in Stone County[58]).

Doc himself shows up in the State Penitentiary census, as shown below:

10th Census of the United States – 1880 – Doc in the Penitentiary
Church of Latter Day Saints Microfilm Series 1254682 Page 51
Residence is State Penitentiary; Jefferson City; Cole Cty, MO   Transcription below

Extract from the top of page 35, showing the beginning of the list of inmates in the Missouri State Penitentiary and the line from page 51 on which "Doc" Gonce (shown as Gonce, A.R.) appears.

My ID	Surname	Name	Age	Implied Year of Birth	Comments
2883	Gonce	A. R.	47	about 1833	

---

56 Church of Latter Day Saints Microfilm Series 1254681, Page 43.
57 Church of Latter Day Saints Microfilm Series 1254683, Page 196.
58 As can be seen in the trial transcripts, there were a number of her Keithley relatives in the area, but I haven't located her living with any relatives that I could identify. Doc's parole record transcription, shown on page 28, supports the assumption that she was still living in Stone County in 1880.

Doc's Parole

Doc was released from the penitentiary on February 28, 1881. His actual penitentiary record at the time of his parole, shown below, provides a fairly detailed physical description of him in 1881.

Penitentiary Record for Abraham Rudolph Gonce (First Visit)		
Missouri State Archives – Prisoner 1685 – February 28, 1881		28 FEB 1881
NUMBER:	1685	
NAME:	A. R. Gonce	
AGE:	46	*This was his age when he entered prison*
NATIVITY:	Tennessee	
HEIGHT:	5 foot 8 1/2 inches	
LENGTH FOOT:	10 1/4 inches	
HAIR:	Gray	
EYES:	Brown	
COMPLEXION:	Dark	
TRADE:	Laborer; Mother lives in Tennessee. Wife in Stone Co. Mo	
MARKS AND SCARS:	High forehead, inclined to baldness, scar in first joint left index finger, 2nd right finger crooked, scar on right thigh above knee, Scar on back - caused by boils, Front teeth left side upper jaw out	*"Mother" refers to Martha "Patsy" Davis who must have still been living; his father Vance Gonce had died on 1 May 1871.*
OFFENSE:	Bigamy	
COUNTY:	Stone	*"Wife" must refer to Martha Keithley, since Mary A. lived in Christian County.*
SENTENCE:	Two years from Aug. 27, 1879	
TERM OF COURT:	Oct. 1879	
WHEN RECEIVED:	Oct. 24, 1879	
EXPIRATION OF SENTENCE:	FULL TIME: Aug. 27, 1881 THREE FOURTHS TIME: Feb. 27, 1881	
REMARKS:	Discharged under 3/4 law Feb'y 28th 1881	

Doc was now almost 48 years old, had been married at least twice, fathered at least ten children, treated countless patients and delivered many babies, served as a Justice of the Peace, developed a short rap sheet, and served a term in the State Penitentiary for Bigamy. This would be enough of a story – if a somewhat cloudy one – for most people, but Doc was apparently just getting started.

Doc returns to Freedom

After his release from prison, Doc moved back to Highlandville with his wife Martha and their son Rolyn, and attempted to gradually rebuild his medical practice. In his absence, however, conditions had changed. Several more physicians were now practicing in the area, including Drs. E. Bedford

Brown, John Collins, and J. H. Fulbright[59]. The most significant change, however, was due to his reputation in Christian County, particularly in Finley Township. His wife Mary was well liked by many people in that area, which included Ozark and Nixa, and they were reluctant[60] to engage his services.

He was able to successfully resume his medical practice, however, and still treated patients in the same general area as before, which ranged more or less from Nixa and Ozark in the north to Ponce de Leon in the west and Walnut Shade in the south.

A little less than a year and a half after his parole, on 2 July 1882, Doc and Martha Keithley's second son (and Doc's eleventh child), Lester Olonzo Gonce, was born. The next two years passed without any recorded incidents.

The Murder of Charlie Keyser

Recall that Alexander Logan, whose second wife Charity had purchased Doc's farm on the White River as he was preparing for his Bigamy trial, had an older daughter Sarah Elizabeth [ID 4110]. By February of 1884, Sarah, who had married Charles Keyser on March 16, 1871, had just had her fifth child. Her husband Charlie, in addition to being a farmer and running a small general store, served as the town's second Postmaster. Charlie and his wife Sarah were both neighbors and patients of Doc's.

On Friday afternoon, the 27th of June in 1884, just before his youngest son's second birthday, Doc shot and killed Charlie. The incident, as reported by a local Ozark stringer, appeared in the Springfield newspaper (the only paper serving the Christian County area at the time) on the following Sunday.

The Springfield Daily Herald – Sunday Morning, June 29, 1884

CRIMES AND CASUALTIES

A Woman's Defamer Shot Dead By Her Husband

The Shooting of Charles Keyser at Ozark, Missouri

Special Telegraph to the Herald

OZARK, Mo, June 28 – About three o'clock yesterday afternoon Dr. A. R. Gonce shot and immediately killed Charles Keyser, a farmer living eleven miles southwest of Ozark. Keyser was considered a good man and law-abiding citizen. Dr. Gonce has served a term in the penitentiary and is said to be a quarrelsome man. Gonce gave himself up and is in jail at this place.

---

59 All three men would be called to testify in his later trial for murder.
60 As Thomas Norman later reminded Doc, "Christian County don't like you much anyway." See his testimony on Green County Archive Sheet (GCAS) 196, transcribed on page 136.

The subtitle "A Woman's Defamer Shot Dead By Her Husband" seems to have no obvious connection to the story about Charles Keyser or to any other story on the page, and apparently must have been warranted by some rumor about the murder that I haven't been able to discover.

We'll discuss some theories about that subtitle and comment on the "quarrelsome man" characterization a little later, but it seems appropriate at this point to first describe the incidents leading to the murder in more detail.

The circumstances that led to the murder of Charlie Keyser had begun a little over a month earlier. Sometime in the early spring, Doc diagnosed Charlie and his wife Sarah with gonorrhea, which at that time was treatable, but not curable, and could eventually lead to infection and even death. There was also then, as now, a social stigma attached to such a diagnosis. Interestingly, during the murder trial, Doc's defense attorney seemed to object to any mention of the victim being Doc's patient[61], although it isn't clear to me why he did that.

On Sunday morning, the 8th of June, Charlie showed up at Doc's front yard[62] and demanded to know why Doc had been spreading such malicious tales about him, suggesting that he and Doc "shoot it out" then and there if Doc wouldn't retract what he had said. Doc said that he didn't wish to "fuss with him." Doc's wife Martha intervened and Keyser left. John Nelson[63] saw

---

61 For example, see my transcription of Green County Archive Sheet (GCAS) 138 on page 178
62 See testimony of Doc's wife Martha Keithley Gonce on GCAS 145; also see Dr. Collins testimony on GCAS 197; these are shown on pages 170 and 135 respectively.
63 See the transcription of John Nelson's testimony (GCAS 165) on page 158.

Doc and Charlie arguing that morning, and said the argument went on for about ten minutes, but he couldn't make out what they were saying.

Doc later told his colleague Dr. John D. Collins about this incident[64], mentioning his diagnosis of "the clap" as the cause, and told Dr. Collins he was sorry he hadn't killed Keyser then, but that if Keyser came back again, he would do so. In Dr. Collins' version of the story, Doc Gonce said that he got Keyser to leave by putting his hand in his back pocket and cocking his pistol. Later testimony seems to indicate that Doc didn't actually have a pistol at that point, so it seems to me this was likely Doc's bravado speaking.

Whether Doc actually told anyone else about the gonorrhea diagnosis is unclear from the trial testimony, although Keyser himself told at least one person that Doc had *said* that about him[65].

According to "Mrs. M. C. Phillips[66]," Doc and his wife Martha's brother Ambrose Keithley were having dinner at her (Phillips') father's tavern in Highlandville sometime between the 11th and 13th. Mrs. Phillips testified that she overheard Doc say, "the Dutch around Highlandville ought to be killed and if he lived long enough he would kill some of them." The defense objected to this testimony, but it was permitted. Interestingly enough, on 15 May 1885, before the trial began, Mrs. Phillips had written a letter[67] to Doc's wife stating that she would "get out of the way" and not testify in the trial if she were given $50. There was also a clear implication that she had not even been asked to testify. The offer of a bribe by itself makes her story somewhat suspect, and Doc certainly knew that Keyser was German, and not Dutch.

Sometime between the 17th and 20th of June on what he described as "a dark, cloudy day", Francis P. Berry[68] was riding on his horse along the road by Keyser's house when he heard gunfire. The sound was close enough that his horse threw him. Berry claimed that the only reason the horse didn't bolt was that Berry's foot was caught in the stirrup[69]. Keyser ran up to him, apologizing profusely, and said that he had shot at him because he thought Berry was Dr. Gonce. Keyser reportedly then said that he intended to waylay Gonce and kill him, and that if Berry said anything about this incident, he would also be killed. The prosecution wasted no time in introducing several

---

64 See the transcription of Dr. Collins testimony (GCAS 197) on page 135.
65 Pleasant Maples, in his testimony, stated this clearly. See my transcription of his testimony (GCAS 158) on page 158.
66 See a transcription of her testimony (GCAS 195) on page 138.
67 The letter introduced by the defense is transcribed on GCAS 160 – see page 159.
68 See my transcription of Berry's testimony (GCAS 159) on page 159. Francis P. Berry was mentioned earlier in this paper on page 10.
69 This sounds like an extremely well trained and docile horse; having one's foot caught in a stirrup after being thrown by a startled horse doesn't usually end so benignly. Could this be one reason the Jury found Berry's story so hard to believe?

witnesses (including Dr. Collins) who testified that Berry was not the sort of person to be believed[70].

On Tuesday June 24th, Pleasant Maples had the conversation[71] alluded to earlier where Keyser asked if Maples had heard the scandalous tale Gonce had told about him. Keyser further said that Gonce had to die. Maples didn't mention this to anyone until after the murder, likely thinking it was bluster.

On Friday morning, the 27th of June, Doc Gonce left Highlandville[72] on horseback to visit a man named George Wilson, a patient of his who lived in the Ponce de Leon area just across the Stone county border. At more or less the same time, Wiley Cloud, a neighbor of Wilson's who knew both Charlie Keyser and Doc Gonce, headed north from Ponce on his way to Highlandville.

At Charlie Keyser's farm, which was roughly half way between Highlandville and Ponce de Leon, both Keyser and Will Larkins[73], his hired hand, had begun plowing the corn fields at around 8:00 am – Keyser in the southeast, and Larkins in the northwest, about 200 yards from Keyser's house[74].

Wiley Cloud arrived at Keyser's farm first, at about 10:00 am[75], and stopped to inquire about purchasing a bottle of German Syrup, apparently used as a medicine. Sarah Keyser, who talked to Wiley, called out to Charlie in the field to ask what he charged for a bottle. They haggled a bit over the price, Cloud saying he could get it cheaper in Highlandville. At about this time, they could see someone coming on horseback down the road from the northeast.

Keyser asked Cloud if he could identify the rider, and Cloud said that he thought it was Doc Gonce. According to Cloud, Keyser responded "God damn him; I said I would kill him and I will do so."

Doc Gonce stopped to ask Cloud how his neighbor George Wilson was doing[76]. As Cloud responded, saying that Wilson was not doing well and was waiting for Doc to arrive, Keyser threatened Gonce, but was prevented by his wife Sarah from doing anything at that time. According to Cloud she said

---

70 See the list of names (GCAS 139) on page 48 of my transcription of the murder trial.
71 See my transcription of Pleasant Maples' testimony (GCAS 158) on page 158.
72 See the Map on page 64 for help in following the day's events.
73 See my transcription of William Larkins' testimony (GCAS 187) on page 142.
74 Since the corn was already growing but not mature at the time, we can only assume that they were clearing out weeds from between the rows. The saying and expectation that corn is "knee high by the fourth of July" seems to have been just as true then as it is now.
75 See my transcription of Wiley Cloud's testimony (GCAS 168) on page 156.
76 See my transcription of Wiley Cloud's affidavit (GCAS 82) and testimony (GCAS 162) on pages 133 and 156.

"don't do that Charley; you will ruin yourself." Both Gonce and Cloud soon left, with Keyser yelling threats at Doc[77].

By about 11:30 that morning, Larkins and Keyser had taken a break from plowing and Larkins, who left at that time, indicated that Keyser was then sitting on the porch with his family[78].

Spenser Smith, who claimed to be traveling north with his invalid wife in a wagon by Keyser's house at around this time, testified[79] that he stopped by Keyser's to water his horses, but Wiley Cloud didn't encounter him, and Mrs. Keyser stated[80] that she didn't remember Smith stopping there that day. Based on the trial testimony, I find it hard to reconcile Smith's statements with other events and testimony of other witnesses, and this is just the first example of many oddities in Smith's story.

A little later, probably after midday, Wiley Cloud again passed by Keyser's house in the opposite direction while returning south to Stone County. He reported having observed some disturbance in the bushes by the road passing Keyser's farm, as if, he said, someone were hiding there[81].

By 2:00 pm, William Larkins had returned to Keyser's farm[82], and he and Keyser resumed plowing. Spenser Smith claims to have left Keyser's around this time but, again, no one else reported seeing him.

After arriving back in Stone County, Wiley Cloud encountered Doc Gonce and told him about seeing what he thought might have been Keyser hiding in the bushes[83].

Fearing that Charlie Keyser was planning to ambush him, Doc decided to arm himself. He asked Thomas Norman, whom he encountered going to dinner, if he could borrow a revolver. Norman refused to loan him any weapon saying, "you're a man who would use it.[84]" Norman suggested that Doc return home by a different route, although I haven't been able to identify what practical route would have been available then, since this area of the country is quite mountainous. Norman also made the statement "Christian County don't like you much anyway,[85]" which seems incongruous in context, but may indicate how Doc's status in the community had suffered due to his recent bigamy, divorce, and incarceration.

---

77   See my transcription of Wiley Cloud's affidavit (GCAS 83 and 84) on pages 134 and 134.
78   See my transcription of William Larkins' testimony (GCAS 187) on page 142.
79   See my transcription of Spenser Smith's testimony (GCAS 178) on page 149.
80   See my transcription of Mrs. Keyser's cross-examination (GCAS 174) on page 152.
81   See my transcription of Wiley Cloud's testimony (GCAS 163) on page 157.
82   See my transcription of Spenser Smith's testimony (GCAS 178) on page 149.
83   See my transcription of Wiley Cloud's affidavit (GCAS 84) and testimony (GCAS 163) on pages 134 and 157.
84   See my transcription of Thomas Norman's testimony (GCAS 196) on page 136.
85   ibid.

Doc eventually was able to borrow a breech-loading shotgun from J. Winn; when Newton Cox ran into Doc in the late afternoon, he observed that Doc was carrying this weapon[86].

Doc then began his return to Highlandville, but stopped off at his eldest son William McClellan Gonce's house, which was about a half mile south of Keyser's farm. According to his daughter-in-law, Doc was obviously disturbed by something. Doc explained that he had armed himself because he was afraid of being ambushed by Keyser[87]. Doc's two oldest grandsons James and Abraham went up the road to see if they could tell where Keyser was; they saw that he was plowing in his field and reported this back to Doc.

Hearing the report from his grandsons, Doc decided that an ambush was unlikely, so he proceeded north, which took him by Keyser's field[88]. It was now between 4:00 and 5:00pm. At her farm, Sarah Keyser was sitting on the porch with her oldest daughter Minnie and saw Doc pass their gate going towards Highlandville. She told Minnie that she was afraid of what might happen, and began heading out towards the gate[89].

It isn't clear what happened when Doc reached the area where Keyser was plowing, but he and Keyser evidently exchanged a few words. Doc said that he asked Keyser whether or not he intended to kill him, and that Charlie replied, "Yes, by God I do."[90] Keyser was standing with his left hand still on the plow handle, but reached back with his right hand. Apparently assuming Keyser was reaching for a pistol[91], Doc, still on horseback, fired the shotgun at least once, hitting Keyser in the chest and left arm. After being shot, Keyser stumbled a bit and then fell to the ground. Doc immediately began riding off towards Ozark, intending to turn himself in to the sheriff there. Larkins, who was plowing in a nearby field, came running and found Keyser's wife turning her husband on his side. Keyser gave a few short gasps and died shortly after Larkins arrived. A shotgun pellet had pierced his heart.

Doc's daughter-in-law Martha reported hearing a shot about fifteen minutes after Doc left her house,[92] tending to confirm the times given above.

Larkins removed Keyser's horse from the plow and set out north to get some relatively nearby neighbors Carter and G. W. Flood to assist him[93].

---

86 See my transcription of Newton Cox's testimony (GCAS 194) on page 139.
87 See my transcription of Martha Sims Gonce's testimony (GCAS 194, 190, 189, & 188) on pages 139 and 140.
88 See my transcription of Martha Sims Gonce's testimony (GCAS 190) on page 139.
89 See my transcription of Sarah Keyser's testimony (GCAS 173, 175, 174, & 176) on pages 151 and 152.
90 See my transcription of this portion of Doc Gonce's cross-examination (GCAS 140) on page 174.
91 Doc made no claim that he actually saw a pistol – just that Keyser reached back like he was going to grab one. See more of his cross-examination (GCAS 141) on page 174.
92 See my transcription of Martha Sims Gonce's testimony (GCAS 189) on page 140.
93 See my transcription of William Larkins' cross-examination (GCAS 186) on page 143.

Spenser Smith, meanwhile, claimed to have heard the report of a gun when he was less than a half-mile north of Keyser's farm[94]; he said that Doc overtook him about eight or ten minutes after the shot. Doc must have mentioned what had happened, because Smith then went to get Flood and William Forbes. This group met Larkins and Carter and proceeded to Keyser's farm. Judge Larkin (apparently no relation to William Larkins) saw and apparently overheard Smith talking to Doc[95], and he and George Clevinger headed to Keyser's around the same time.

Spenser Smith claims all this took place at about 3:00pm, which meant that he had only gone about half a mile in the hours since he claimed to have left Keyser's. Other witnesses seem to put the gunfire and Keyser's death somewhat later, meaning Smith's progress must have been extremely slow. Throughout the testimony, it is apparent that there are many discrepancies between Spenser's time-lines and everyone else's; indeed, it could be argued that his own timelines seem internally inconsistent.

D. J. White, on his way south from Highlandville at around 4:00 pm, met Doc Gonce coming north about ¼ mile north of Keyser's. Doc reportedly told him "you will find a dead man down the road." White had heard in Highlandville that Keyser had attempted to kill Doc and, ascertaining that the deceased was indeed Keyser, asked if Doc had killed him. Doc replied "yes," he "had killed the damn son of a bitch."[96]

When the group arrived at Keyser's, they began examining the land, the body, the clothes, etc[97]. William Forbes found a plow wrench in Keyser's right pocket, and tobacco in his left pocket.[98]

Based on his original Affidavit for Continuance, Doc had apparently been told by Spenser Smith that Smith had seen someone possibly remove a weapon from Keyser's pocket and return it to the house[99], but I found no record of Smith's testifying to this at the trial. I am assuming that what Smith may have seen was William Forbes removing the plow wrench from Keyser's right pocket[100]. It is certainly possible that he learned later that what was found was a wrench, but no explanation was presented at the trial for why such an item would have been removed that I could find.

---

94 See my transcription of Spenser Smith's testimony (GCAS 177 and 178) on page 149.
95 See my transcription of Judge (Judge is his name, not his profession) Larkin's testimony (GCAS 178) on page 149.
96 See my transcription of D. J. White's testimony (GCAS 169) on page 153.
97 I have been unable to learn if this was common practice, or the residents of the Highlandville area were all just anachronistic CSI wannabes.
98 See my transcription of William Forbes' testimony (GCAS 181 and 184) on pages 144 and 145. Pay particular attention to the idea that a plow wrench or clovis pin was found in Keyser's pocket.
99 See my transcription of Doc's affidavit (GCAS 62) on page 125.
100 See my transcription of William Forbes' testimony (GCAS 181 and 184) on pages 144 and 145.

Each of those present when Keyser's body was being examined seems to have acknowledged the presence of most of the others but, curiously, no one mentioned Spenser Smith's "invalid wife," who he had said was traveling with him.

Two or three hours after the murder[101], Doctors E. B. Brown and Fulbright arrived to examine the body. Dr. Brown determined that there were 44 holes in the body from No. 2 shot, but that none of these were in the right arm[102]. He determined by probing the wound tracks that a single one of the pellets that had entered around Keyser's nipple continued into his heart and would have caused "almost instant death." Dr. Brown further stated "If the right arm was hanging by the side from the [*illegible*] of the shot, some of them (i.e. the pellets) would have struck the arm," although this testimony was struck out[103]. Dr. Fulbright testified that, based on the "inward, downward, and backward"[104] wound pattern, the shooter must have stood facing the victim and to his right. The defense objected to all of this testimony, claiming none of it was scientific or factual. Here again I don't understand why the defense objected, since the testimony seems to support Doc's contention that Keyser must have had his arm behind him (or at least back along his right side) when the gun was fired – thus lending some credence to Doc's claims of self-defense. The Indictment[105] itself says the wounds were inflicted "upon the right side of the said Charles Keysser."

As far as I can determine, there were no newspapers in the local areas where Doc Gonce lived and practiced, and the Springfield Daily Herald seemed to have served the entire area where Doc lived and worked, so it is appropriate to comment on their reporting of the murder in the article illustrated and transcribed above.

The first header for the article, "A Woman's Defamer Shot Dead By Her Husband" would seem to suggest that Charlie Keyser was killed by Doc because Charlie had defamed Doc's wife Martha Keithley. If this is the case, it seems a little odd that there isn't anything in the trial records or other contemporary sources mentioning or even suggesting such defamation.

If, however, one assumes that the author (or his editor) had meant to say "A Woman's Defamer Shoots Her Husband Dead," which some of those I've corresponded with *speculate*[106], another scenario presents itself.

---

101 See my transcription of Judge Larkin's testimony (GCAS 181) on page 144.
102 See my transcription of Dr. Brown's testimony (GCAS 184) on page 145.
103 See my transcription of Dr. Brown's testimony (GCAS 182) on page 146.
104 See my transcription of Dr. Brown's testimony (GCAS 184) on page 145. This seems perfectly consistent for the results of a shot from someone on horseback.
105 See my transcription of the Indictment (GCAS 57) on page 120.
106 Note the word "speculate." There is no evidence I am aware of to support this contention, although it does make more sense than the implied meaning of the reporter's header.

This speculative but intriguing scenario can be summarized as follows:

> Charlie's difficulties with Doc's diagnosis initially revolved around his belief that, since he had never cheated on his wife Sarah, he couldn't possibly have contracted a venereal disease. When, after a little thought, he realized that there was, in fact, at least one possible explanation[107], his approach to dealing with this realization was to assume that Doc was indirectly defaming Sarah's reputation.

As for the implication in the article that Doc was "said to be a quarrelsome man," it is interesting that the trial records show many witnesses testifying that Charlie Keyser was certainly "quarrelsome," but none that referred to Doc Gonce in any similar fashion[108]. When describing Keyser, witnesses used the terms "loud spoken man" (Wiley Cloud; see GCAS-163[109]), "quarrelsome man" (Pleasant Maples; see GCAS-158[110]), "overbearing, high-tempered man" (Wm. F. Brown, a former Justice of the Peace; see GCAS-148[111]), "quarrelsome high-tempered man" (Frank Kentling; also on GCAS-148), "quarrelsome dangerous man" (Martin Blyen; see GCAS-149[112]) and "quarrelsome and dangerous man" (J. W. Kirk; see GCAS-143[113]).

Doc Gonce was indicted by the Christian County Grand Jury for Murder in the 1st Degree on 27 August 1884, and his trial in Christian County began a few days later. He formally pled "not guilty" on September 2nd, and filed for a Continuance, which was granted[114]. He returned to Court at the opening of the next session, and filed for a Change of Venue on 23 February 1885, which was also granted.

In January of 1885[115], Doc's wife Martha gave birth to their third and last child together, a daughter named Anna Belle.

It isn't very clear to me why, if the purpose of the Change of Venue were to avoid local prejudices, a move to Greene County would have had any discernable effect. The Greene County Circuit Court met in Springfield, not much further up the road from Ozark than Doc normally traveled in his daily

---

107 …and, if Charlie had indeed been completely faithful to Sarah, there was really only one explanation.
108 This is certainly not to suggest that Doc himself was not quarrelsome, only that the contrast between Charlie and Doc implied by the reporter was likely minimal. Doc's actions during his earlier Bigamy trial certainly suggest at least the possibility of temper tantrums on his part.
109 Refer to transcriptions on page 157.
110 Refer to transcriptions on page 158.
111 Refer to transcriptions on page 169.
112 Refer to transcriptions on page 169.
113 Refer to transcriptions on page 171.
114 See my transcription of Doc's affidavit (GCAS 60) on page 123.
115 This date was reported on the 1900 census (NARC t623 Roll 474 Page 9a). Doc was in jail continuously from the time of the murder in June 1884. Martha was said to have attended the murder trial with all three of her children (The Atchison, Kansas Daily Globe report of June 11, 1885).

business. The Springfield paper served both areas and, as we know from the history of the Highlandville area, this was a heavily traveled corridor in an otherwise very mountainous region. Nonetheless, the trial in Springfield began, first with another continuance, and then in earnest on the 4th of June, 1885. Transcripts of the trial are shown in Section III beginning on page 113.

Toward the end of the trial, Doc's defense attorney introduced testimony by two persons that the Juror J. D. Bryant had expressed an opinion as to Doc's guilt prior to the trial. J. P. Simpson[116] testified that Bryant had said Doc "ought to be hung," and George A. Porter[117] related that Bryant had said, "Gonce was guilty of murder and ought to be hung for it." Porter, by the way, was an ex-police officer. Once Bryant swore that neither of these reports was true, the court accepted this.

The questions posed to witnesses by the juror J. C. Mitchell during the trial[118] also seem to me to show a decided lack of impartiality.

At the conclusion of the trial, the jury returned their verdict:

"We the Jury find the defendant guilty of murder in the second degree and assess his punishment at imprisonment for the term of 30 years in the Penitentiary. – W.L. White Foreman, and at the instance and request of the Defendant, the names of the jurors of said Jury were called by the Clerk, and asked, If this was his verdict; each and everyone of said jurors answering for himself in the affirmative"[119].

The end of the trial and the guilty verdict were reported as far away as Atchison, Kansas. I have been unable to locate any extant copies of the Springfield Daily Herald for 1885, but a copy of the story that appeared in the Atchison Globe on June 11, 1885 is shown below and on the next page.

The Atchison Globe; Atchison, Kansas

SPRINGFIELD, MO., June 11

The trial of Dr. A. R. Gonce, charged with the murder of Charley Keyser near Highlandville, Christian County, one year ago, began in the circuit court at this place one week ago and terminated last evening, when the case was given to the jury who agreed on a verdict of guilty of murder in the second degree and fixed the prisoner's punishment at thirty years' imprisonment in the penitentiary. The homicide grew out of an old feud between the two men, which culminated on the 27th of last June, at which time Gonce rode up to the field where Keyser was plowing and shot him dead with a shotgun. Gonce was immediately arrested, and since that time has been confined in the jail at this place. His wife and three little children were present with him during the trial. Gonce served one term in the penitentiary a few years ago on the charge of bigamy.

---

116 See my transcription of Simpson's testimony (GCAS 117) on page 70.
117 See my transcription of Porter's affidavit (GCAS 113) on page 67.
118 Apparently, Jurors were permitted to ask questions of witnesses in Missouri in those days. As an example, see GCAS 144, transcribed on page 171, where he sounds like a prosecutor rather than a supposedly impartial juror.
119 Greene County, Missouri Archives: Book 27, Page 140; also see GCAS 86.

The feud, of course, was not as "old" as the article implies, and Doc actually turned himself in, but the reporting here seemed more factual than the earlier report in the Springfield Daily Herald.

After several attempts at a reversal of the verdict or a new trial[120], Doc entered the penitentiary to begin serving his sentence on 15 June 1885.

Due to, among other things, the destruction of the 1890 censuses by fire, the whereabouts of Doc's families during this period are not clear, but later records seem to indicate that they all remained in the same general area.

In July of 1893, just over eight years after entering prison, Doc managed to obtain a pardon from then Governor W. J. Stone. Doc was then sixty years old. The rationale for his pardon seems suspect, given his activities after his release, but the extant records relating to the pardon should be permitted to speak for themselves. The first is a report from the Penitentiary's physician, testifying to Doc's obviously deteriorating physical condition

Physician's Letter to Governor regarding Pardon

Office of Physician
Missouri State Penitentiary

Jefferson City, MO: July 12, 1893

Hon. W. J. Stone:
Governor:

I have today examined A. R. Gonce and find him afflicted with infirmities and damage of heart. He has been in hospital for about two years. He now more than when admitted is unable to walk or even to stand without support and then only for a few minutes. I have filled out regular [blank?], which is attached.

Respt,

J. L. Hayes, MD

On a separate pro-forma document dated 11 July 1893 and submitted with the Pardon application, J. L. Pace, the Warden at the time, simply stated "Conduct Good." This document otherwise gave the same details provided in the Penitentiary Record transcribed below.

These recommendations proceeded through channels, with a final endorsement of the recommendation for pardon coming from the Board of Inspectors.

---

120 ... all of which are covered in Section III of this book.

Board of Inspector's Endorsement to Governor regarding Pardon
Date Unknown; approximately 12 July 1893

MISSOURI STATE PENITENTIARY
OFFICE OF PRISON PHYSICIAN
CITY OF JEFFERSON

189__

To the Honorable the Board of Inspectors of the Missouri State Penitentiary:

    Gentlemen: In compliance with the provisions of section 9265 of the Revised Statutes of Missouri, 1889, I hereby certify that *A. R. Gonce* a convict, (Registered No. *5018*) now confined in the Hospital of this institution is afflicted with *Chronic functional disease of heart and rheumatism* a disease of such character as to be incurable, and that further confinement will necessarily greatly endanger or shorten his life.

    The prison record of the convict above referred to is hereto attached.

    Very Respectfully Sumitted,

J. L. Thorpe, Acting
Prison Physician.

TO THE GOVERNOR:

    We, the undersigned, Inspectors of the Missouri State Penitentiary, hereby recommend the pardon of the above mentioned convict upon the facts stated in the certificate of the Prison Physician.

Lon V. Stephens
State Treasurer.

R. F. Walker
Attorney-General.

State Auditor.
Comprising the Board of Inspectors.

12 July 1893 Pardon by Governor

#315

Pardon of

A. R. Gonce

Sentenced at the

May Tr 1885 of the Circuit Ct Greene Co

30 years for

Murger[121] 2nd Degree

E/74

and Pardon issued

To Secretary State:

On the recommendations of the prison physician & Inspectors, & also of the Warden and other officials of the penitentiary, who inform me that the within named convict has now been in the hospital for some two years and because he is now an old and broken man, after many years imprisonment and because his son-in-law L. J. Chrisman agrees to take and care for him, I do hereby pardon said A. R. Gonce. Issue habeus accordingly.

(signed) W. J. Stone, Gov.

---

121 Yes, it really says "Murger" quite clearly; as can be seen on the image above right.

Doc's penitentiary record is shown below. It is interesting to compare some of the particulars to those reported on his prison record from 1881 shown on page 28. What was earlier described as "gray hair" was now "dark and wavy," an interesting progression. His complexion was now "ruddy" rather than "dark," not surprising after eight years in confinement, and he was now recognized as a physician rather than simply a laborer.

Penitentiary Record for Abraham Rudolph Gonce (Second Visit)		
Missouri State Archives – Prisoner 5018		12 JUL 1893
NUMBER:	5018	
NAME:	A. R. Gonce	
AGE:	54	*Doc was actually 52 when he entered the penitentiary and just over 60 when he was released.*
NATIVITY:	Tennessee	
TRADE:	Physician	
HEIGHT:	5 foot 8 1/2 inches	
LENGTH FOOT:	10 1/2 inches	
HAIR:	Dark and Wavy	
EYES:	Brown	
COMPLEXION:	Ruddy	
WHISKERS WORN:	Full Beard	
RELIGION:	None	
HABITS OF LIFE:	Temperate	
EDUCATION:	Reads and Writes	
FORMER IMPRISONMENT: One Term in MO Pen		
MARKS AND SCARS: Parents dead, Wife and family at Highlandville, Christian Co MO. Head bald. Scar on right eyebrow, Small scar lower part left face, Small scar left shoulder, Little finger left hand Crooked - Weight		*"Wife" refers to Martha Keithley, since Mary A. lived in Christian County.*
OFFENSE:	Murder 2d Degree	
COUNTY:	Greene	
SENTENCE:	Thirty years from June 15, 1885	
TERM OF COURT:	May 1885	
WHEN RECEIVED:	June 6, 1885	
EXPIRATION OF SENTENCE: FULL TIME: June 15, 1915 THREE FOURTHS TIME: Dec 15, 1907		
REMARKS:	Pardoned by Gov. Stone July 12 - 1893	

During his incarceration, his wife Martha Keithley divorced him, although she is still listed in the Penitentiary Record as living with her family in Highlandville. In 1893, she moved to Kansas, although I have been unable to determine the exact dates for either of these actions or whether they were simultaneous or directly related to Doc's impending release.

Northern Christian County now had its own newspaper, which dutifully, if a little floridly, reported Doc's pardon:

Dr. A. R. Gonce Pardoned out of the Penitentiary to Die	
The Christian County Republican Exact Date Unknown	July 1893[122]
After years of weary, almost hopeless waiting, Dr. A. R. Gonce, once so well known in Ozark, is again free from the restraints of prison life, having been pardoned out of the penitentiary, where he was confined for nearly ten years for the murder of Charles Kaiser, who lived a short distance south of Highlandville in this county. The reader of the REPUBLICAN remembers the history of the crime. A slight difficulty on the morning of the fatal day between Gonce and his victim seemed but a slight provocation for the bloody deed that followed. Gonce rode all the way to Ponce De Leon that morning after the little quarrel with Kaiser. There he borrowed a gun, as ugly a shooting iron as was ever exhibited in court, and loaded it with a heavy charge of shot. Putting the gun across his saddle front Gonce turned the head of his horse homeward and rode about eight miles before he reached Mr. Kaiser's place. Kaiser was plowing in the lane, through which Gonce aimed, and perhaps unmindful of the peril, without dismounting or checking the pace of his horse, aimed and fired and killed Kaiser who was at the plow handles. It was a shooting crime, and the jury had a strong leaning toward the gallows when the case went to trial in Greene County on a change of venue. Ninety-nine years in the penitentiary seemed a reasonable compromise to the jurors that urged the death penalty, and Gonce was sent up for life as everyone supposed. He had been in the penitentiary once before but had not learned to like the place. He longed to be out and kept fighting for liberty. He has written many graphic letters for the newspaper, detailing as far as a prisoner is allowed to go, the horrors of penitentiary life. The late convict is now a confirmed invalid, having consumption well defined. His son-in-law, Fayette Chrisman has agreed to become the old man's support during his last days. Chrisman and J. J. Burton went to Jefferson City Monday[123] to bring home the doctor. The shooting happened about 1884.	*Actually it was no more than eight!* *As is often the case with this type of reporting, the story was written without benefit of much, if any, research.* *...actually for 30 years.* *...for Bigamy, between 24 Oct 79 to 28 Feb 81.* *Lafayette J. Chrisman married Doc's daughter Mary Ellen (Ella) Gonce in June 1876.*

Based on the examination of the prison Doctor and the Governor's conclusions after reviewing the findings of his prison inspection board, we are left with the impression that parolee Abraham Rudolph Gonce, now slightly more than 60 years old, was infirm, a cripple, and possibly close to death. Dr. Hayes, the prison physician, said that Doc had heart damage and

---

122 As near as I can determine, there are no extant original or microfilm copies of the Christian County Republican from this period in any Archive or Library in the United States. If anyone knows of one, I would appreciate knowing about it. This transcription of the article was provided by another Gonce researcher.

123 The first Monday after the 12 July 1893 date mentioned above was 17 July 1893. If this is the case, the article must have appeared in the Christian County Republican shortly after the 17th of July.

was unable to walk or even stand without support, and then only briefly. Governor Stone referred to Doc as an old and broken man.

Doc's Resurrection and New Marriage

Once released, however, Doc seems to have made an immediate and quite remarkable recovery[124]. Doc immediately moved to Kirbyville in southern Taney County and moved in with Charity Logan, who was now a 44 year-old widow. Because they were married[125] on July 26th, a mere nine days after Doc's release, we can only assume that they must have had some contact or correspondence during Doc's incarceration. Charity was still living on the farm by the White River that she had purchased from Doc and his first wife Mary some sixteen years earlier. What prompted Charity to consider marriage with the now "crippled, old and broken man" who had killed her stepdaughter's husband seems to be a mystery. One has to wonder what her relationship was with her older stepdaughter Sarah Keyser at this time, and whether Sarah knew of or approved of the marriage.

Third Divorce

Within less than two years, however, it became apparent to Charity that Doc's main interest in the marriage was in having her deed the White River farm property back[126] to him, and she subsequently divorced him in 1895[127].

"Doc" apparently didn't remain alone for very long after Charity left him. In June of 1896, at age 63, he had another daughter, Aria E. Gonce [ID 3999], with an 18 year-old named Susan T. Hargrove [ID 3998]. Susan was the youngest of nine children of William [ID 2879] and Lucinda [ID 4083] Hargrove, who had also migrated from Tennessee to Missouri in about 1869[128], but there is no indication whether Doc had known William Hargrove when they lived in Tennessee during their childhoods[129].

At some point, likely around the early part of 1896, Doc apparently began selling liquor. He had done this much earlier in his career although, at the time, being a recognized physician, he was able to color it with blackberry juice and pass it off as medicine[130]. Now, however, his liquor sales seem to have brought him in confrontation with the authorities on a regular basis throughout 1896. Records of his arrests for selling liquor in Taney County without a license can be found[131], but are not reproduced here.

---

124 Sadly for him, the Academy Award hadn't been invented yet.
125 "Missouri Marriages 1851-1900"; Jordan Dodd; Liahona Research
126 See page 32 of the book "The Granny Woman of the Hills" by Ella Ingenthron Dunn, a portion of which is reproduced on page 52.
127 Missouri Judicial Index: Stone County Box 11 (Microfilm No C 37195), Folder 77, Case 48
128 This is based on the ages and birthplaces of their children as reported on the 1880 Census; LDS Microfilm Series 1254738, Page 10.
129 Abraham Rudolph Gonce was less than two years older than his new bride's father.
130 The Ozark Headliner; 16 August 1973; page 1. This article is transcribed on page 52.
131 Missouri Judicial Index (Microfilm No C 37193): Taney County Box 3, Folder 76, Case 6; ibid Folder 77, Case 5; ibid Folder 78, Case 13; and in Box 4, Folder 3, Case 3.

Doc and Susan T. Hargrove married on 9 June 1897[132], a year or so after the birth of their first child Aria. They settled in Jasper Township[133] and their second child, another daughter, Cora B. Gonce ID 4000, was born in March of 1899.

12th Census of the United States – 1900
National Archives Microfilm Series t623 Roll 905 Pages 10b & 11a
Residence is Jasper Twp; Taney County; Missouri   Transcription below

Abraham Rudolph Gonce with his last wife and their first two children in 1900; Aria is on the bottom of page 10b and Cora is at the top of page 11a. (Many lines have been removed from the top image to save space)

My ID	Surname	Name	Age	Month and Year of Birth
2883	Gonce	Abraham R.	67	May 1832
3998	Gonce	Susie H.	21	Mar 1879
3999	Gonce	Aria E.	3	Jun 1896
4000	Gonce	Cora B.	1	Mar 1899

On 8 April 1899, a month after Cora's birth, Doc's second wife Martha A. Keithley died in the town of Sterling in Rice County, Kansas.

---

132 These dates are based on "Marriage Records, Stone County, Missouri 1851 – 1900"; Loren Loden; Volume 7 - No. 7 and the 1900 Census National Archives Microfilm Series t623, Roll 905, Page 10b.
133 Taney County, Missouri

On 10 November 1900, too late to appear in the earlier census, James Tilford Gonce [ID 4001], Doc and Susie's first and only son, was born.

Two more daughters, Myrtle [ID 4002], and Nora [ID 4003], were born in about 1903 and 1907 respectively. The 1910 Census indicates that Susie is the mother of 5 with 5 living, suggesting they had no other children.

Thirteenth Census of the United States – 1910
National Archives Microfilm Series t624 Roll 827 Page 3a
Residence is Swan Township; Taney County; Missouri

This was the last census in which Doc and Susie appear, and shows all five of their children.

My ID	Surname	Proper Name	Age	Implied Year of Birth
2883	Gonce	A.R.	76	about 1834
3998	Gonce	Susie	30	about 1880
3999	Gonce	Ora (actually Aria)	13	about 1897
4000	Gonce	Cora	11	about 1899
4001	Gonce	James T.	9	about 1901
4002	Gonce	Myrtle	7	about 1903
4003	Gonce	Nora	3	about 1907

From Left to Right: Cora B. Gonce [ID 4000], Aria E. Gonce [ID 3999] and Doctor Abraham Rudolph Gonce
(Credit for this photograph is given in the article quoted on page 52.)

In spite of the significant difference in their ages, Susie, then only about 32 years old, died before Doc did. Her tombstone gives her year of death as 1911, consistent with Abraham's death certificate[134], which lists him as a widower at the time of his death in 1912.

Death Certificate of Doc Gonce

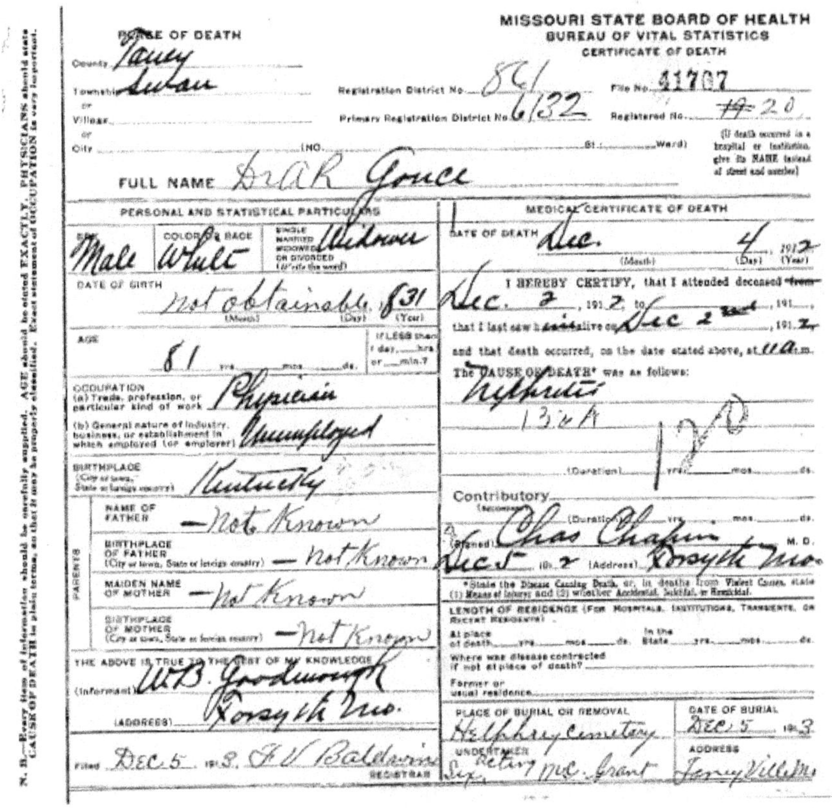

MISSOURI STATE BOARD OF HEALTH
BUREAU OF VITAL STATISTICS
CERTIFICATE OF DEATH

PLACE OF DEATH
County Taney
Township Swan
Registration District No. 861
File No. 41707
Primary Registration District No. 6132
Registered No. 20

FULL NAME Drak Gonce

PERSONAL AND STATISTICAL PARTICULARS
Sex Male
Color or Race White
Single, Married, Widowed or Divorced: Widower
Date of Birth: not obtainable 831
Age: 81 yrs.
Occupation (a) Trade, profession, or particular kind of work: Physician
(b) General nature of industry, business, or establishment in which employed (or employer): Unemployed
Birthplace: Kentucky
Name of Father: Not Known
Birthplace of Father: Not Known
Maiden Name of Mother: Not Known
Birthplace of Mother: Not Known
The above is true to the best of my knowledge
(Informant) W.B. Goodnough
(Address) Forsyth Mo.
Filed Dec 5 1913 F.W. Baldwin Registrar

MEDICAL CERTIFICATE OF DEATH
Date of Death: Dec. 4, 1912
I HEREBY CERTIFY, that I attended deceased from Dec. 2, 1912, to Dec 2nd, 1912, that I last saw h alive on Dec 2nd, 1912, and that death occurred, on the date stated above, at 11 a.m.
The CAUSE OF DEATH was as follows:
Nephritis
Contributory
(Signed) Chas Chapin M.D.
Dec 5, 1912 (Address) Forsyth Mo.
Place of Burial or Removal: Helphrey Cemetery
Date of Burial: Dec 5 1913
Undertaker: Retired Mc Grant
Address: Taneyville Mo.

Death Certificate of Abraham Rudolph Gonce showing his death from Nephritis (Kidney Inflammation). Note that the filing and burial occurred almost a year after his death. Doc was only 79 years old, not 81.

A transcription of Doc's death certificate is provided on the next page. It should be pointed out that the date of filing and the date of burial are shown to be a year after the date of death, but I haven't been able to determine whether this is a clerical error or indicates some actual delay in the burial.

134 Shown below and transcribed on the next page.

Missouri State Board of Health; Bureau of Vital Statistics Swan Township – Taney County			
Registration District No	861	File No	41767
Primary Registration District No	6132	Registered No	20
FULL NAME	Dr. A. R. Gonce; Male White Widower, born 1831 in Kentucky; age 81; unemployed Physician; parents names and birthplaces unknown.		
Date of Death	Dec 4, 1912	Cause of Death	Nephritis
Date Filed	Dec 5, 1913		
Date of Burial	Dec 5, 1913	Place of Burial	Helphrey Cemetery

Doctor Abraham Rudolph Gonce and his final wife Susan T. Hargrove are buried in the Helphrey Cemetery, which is located on County Road AA just north of Taneyville in Taney County. Their graves are side by side in plot T24N-R19W-S22, and marked "Dr. A. R. Gonce; 1912" and "S. T. Gonce; 1911"

"Doc" and Susie's tombstone

Aside from the postscripts and miscellany immediately below, this ends the biography of my third-cousin-four-times-removed. Sections II and III provide transcripts of his trials for Bigamy (page 73) and Murder (page 113). Section IV on page 209 discusses some of Doc's outlaw descendants whose exploits seem to represent a legacy of sorts, and Section V on page 243 gives details of the Bright Murders[135].

---

135 Doc's son Lester Olonzo Gonce married Sarah Jane Bright, whose father shot and killed her mother and who was subsequently hanged by a vigilante mob for that crime.

Postscripts

Obituary of Mrs. Sarah E. Keysser	No image
Christian County Republican 30 October 1925	Oct 1925
Mrs. Sarah E. Keysser, aged 78 years, 11 months and 6 days, died at her home, 3 miles southwest of Highlandville on Saturday, October 4, 1925. Funeral services were held at the Highlandville Christian church at 1:00 o'clock p.m. Monday, conducted by Rev. James W. White with interment in the I.O.O.F. cemetery at Ozark, beside her husband, Chas. Keysser who, it will be remembered by old-timers, was killed by Doc Gonce nearly 40 years ago. The deceased was a sister of the late G.W. Logan of Ozark and leaves one brother, John Logan, living in Arkansas. She leaves one son and four daughters, besides many grandchildren and other relatives.	*Sarah was the daughter of Alexander Logan and his first wife. He later married Charity Wiggins. The irony is that Charity married "Doc" after he was paroled for killing her stepdaughter Sarah's husband.*

Note that the spelling of the surname Keysser differs from the spelling used in the Christian County centennial book referenced earlier. "Nearly 40 years ago" implies a date after 1885 but, as mentioned above, Bright Nicholson replaced Charlie Keyser as Postmaster in 1884, so this may have been a "canned" obituary prepared prior to Mrs. Keysser's death.

Rolyn and Myrtle Gonce

Although Doc's second wife Martha Keithley had left Missouri for Kansas in 1893, ten years prior to the birth of Doc and Susie's daughter Myrtle, at least one of her sons must have remained in Missouri. It is otherwise difficult to explain how Susie's daughter Myrtle, who wasn't born until 1903, came to know Martha's son (and Myrtle's half-brother) Rolyn.

Myrtle was known to be living with Rolyn, twenty-five years her senior, in Oklahoma at the time of the 1930 census[136]. It is interesting to speculate on how this came about, but I have as yet uncovered nothing that would provide a clue. Nonetheless, they must have known each other in Missouri.[137]

Headstone for Rolyn Gonce, son of Martha Keithley, and his half-sister Myrtle, daughter of Susan Hargrove in the Odd Fellows Cemetery in Ponca City, Kay County, Oklahoma.

---

136 National Archives Microfilm Series t626 Roll 1909 Page 8a.
137 It seems way too far-fetched to suppose that they both moved to Oklahoma and met there. There is a photograph of Rolyn on page 62.

Miscellany

Some miscellaneous mentions of "Doc" in other publications follow:

Aunt Charity's Visit		
	Excerpted from **The Granny Woman of the Hills** by Ella Ingenthron Dunn Copyright 1978 by Elmo Ingenthron published by The Ozarks Mountaineer, Star Rt. 3, Branson, MO. 65616	Late 1893 or Early 1894
Background: A "Granny Woman" was generally a knowledgeable older woman who could be relied upon for support in crises, and often served as a mid-wife.		
From page 31: Father came in and told mother Aunt Charity Logan was coming. We younguns always ran out to meet her when she came. She was a very special person in our young lives, but I decided to look at Aunt Charity closer than usual this time. She said 'Ellie, ain't youse ever seed me afore?' I said, "Yes, Aunt Charity, I seed you every time you came down here, but guess I'm gladder to see you this time." ... From page 32: Aunt Charity married a doctor who lived at Kirbyville and had a nice white house. His name was Doc Gonce and I never knew if he practiced medicine or "Doc" was the name he went by. Anyway he wanted her to deed him her river farm on White River and she refused, so she moved back to the farm. She had five boys and two girls and had made a living alone with the children's (sic) help ever since their own father died and she never tried marriage again.		*This is Charity Elizabeth Wiggins, widow of Alexander Logan, and third wife of Doc Gonce.* *The middle of the chapter has no mention of "Doc" Gonce.*

Pioneer Doctor: The True Story of Pioneer, Dr. Abraham R. Gonce		
Excerpted from The Ozark Headliner; 16 August 1973; Page 1		
	Written by A. F. (Derry) St. Clair, Spokane, Missouri (presumably copyrighted, but not explicitly stated)	
The old timers don't seem to know when he was born or where. Most old settlers migrated to Missouri before the Civil War. About all came in wagons from Kentucky, Tennessee and West Virginia to homestead in Missouri. Dr. Gonce probably came from one of these three areas. He took his first wife about one hundred years ago. Her name was Martha Frazier. To this union were born eight children. He lived a lot of his life in northern Taney County and southern Christian County. He maintained an office in Walnut Shade and another in Day, both in Taney County as well as offices in		*There are quite a few errors and omissions in this account, but it has some interesting anecdotes.* *Doc was born in Tennessee.* *I can't substantiate that Martha was Mary's real name.*

Pioneer Doctor: The True Story of Pioneer, Dr. Abraham R. Gonce

Excerpted from The Ozark Headliner; 16 August 1973; Page 1

Written by A. F. (Derry) St. Clair, Spokane, Missouri (presumably copyrighted, but not explicitly stated)

Highlandville and Ozark, these two were in Christian County.

He had a drug store and office in Walnut Shade. The business was in a log building. The property belonged to Dave Smith. Dave was the first merchant in Walnut Shade.

Asa St. Clair worked in the drug store. Asa was the pharmacist. The doctor and Asa made moonshine whiskey. They would color the stuff with blackberry juice.

Dr. Gonce called the moonshine his tonic for the sick. When he went to see the sick, he would fill his pill bag with colored pills and a bottle of tonic. He would soon have his patient on his feet and feeling fine again.

I'm sure his political party was on the Republican side. In those days, a doctor who had been a Democrat would have little business.

About 1900, Doc bought the store at Day, MO. He bought the store and post office from H. S. Cook. At that time, the Post Office always went with the store. In 1902, Rose O'Neill began building on her famous 17-room home after she married Harry Leon Wilson. Rose sent the hired man to Doc's store after some finishing nails. Doc's reply was, "I don't know what she wants with finishing nails. She just started the building last week." That was in the old days when the Whacker-Dam Mill was in operation.

There came a day when Martha Gonce, mother of eight, passed away and went to receive her eternal reward. Doc Gonce, like most men, thought he couldn't get along without a cook. So he married Matt Keithley. She was a sister of Honce Keithley, a good woman and real nice looking. They had three children. Doc gone into some kind of legal trouble, and Matt wouldn't live with him any more because of the crime.

In those early days, they had a Justice of the Peace and Constable. They held court in their own neighborhood. When Doc got into this trouble, Ike Cupp was Justice of the Peace. Babe Weatherman was Constable. They were trying Doc Gonce at the old log cabin on Bull Creek. at the Sim Cupp homestead. They paneled the jury, got set for the trial. Mr. Cupp gave the court a coffee break for fifteen minutes before they started. The doctor and the constable had a few words. It ended with a shootout, though no one was injured. When Mr. Cupp was ready to proceed with the trial, the jurors had all gotten scared and ran off. The Justice of Peace had to reschedule the trial date.

Well, it was time for the doctor to go looking for a third wife. He soon married a young woman by the name of Susie. I don't know her last name. The doctor and his third wife had four children. Then, the doctor was the father of fifteen children. You can see in this photograph the two beautiful little daughters standing beside their

Doc had nine children with Mary, but one died before they went to Missouri.

Asa is presumably related to the author.

Mary actually didn't die until later. Doc was charged with Bigamy when he married Matt.

This apparently describes the Bigamy trial in May 1877. Here, the author skips a murder, the trial, the penitentiary term, marriage to Charity Logan, etc.

Susan Hargrove, who was at least Doc's fourth wife.

Pioneer Doctor: The True Story of Pioneer, Dr. Abraham R. Gonce	
Excerpted from The Ozark Headliner; 16 August 1973; Page 1	
Written by A. F. (Derry) St. Clair, Spokane, Missouri (presumably copyrighted, but not explicitly stated)	

father's side. These two were the youngest of the last family. Their names were Cora and Nova.

I'm sure you will agree that Abraham was a good name for the doctor. He was more than 90 years old when the last one was born. Lo and behold, the doctor outlived all three wives. God said in the beginning - multiply and replenish the earth, the old timers did what God said, most families raising from 9 to fifteen children.

Actually, he was 76.

Delivering babies was, of course, a good business for the doctor. Of course, the doc had plenty of competition. The midwives had a big part in this work. I will mention a few: Grandma Cupp and Martha Dever and Ann Cupp and many others. The midwives charged three dollars. The doc charged five dollars. But, of course, the doc needed help. He couldn't do it all.

Other midwives were Charity Logan, Eliza Ann Cornelison Ingenthron and Ella Ingenthron Dunn.

The last time I saw Doc Gonce was at the 4th of July celebration at the Ball Nash place in 1910, sitting on a rail fence smoking a cog pipe. That was in the horse and buggy days. The horses were tied to the rail fence that he was sitting on. Some kids threw firecrackers among the horses. They ran back, took the old doctor for a ride on the rail fence. He got up on his hands and knees, found his pipe and went on smoking. It was a good show.

Interesting anecdote that paints a different physical picture than the pardon documents!

The doctor's third wife passed away in 1911. The doctor went to board with the Lum Davis family then. I believe they called Mrs. Davis "Ann". The doctor and Ann had a few words at the dinner table one night. I believe the doc made fun of her cooking. Ann grabbed him by the hair, threw his head back and told him not to make fun of her cooking again or she would cut his throat from ear to ear. Of course, she had her butcher knife in her hand at the time.

This refers to Susan Hargrove, who was at least his fourth wife. I haven't identified the Davis family.

Well, it finally came time for Dr. Abraham Gonce to pass on to the great beyond. He was buried beside his third wife in Helphrey Cemetery at Taneyville, MO in 1912. There are no dates on his marker, only the date of his death. The doctor lived a lot longer than three score and ten that ninth Psalms tells about. He was near a hundred, I am sure. Where the doctor will spend eternity, we do not know. We are not the judge. We don't know whether the thief on the cross was saved or not. It was his choice. I believe as long as we have breath in our body, we have a chance to repent if we will. I believe Acts2 - 20th & 21st will verify that statement for me.

Another good anecdote.

He was actually 79 years and 7 months old.

I have had the privilege and pleasure down through the years of meeting several generations of the Gonce family. All were well groomed, nice looking and of above average intelligence. This photo was furnished by Sadie Friend of Nixa, MO, submitted by A. F. "Derry" St. Clair. This is only a short sketch of the story of Dr. Abraham R. Gonce. Any one could do a little research work and

This probably isn't

Pioneer Doctor: The True Story of Pioneer, Dr. Abraham R. Gonce	
Excerpted from The Ozark Headliner; 16 August 1973; Page 1	
Written by A. F. (Derry) St. Clair, Spokane, Missouri (presumably copyrighted, but not explicitly stated)	
write a real book about the doctor. All you readers be good and have fun.	that "real book," but it's a shot ...

Dr. Heck regarding Abraham Rudolph Gonce	
Descendants of Hezekiah Davis I by Arch O. Heck, PhD Copyright 1965 by Arch O. Heck, Columbus, Ohio	
From page 32: Abraham R. Gonce was born in 1829; he married; Abraham was an M.D.; he went to Kentucky to practice medicine; he was also in Maryland. Writing from Jefferson City, Missouri, June 21, 1891, he says "My father was Vance Gonce. - - my mother was a Davis, a sister of Hezekiah and all the six brothers. We lived in Clinch Valley. The Davis's lived four miles south west of Rogersville. Mother was also a sister to Mrs. Sukie Pearson, the mother of Jackson Pearson - - - I read medicine for three years in Rogersville under Doctors Walker and Carmichael - - Ex-sheriff Joe Dodson of Green County, Missouri, is a cousin of mine on my mother's side and his mother's too".	Born 3 May 1931 There is no evidence "Doc" was ever in Maryland. Jefferson City is technically correct, since in June 1891, "Doc" was in the Penitentiary there after his murder conviction.

Doctor John D. Collins regarding Abraham Rudolph Gonce	
Posted in response to questions on Gonce internet forum	12 MAR 2002
A note to follow-up on the "Doc" Gonce murder story: my great-grandfather, Dr. John D. Collins, son of John Collins of Selmore, appears to have first practiced a bit in Ozark as well as in Highlandville, where both he and Gonce seem to have been practicing at the same time; Gonce's being sent to prison apparently left Highlandville without another doctor, so Dr. Collins became the sole doctor for most of the period until his 1901 death. Although the little centennial book "Christian County: Its First 100 Years" claims Collins moved to Highandville after Gonce killed Keyser[138], in fact, Collins was already in Highlandville at the 1800[139] census, and some early birth records (incomplete) from the 1880s show both Gonce and Collins delivering babies in the early 1880s. Michael Dunn (great-grandson of Dr. John D. Collins)	I haven't located any birth records, but see no reason to doubt this report.

---

138 He is referring to page 172 of the Christian County Centennial book referenced earlier.
139 This was undoubtedly a typo in the e-mail; Dr. Collins first appeared in the area in the 1880 census.

Doctor John D. Collins regarding Abraham Rudolph Gonce	
Posted in response to questions on Gonce internet forum	12 MAR 2002
Comment: It is evident from Dr. Collins' testimony in Dr. Gonce's murder trial that the two knew each other prior to the murder. It is possible that the authors of the Christian County history confused the murder sentence with Doc Gonce's earlier sentence for bigamy, which fits their timeline much more neatly.	

Malpractice ?	
From Effie Davis Morrow of Springfield MO	
"Hillard Davis (Tom Davis' son--Tom's parents were Willie and Elizabeth) told me that Doc Gonce killed great grandmother Elizabeth with some medicine that ate her stomach out. Hillard remembers his dad telling him."	*This web posting sounds intriguing, but I've located no evidence to support it.*
Comment: I have been unable to identify any of these Davises or connect them to any other Davises mentioned in this history.	

From another posting: "There is considerable data in the pension file of James W. Sims (probably a relative of Martha Ann Sims, Doc's daughter-in-law) about a Dr. Gonce, who was convicted of killing a man and sentenced to life imprisonment[140]. Served 10 years, was discharged."

---

140 He was actually sentenced to thirty years for the murder, and was pardoned after eight years and one month.

Doc's Year of Birth

Because there is some discrepancy in the year-of-birth given for Abraham Rudolph Gonce, I have collected all the references I am aware of that provide an age or year of birth into the following table. This should, I believe, buttress the case that he was born in May 1833 as stated on the 1900 U.S. Census, rather than in 1829, as given in several genealogical books.

Doc Gonce's Year of Birth				
Year	Age	Implied Birth Year	Census or Other Reference	Comments
1 Jun 1840	5 to 9	In [1831-1835] bracket	NARC Series m704 Roll 526 Page 236	With Vance and Martha
1 Jun 1850	21	about 1829 ±1	NARC Series m432 Roll 882 Page 313	Wife Mary; no children
			Did he "fudge" his year of birth in 1850 in order to appear older so that he could study medicine with Drs. Walker and Carmichael, or because Mary was really two years older than he was?	
1 Jun 1860			Cannot Locate Abraham or his 6 year old son Arthur in 1860	Remainder of family is in Hawkins County, TN
1 Jun 1870	38	about 1832 ±1	NARC Series m593 Roll 769 Page 388	Wife Mary; 6 children
1879	46	about 1833 ±1	Penitentiary Record – Prisoner 1685	
1 Jun 1880	47	about 1833 ±1	LDS Series 1254682 Page 51	In Missouri State Pen
Jun 1885	52	about 1833 ±1	Greene County Archives – sheet 154	Murder Trial Testimony
16 Jun 1885	54	about 1832 ±1	Penitentiary Record – Prisoner 5018	
1 Jun 1890			None extant	1890 Census Destroyed
1 Jun 1900	67	May 1833 specified	NARC Series t623 Roll 905 Page 10b	Wife Susie; 2 children
15 Apr 1910	76	about 1834 ±1	NARC Series t624 Roll 827 Page 3a	Wife Susie; 5 children
4 Dec 1912	81	about 1831	Taney County Death Certificate 41767	Widower
"Doc" Gonce was very likely born in 1833, not 1929 as some secondary sources suggest.				

Further, there is considerable extant evidence that Abraham Rudolph Gonce's older brother Hezekiah Gonce was born in October of 1829, implying that Doc could not have been born before the latter part of 1830. Consider the following data from the cited references:

Hezekiah Gonce's Year of Birth (Doc's Older Brother)					
Year	Age	Implied Birth Year	Census or Other Reference	Comments
1 Jun 1830	<5	In [1826-1830] bracket	NARC Series m019 Roll 178 Page 71	With parents Vance and Martha Gonce
1 Jun 1840	10-14	In [1826-1830] bracket	NARC Series m704 Roll 526 Page 236	With Vance and Martha
1 Jun 1850	21	about 1829 ±1	NARC Series m432 Roll 882 Page 320	With Vance and Martha
1 Jun 1860	28	About 1832	NARC Series m653 Roll 1255 Page 14	With wife Parmelia and 2 children
1 Jun 1870	38	about 1832 ±1	NARC Series m593 Roll 1535 Page 28	With wife Chaney and 2 children
1 Jun 1880			Haven't Located	
1 Jun 1890			None extant	1890 Census Destroyed
1 Jun 1900	70	Oct 1829 specified	NARC Series t623 Roll 1577 Page 8	With wife Chaney

Abraham Rudolph's older brother Hezekiah Gonce was born in October 1829, making it very improbable that Doc was also born in May 1829.

Known Children of Abraham Rudolph "Doc" Gonce

A full list of Abraham Rudolph Gonce's known children is given below, showing the mother of each.

Name [married]	ID	Birth Date	Birth Place	Mother	1860	1870	1876	1880	1900	1910	1920	1930
William McClellan (Mac)	3480	Aug 1851	Hawkins Cty TN	Mary A. Frazier (?) (3320)	•	•	•	•				
Arthur Davis	3318	12 May 1854	Hawkins Cty TN	Mary A. Frazier (?) (3320)	?	•	•	•				
Nancy	3848	about 1856	TN	Mary A. Frazier (?) (3320)	•							
Martha E. [Smith]	3532	about 1856	TN	Mary A. Frazier (?) (3320)	•	•	•	•	?	?	?	?
Mary Ellen (Ella) [Chrisman]	3533	about 1860	TN	Mary A. Frazier (?) (3320)	•	•	•	•	?	•		
Olive Alice [Johnson/Brock]	3534	about 1864	IN	Mary A. Frazier (?) (3320)		•	•					
Thomas Jefferson	3535	8 Jan 1866	IN	Mary A. Frazier (?) (3320)		•	•	?	•	•		
Laura Alice	3536	about 1869	MO	Mary A. Frazier (?) (3320)		•	•	•				
Benjamin Franklin	3688	about 1872	MO	Mary A. Frazier (?) (3320)			•	•	?	•		
Rolyn [141] [142]	4161	23 Sep 1877	MO	Martha A. (Matt) Keithley (4007)					?	?	?	?	•
Lester Olonzo	4073	2 Jul 1882	MO	Martha A. (Matt) Keithley (4007)						•	•	•	•
Anna Belle [Elstun/Heter]	4172	Jan 1885	MO	Martha A. (Matt) Keithley (4007)					•	•	?	?
No Children Known	-----	-----	-----	Charity E. Wiggins Logan (3473)								
Aria Edith [Austin]	3999	Jun 1896	MO	Susan T. Hargrove (3998)					•	•	?	?
Cora B. [Blevins]	4000	Mar 1899	MO	Susan T. Hargrove (3998)					•	•	?	?
James Tilford	4001	10 Nov 1900	MO	Susan T. Hargrove (3998)					•	?	•	
Myrtle See 2nd note under Rolyn above	4002	about 1903	MO	Susan T. Hargrove (3998)						•	?	•
Nora	4003	about 1907	MO	Susan T. Hargrove (3998)						•	?	?

Abraham Rudolph "Doc" Gonce seems to have had at least seventeen children with at least three of his wives.

---

141 In their report of Doc's murder trial, the Atchison (Kansas) Globe of Thursday June 11, 1885 reported "his wife and three little children were present with him during the trial." The number of children is also based on a Gonce forum posting by Doreen Kuhlmann on 6 January 2002; she wrote "In 1877 he had married one of our relatives Martha A. (Matt) Keithley," and she later referred to their three children.

142 Doc's second last child Myrtle Gonce was living in Oklahoma at the time of the 1930 census (National Archives Microfilm Series t626 Roll 1901 Page 1a) in the household of Rolyn Gonce, a brick mason who was born circa 1878; she is listed as his sister. Rolyn's World War I Draft Card lists Lester, also living in Kansas at the time, as his brother.

Some of the detail in the list above is based on a certain level of inference and speculation, particularly with regard to the children of Mary A. Frazier. At first blush, the various extant documents I have located and presented that identify Mary A. Frazier's children seem inconsistent. The table below is provided, therefore, to support the inferences[143] I have made from these documents. A pair of columns is shown for each of the sources mentioned in this document, and the children are listed sequentially in each column along with the years of birth implied by the document.

Doc's Children with Mary A. Frazier as reported in Various Documents									
1860 U.S. Census		1870 U.S. Census		1876 Missouri		1877		1880 U.S. Census		My ID
Name Given	Age – Birth Year	Name Given	Age – Birth Year	Name Given	Ranges: of Age & Birth Years	Name Given	Name Given	Age – Birth Year	
William M. Gaunce	9 – 1851	William Gonce	18 – 1852	Mack Gonce	21-45 – 1831-1855	Wm. M. Gonce			3480
		Arthur Gonce	17 – 1853	Arthur Gonce	21-45 – 1831-1855	Arthur Gonce	Arthur Gonce	26 – 1854	3318
Nancy Gaunce	4 – 1856								3848
Martha Gaunce	4 – 1856	Martha E. Gonce	14 – 1856	M. E. Gonce	18-21 – 1855-1858	Martha E. Gonce			3532
Mary Gaunce	0.5 – 1859	Mary E. Gonce	10 – 1860	Ollie Chrisman	10-18 – 1858-1866	Ella Gonce	Ella Chrisman		3533
		Alice Gonce	6 – 1864	O. A. Gonce	10-18 – 1858-1866	Olive Gonce			3534
		Thomas Gonce	4 – 1866	T. B. Gonce	10-18 – 1858-1866	Thomas Gonce	Thomas Gonce	14 – 1866	3535
		Laura A. Gonce	1 – 1869	L. A. Gonce	<10 – 1866-1876	Alice Gonce	Alice Gonce	11 – 1869	3536, not 3534
				B. F. Gonce	<10 – 1866-1876	Benjamin Gonce	Benjamin Gonce	8 – 1872	3688

In the 1870 census, for instance, Alice is clearly older than Thomas, but in the Divorce Decree of 1877, Alice is shown after Thomas (therefore

---

143 Of course, if anyone is aware of documents that would prove or disprove these inferences, I would appreciate knowing that.

probably younger), and the name Olive appears before Thomas. Mary Ellen Gonce, known as Ella, married L. J. Chrisman, and is shown on the 1876 Missouri Census as Ollie Chrisman.

Olive, in the 1877 Divorce Decree, cannot be Mary Ellen/Ella/Ollie, tempting as that assumption is, because Ella is shown separately. Therefore, Olive must be the first name of the Alice shown in the 1870 census; this seems to be supported by the entry of O. A. Gonce in the 1876 Missouri Census.

Since the name Olive (middle name Alice) is shown in the Divorce Decree, and an Alice appears after Thomas, it seems reasonable that this second Alice is not the same one that appears in the 1870 Census.

Since the name Laura does not appear in the Divorce Decree, I have concluded that the name Laura A. Gonce is likely Laura Alice Gonce, and that she began to be called by her middle name in this period.

Since two of Mary's daughters appear to have been given the middle name of Alice, and since I know of no relative of their father's who is named Alice, this might suggest that Mary A. Frazier's middle name might also have been Alice and/or that her mother or grandmother's name may have been Alice. This might help in identifying Mary's family in Tennessee, an endeavor with which I have not yet had any success.

For the most part, Doc's descendants seem to have been unaffected by his foibles, but three of his children and several of his later descendants also seem to have strayed from the straight and narrow.

Doc's ninth child Benjamin Franklin Gonce [ID 3688] was charged with felonious assault on Bud Boswell in 1893[144], but I haven't followed up on this to determine the circumstances. He would have been 21 years old at the time.

Doc's eleventh child Lester Olonzo Gonce was charged with (but acquitted of) murder, and his sons Forrest[145] [ID 4096], Vollie Vernon[146] [ID 4097], and Lester[147] (aka Chet) [ID 4098], served time in the Colorado State Penitentiary. Details of the exploits of these grandsons of Doc's are given in Section III.

Doc's fifteenth child James Tilford Gonce [ID 4001], who was later known as Tilford J. Gonce, was divorced by his wife Ruth [ID 4044]; after this, he left Kansas City Missouri, checked into a hotel in Joplin Missouri and, on 21 April 1942, committed suicide by swallowing strychnine[148].

---

144 Missouri Judicial Microfilm C37192, Box 2, Folder 45, Case 213
145 Inmate Number: 13596; Colorado State Penitentiary Index 1871-1973
146 Vollie was a guest of the facility twice. He was Inmate Number 18596 and, later, Inmate Number 20257; Colorado State Penitentiary Index 1871-1973
147 Inmate Number: 16472; Colorado State Penitentiary Index 1871-1973 (records available from CO State Archives)
148 Missouri Death Certificate 14610, filed 5 May 1942 in Joplin, Jasper County, Missouri.

Finally, Doc's second great grandsons Fain and Richard Gonce (descendants of Doc's first son William McClellan Gonce [ID 3480]) were convicted in Nevada of armed robbery and kidnapping. Details of these brothers' exploits are also given in Section III, beginning on page 236, "The Senior Citizen Burglars of Nevada."

Martha Ann Keithley
6 May 1858 - 10 Apr 1899
Doc's second wife[149]

Rolyn Gonce
23 Sep 1877 - 1938
Doc's tenth child

Lester Olonzo Gonce
2 JUL 1882 - 25 DEC 1957
Doc's eleventh child

Martha's first son Rolyn was married to Minnie White in 1920, but I am unaware of any children. Lester Olonzo and his family are described in detail beginning on page 209 "Doc Gonce's Outlaw Descendants."

Anna Belle Gonce
Jan 1885 -
Doc's twelfth child

Anna Belle Gonce
Jan 1885 -
Doc's twelfth child

Anna Belle Gonce
Jan 1885 -
Doc's twelfth child

Doc's twelfth child – his third and last with Martha Ann Keithley – was Anna Belle Gonce, shown above at three different ages. Anna Belle was

---

149 There is another photograph of Martha on page 209.

married four times, and lived her adult life in Kansas. Anna was the mother of a son and three daughters who were born between 1902 and 1910.

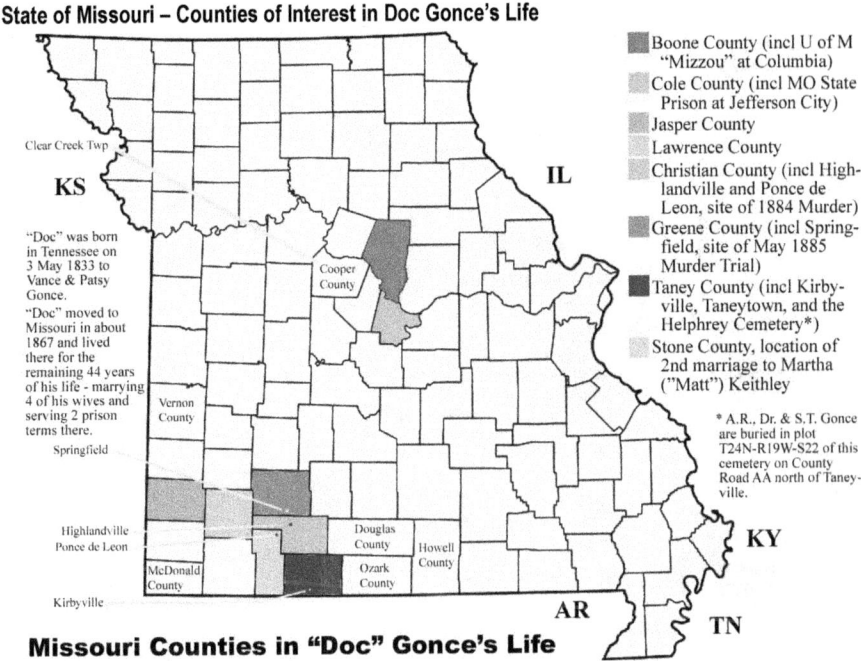

Map showing Missouri Counties of Interest in "Doc" Gonce's Life

Southern Missouri – Important Towns and Locations in Doc Gonce's Life

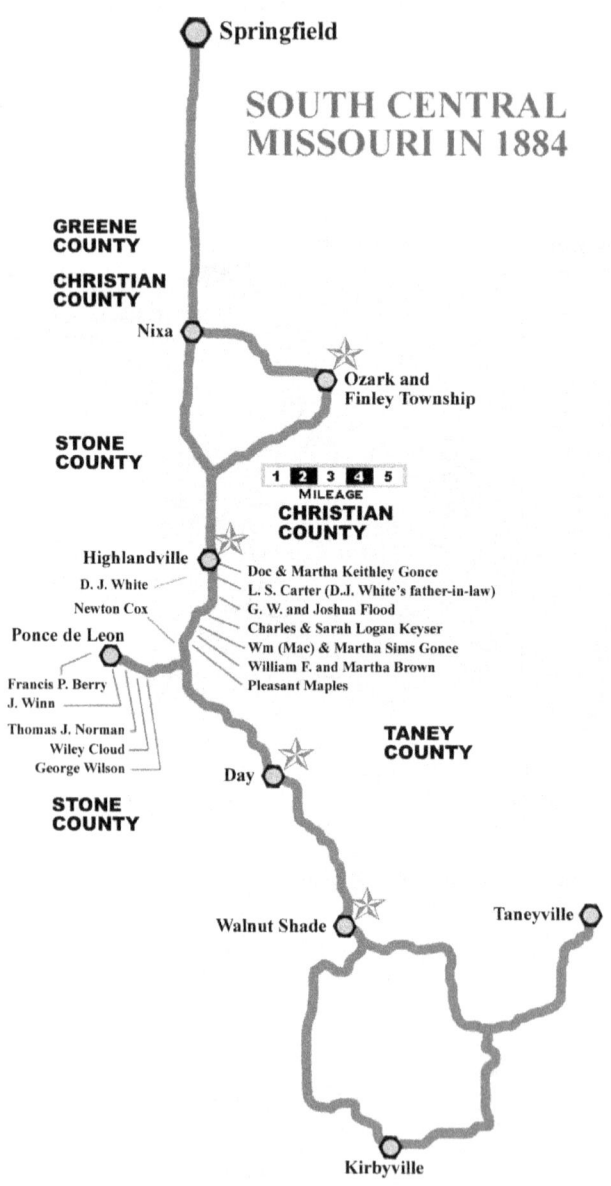

Location of the farms and residences indicated are approximate.

This map shows more details of the area in which Doc Gonce lived and worked at the time of Charlie Keyser's murder. Doc and his then wife Martha (Matt) Keithley Gonce, lived in Highlandville. Earlier, while married to his first wife Mary, he lived in Finley Township, which is just outside Ozark to the north. Doc's offices are marked with stars. The approximate locations of his neighbors between Highlandville and Ponce de Leon are indicated in order to follow the events of 27 June. The routes shown between various pairs of towns are an approximation, since I have been unable to locate any contemporary maps of this particular area. The routes are, by necessity, similar to present day highways due to the terrain, but there are some differences based on the documents I've reviewed. The key to understanding some of the testimony in the murder trial is that Charlie Keyser's farm was on an east-west section of an otherwise north-south road.

Chronology of Events in the Life of Abraham Rudolph Gonce

Date	Event	Notes and/or Sources
abt 1831	Future wife Mary A. (3320 - unknown surname, possibly Frazier) is born in Tennessee	1860 and 1870 Census references below refer to her age
3 May 1833	Abraham Rudolph born to Vance Gonce (2881) and Martha Patsy Davis (2882)	Some sources say 1829, but this can't be correct (see Hezekiah)
1 Jun 1840	6th US Census: Vance - ARG accounted for as "1 White Male; age 5-9 (1831-1835)"	NARC Series m704 Roll 526 Page 236
29 Oct 1846	Sarah Elizabeth Logan (4110) born to Alexander Logan (4108)	
abt 1848	Per some sources, ARG marries Sarah Nancy Fraizer (2884) [Doubtful to me]	This might be the same person as Mary A. (3320); see 28 Mar 1850.
abt 1849	Charity Elizabeth Wiggins (3473), future wife of Alexander Logan (4108) and ARG (2883), born; mother unk.	NARC Series m593 Roll 769 Page 391
28 Mar 1850	ARG, age about 17, marries Mary A. (3320), age about 19	From Mary's Affidavit in 1879 Divorce Proceedings
1 Jun 1850	7th US Census: "Abram" (farmer) & wife Mary in Dist 2, Hawkins Cty, TN	NARC Series m432 Roll 882 Page 313 (Age 21 vs 17) (19)
1 Jun 1850	Dr. Hugh Walker and family living in District 10; Hawkins Cty TN	NARC Series m432 Roll 832 Page 384
1 Jun 1850	Dr. A. Carmichael and family living in District 10; Hawkins Cty TN	NARC Series m432 Roll 832 Page 385
Aug 1851	William McClellan (Mac) Gonce (3480) born in Tennessee	Mother is Mary A. (3320)
Jan 1854	Doctor John D. Collins born; he took over Doc Gonce's patients after the murder arrest in 1884. Dr. Collins also testified in Doc's murder trial.	
12 May 1854	Arthur Davis Gonce (3318) born in Rogersville, Tennessee	Mother is Mary A. (3320)
o/a 1854	ARG "reads medicine" with Drs Walker and Carmichael in Rogersville, TN	3 year apprenticeship per 21 Jun 1891 letter to Arch O. Heck
abt 1856	Nancy Gonce (3848) born in Tennessee (per 1870 census)	twins? Mother is Mary A. (3320)
abt 1856	Martha E. Gonce (3532) born in Tennessee (per 1870 census)	twins? Mother is Mary A. (3320)
guess 1857	Sarah Logan, first wife of Alexander Logan (4108) and mother of Sarah Elizabeth Logan (4110) dies.	
abt 1859	Mary Ellen Gonce (3533) born in Tennessee (per 1870 census)	Mother is Mary A. (3320) - NARC Series m653 Roll 1255 Page 14
guess 1860	ARG possibly begins practicing medicine in Kentucky in this period	Arch O. Heck book, page 32
guess 1860	ARG possibly practices medicine in Maryland during this period	Arch O. Heck book, page 32 **VERY DOUBTFUL TO ME**
1 Jun 1860	8th US Census: Mary A. (listed as a widow), son Wm & 3 daughters living near ARG's older brother Hezekiah in Tennessee	NARC Series m653 Roll 1255 Page 14 (Mary 28)

Chronology of Events in the Life of Abraham Rudolph Gonce

Date	Event	Notes and/or Sources
1 Jun 1860	8th US Census: Cannot locate ARG or son Arthur Davis in this Census	Ages should be about 27-28 & 6 respectively
28 Aug 1861	ARG, as "Doc Gonce", age 28, probed for bullet in Samuel Marion Davis with "a long rusty hat pin" in Stone County, MO	See details on page 8
guess 1863	ARG reunites with Mary A. and settles the family in Indiana	
abt 1864	Alice Gonce (3534) born in Indiana (per 1870 census)	Mother is Mary A. (3320)
abt 1865	Alexander Logan (4108) marries Charity Elizabeth Wiggins (3473); Charity is about 16; Alexander's daughter Sarah Elizabeth Logan (4110) is about 19.	Doc later killed Sarah's husband (see 16 Mar 1871 & 27 Jun 1884) and eventually married Charity.
8 Jan 1866	Thomas Jefferson Gonce (3535) born in Indiana (per 1870 census)	Mother is Mary A. (3320)
guess 1867	ARG and family move to Missouri	
23 Jan 1868	ARG serving as Justice of the Peace in marriage of John Benham to Julia Dennis in Stone County, MO	See page 10
20 Oct 1868	ARG recorded as Curator of Estates for several minor heirs of Caleb Harris	See page 10
mid 1868	Charges filed in assault against Albert A. Gonce (unidentified, but not the Albert Anderson Gonce who was the son of William McClellan Gonce and Martha Ann Sims or the Albert Anderson Gonce who was the son of John Wisdom Gonce and Jane Julia Lovell). Both of these Alberts were born much later.	Stone County Court Records Box 1; Folder 34; Case 8 I haven't identified Albert A. Gonce, but assume he is related.
abt 1869	Laura Alice Gonce (3536) born in Missouri (per 1870 census)	Mother is Mary A. (3320)
1 Jun 1870	9th US Census: ARG, wife Mary A & 6 children living in Finley Twp, Christian Cty, MO	NARC Series m593 Roll 769 Page 388 (Age 38 & 39)
1 Jun 1870	9th US Census: Doc's oldest son Mac, 18, and his wife Martha (Sims) living in Howell Twp, Howell Cty, MO	NARC Series m593 Roll 780 Page 485
16 Mar 1871	Charles G. Keyser (4111) marries Sarah Elizabeth Logan (4110), daughter of Alexander Logan; Wm. F. Brown, J.P. presiding, in Christian Cty, MO	
abt 1872	Benjamin Franklin Gonce (3688) born in Missouri	Mother is Mary A. (3320)
1872	ARG is listed among the citizens of Ozark as a Doctor	WRVQ, v2, #10; see page 12
1875	ARG listed as paying land taxes on 2 lots (Ozark Block 7, Lot 2 & Ozark block 8, part of Lot 2)	Christian County Tax Records; see page 13
1875	ARG listed with J. L. Robberson as paying land taxes on 6 lots (Ozark Block 16, Lots 1-2 & Ozark Old Town block 6, Lots 18-21)	Christian County Tax Records; see page 13
Jun 1876	Missouri Census: Doc, Mary A. and five children living in Finley Township near their daughter	Missouri Census for 1876; Finley Township; pg 16
Jun 1876	Missouri Census: Arthur and William Gonce and their families living in Finley Township	Missouri Census for 1876; Finley Township; pg

Chronology of Events in the Life of Abraham Rudolph Gonce

Date	Event	Notes and/or Sources
17 Oct 1876	ARG abandons Mary; moves in with Martha Ann (Matt) Keithley (4007)	Based on Divorce Petition
1 Nov 1876	ARG and Martha Ann Keithley married in Arkansas	Based on Bigamy Trial testimony
Feb 1877	ARG and Martha Ann Keithley return from Arkansas to Stone County Missouri	Based on Mary's Bigamy Trial testimony (B4F17C44-35)
26 Mar 1877	ARG marriage to Martha Ann (Matt) Keithley (4007) "without Missouri" in Arkansas is filed in Missouri	See 1 Nov 1876 above.
5 Apr 1877	Bigamy (Mary A/Martha) charges filed against ARG in Stone County Circuit Court	Stone County Court Records Box 4; Folder 2; Case 3, pp 25 & 26
6 Apr 1877	Based on Bigamy indictment, an Arrest Warrant is issued for ARG	Stone County Court Records Box 4; Folder 2; Case 3, pp 23 & 24
10 Apr 1877	ARG marries Martha Ann Keithley (4007) again, this time in Missouri, Westley Henry presiding	Stone County, MO Marriages 1851-1900; v7, no 7
late Apr 1877	ARG arrested and confined in jail.	(between 11 & 29 April)
30 Apr 1877	After his arrest, ARG posts first of several $500 Recognizance Bonds to remain free until Bigamy Trial. This bond co-signed by Amos S. Kelly.	Stone County Court Records Box 4; Folder 2; Case 3, pg 1; see transcription on page 80.
30 May 1877	A.R. and Mary A. Gonce sell land in Taney County to Charity Elizabeth Logan, wife of Alexander Logan and step-mother of Sarah Logan Keyser.	Taney County Deed Book 3; see transcription on page 81.
	Doc goes into hiding.	
31 Aug 1877	First Subpoenas issued for Bigamy Trial, now scheduled for February 1878 court session	Stone County Court Records Box 4; Folder 2; Case 3, pp 4 & 5
23 Sep 1877	Son Rolyn Gonce (4161) is born in Missouri	Mother is Martha Keithley (4007)
Oct 1877	ARG does not appear for his Bigamy Trial	
17 Dec 1877	Based on information that ARG fled to Barry County, an Arrest Warrant is issued to the Sheriff there.	Stone County Court Records Box 4; Folder 2; Case 3, p 14
Feb 1878	ARG Trial for Bigamy rescheduled to begin in Galena, Missouri. ARG is again a no-show. Trial postponed.	Court due to be in session on fourth Monday of February.
Fall 1878	ARG returns to Taney County and is again arrested and placed in jail.	
26 Sep 1878	Mary petitions for Divorce	Stone County Court Records Box 4; Folder 17; Case 44, pg 35
26 Sep 1878	Doc files Denial of all the allegations in Mary's Petition for Divorce	Stone County Court Records Box 4; Folder 17; Case 44, pg 34
26 Sep 1878	Divorce Decree and custody of minor children granted to Mary A. (3320) by Judge J. Frank Seaman	Stone County Court Records Box 4; Folder 17; Case 44, pp 32 & 33
Jan 1879	Barry County Sheriff returns arrest warrant noting that Doc could not be found in that County	See 17 Dec 1877 entry.
1 Feb 1879	Bigamy Trial preliminaries begin in "old log cabin on Bull Creek" with Justice of the Peace Cupp.	
1 Feb 1879	Altercation in courtroom with Alexander Osborn; Doc re-confined in jail	Stone County Court Records Box 4; Folder 10; Case 26, page 8.

Chronology of Events in the Life of Abraham Rudolph Gonce

Date	Event	Notes and/or Sources
24 Feb 1879	ARG is again arrested and confined to await trial for Bigamy in February Circuit Court session	Stone County Court Records Box 4; Folder 2; Case 3, page 17
25 Feb 1879	ARG posts second of several $500 Recognizance Bonds and is released.	Stone County Court Records Box 4; Folder 2; Case 3, page 18,19,20
26 Feb 1879	Based on 1 Feb 1879 incident, Deadly Weapons charge filed against ARG in Stone County Circuit Court; new arrest warrant issued for ARG same day.	Stone County Court Records Box 4; Folder 10; Case 26, pp 8 & 6
26 Feb 1879	Based on 1 Feb 1879 incident, Felonious Assault charge filed against ARG in Stone County Circuit Court; new arrest warrant issued for ARG same day.	Stone County Court Records Box 4; Folder 10; Case 26, pp 16 &14
28 Feb 1879	Motion to Quash Deadly Weapons charge accepted by Court	Stone County Court Records Box 4; Folder 10; Case 26, page 10
28 Feb 1879	ARG posts third of several $500 Recognizance Bonds, this related to Felony Assault charges.	Stone County Court Records Box 4; Folder 10; Case 26, page 4
Mar 1879	ARG's future wife Susan T. Hargrove (3998) is born in Missouri to William & Lucinda Hargrove	NARC Series t623 Roll 905 Page 10b (1900 Census)
15 Mar 1879	ARG posts fourth of several $500 Recognizance Bonds	Stone County Court Records Box 4; Folder 2; Case 3, page 22 & 21
22 Apr 1879	ARG posts fifth of several $500 Recognizance Bonds	Stone County Court Records Box 4; Folder 2; Case 3, page 7
24 Apr 1879	ARG released from Jail by Sheriff T. L. Giles after fifth Recognizance Bond posted	Stone County Court Records Box 4; Folder 2; Case 3, page 12
26 Aug 1879	ARG Trial for Bigamy begins in Galena, Missouri. See transcripts in section II beginning on page 73	Stone County Court Records Box 4; Folder 17; Case 44
28 Aug 1879	ARG Convicted of Bigamy in Stone County, MO.; sentenced to two years in the State Penitentiary.	Stone County Court Records Box 4; Folder 17; Case 44, p 20
29 Aug 1879	ARG escapes and is believed to have fled the County.	
15 Sep 1879	$150 Reward offered by Governor for capture of escaped fugitive A. R. Gonce, convicted of Bigamy	State of Missouri Register of Civil Proceedings 1879-1882, p. 89
24 Oct 1879	ARG enters Missouri State Penitentiary in Jefferson City, MO after conviction for Bigamy	Prisoner # 1685, age 46; 5'8.5"; gray hair; brown eyes
1 Jun 1880	10th US Census: ARG in State Penitentiary; Jefferson City, Cole County, Missouri	LDS Series 1254682 Page 51 (Age 47)
1 Jun 1880	10th US Census: Mary A. Gonce (3320), age 46, divorced living w/children Thomas, 14, Alice, 11, and Benjamin, 8, in Finley Twp, Christian County, MO	LDS Series 1254681 Page 52
1 Jun 1880	10th US Census: Alexander Logan and wife Charity Elizabeth Wiggins Logan (3473) and family living in Newton Twp, Taney County, Missouri	LDS Series 1254738 Page 242
28 Feb 1881	ARG released from Prison under 3/4 term law; since this was calculated from his sentencing he actually only served 16 months and 4 days.	Penitentiary Record: Prisoner #1685, shown on page 28
2 Jul 1882	Son Lester Olonzo Gonce (4073) is born in Missouri	Mother is Martha Keithley (4007)

Chronology of Events in the Life of Abraham Rudolph Gonce

Date	Event	Notes and/or Sources
? late 1882	ARG reopens medical practice in Highlandville, Christian County, MO	LOOK for Highlandville Birth Records w/his name
Jun 1884	ARG diagnoses Charlie Keysser with Gonorrhea	
15 Jun 1884	Charlie Keysser goes to ARG's House and demands retraction; offers to duel	
27 Jun 1884	ARG murders Postmaster Charlie Keyser in Ponce de Leon; Christian County, MO	
27 Aug 1884	ARG Indicted by Christian County Grand Jury for 1st degree Murder	
29 Jun 1884	Murder reported in the Sunday Morning Springfield Daily Herald	
30 Aug 1884	ARG enters Not Guilty plea based on self-defense	
2 Sep 1884	Continuance granted until February 1885 court term	
23 Feb 1885	ARG given Change of Venue to Greene County due to prejudicial atmosphere in Christian County	See Section III – "Murder Trial Transcriptions" beginning on page 113 for detailed information on all of these events.
Early 1885	Doc and Martha's third and last child Anna Gonce (4172) is born.	
May 1885	At time of Murder Trial, ARG was married to Martha Keithley (4007); she and Doc's oldest son William McClellan (3480) testified	
1 Jun 1885	Motion for Continuance granted because of missing witness Wiley Cloud	
4 Jun 1885	Murder trial begins in Greene County	
13 Jun 1885	Motion for new trial entered and denied	
15 Jun 1885	Verdict returned: Guilty of Murder in the 2nd degree; sentence of 30 years. ARG convicted of Charlie Keyser's murder in Greene County, MO	
16 Jun 1885	ARG enters Missouri State Penitentiary after conviction for 2nd degree Murder; sentenced to 30 years.	
abt 1886	Martha Keithley divorces ARG and moves out of state	Timing Uncertain
21 Jun 1891	ARG known to be living in Jefferson City, Missouri (IN PENITENTIARY)	Letter transcribed and quoted by Arch O. Heck
12 Jul 1893	ARG released from Penitentiary - Pardoned by Governor Stone as an invalid due to consumption	
14 Jul 1893	"Doc Gonce" lived in "a nice white house in Kirbyville" (Taney County)	Ingenthron-Dunn, pg 32
26 Jul 1893	ARG marries the widow Charity E. Logan, age about 44, in Taney County, Missouri (likely to get land back)	MO Marriages 1851-1900; Book 2, page 56
abt 1894	Charity Logan returns to White River farm after refusing to deed it over to ARG	Ingenthron-Dunn, pg 32
1895	ARG and Charity Logan are divorced	Taney County Court Records Box 11; Folder 77; Case 48

Chronology of Events in the Life of Abraham Rudolph Gonce

Date	Event	Notes and/or Sources
1895	ARG, now 62, takes up with 17 year old Susie Hargrove (3998), daughter of William and Lucinda Hargrove.	
late 1895	ARG purchases Drug Store "the Day Store" in Kirbyville (not in Day?) from H.S. Cook and converted it into a saloon	
abt Apr 1896	ARG charged with distributing liquor without a license in Taney County	Taney County Court Records Box 3; Folder 76; Case 6
abt May 1896	ARG charged with distributing liquor without a license in Taney County	Taney County Court Records Box 3; Folder 77; Case 5
Jun 1896	Aria E. Gonce (3999) is born in Missouri	Mother is Susie Hargrove (3998)
Jul 1896	ARG charged with distributing liquor without a license in Taney County	Taney County Court Records Box 3; Folder 78; Case 13
abt Oct 1896	ARG charged with distributing liquor without a license in Taney County	Taney County Court Records Box 4; Folder 3; Case 3
9 Jun 1897	ARG, age 64, marries Susan T. Hargrove (3998), a 19 year old with whom he already had a daughter.	NARC Series t623 Roll 905 Page 10b (1900 Census, m 3 yrs)
Mar 1899	Cora B. Gonce (4000) is born in Missouri	Mother is Susie Hargrove (3998)
8 Apr 1899	Martha A. Keithley-Gonce May (4007) dies in Kansas	Town of Sterling in Rice County
1 Jun 1900	12th US Census: ARG, Susie, Aria and Cora living in Jasper Twp, Taney Cty, MO	NARC Series t623 Roll 905 Page 10b (Age 67-May 1833)
abt 1901	James Tilford Gonce (4001) is born in Missouri (known later as Tilford)	Mother is Susie Hargrove (3998)
abt 1903	Myrtle Gonce (4002) is born in Missouri	Mother is Susie Hargrove (3998)
abt 1907	Nora Gonce (4003) is born in Missouri	Mother is Susie Hargrove (3998)
15 Apr 1910	13th US Census: ARG, Susie and 5 children living in Swan Twp, Taney Cty, MO	NARC Series t624 Roll 827 Page 3a (Ages 76 & 31)
4 Jul 1910	ARG attends celebration at the "Ball Nash Place"; he is knocked off fence by horses; he gets up, retrieves his pipe, and continues ...	Ozark Headliner article by A.F. (Derry) St. Claire; see page 52
1911	Susan Hargrove Gonce dies at about age 32. "Doc" is about 80.	Based on year of death given on her tombstone
late 1911	ARG boards with "Lum and Ann Davis" (whom I can't identify) after Susie's death; Ann threatens Doc after he insults her cooking.	Ozark Headliner article by A.F. (Derry) St. Claire; see page 52
4 Dec 1912	Abraham Rudolph Gonce dies in Missouri - Death Certificate lists him as a Widower, confirming that Susan had already died	See page 49
5 Dec 1913	"A.R. Gonce (1912) Dr." and "S.T. Gonce (1911)" are buried at T24N-R19W-S22 in Helphrey Cemetery, Taneyville, Taney County, MO	Because of year, I assume these are reburials, but have no further information to confirm that.
4 Oct 1925	Sarah E. Keysser (4110 - widow of Charles) dies, age 78, 11 m, 6 d, near Highlandville.	Obituary says nearly 40 years after husband's murder, but it was actually over 41 years.

Section II:
Bigamy Trial
Transcriptions

5 April 1877 – 24 October 1879

Bigamy Trial Transcriptions

Preface

Some familiarity with Abraham Rudolph Gonce's rather bizarre but interesting life, described earlier, will be useful in putting the records transcribed in this document into context. Briefly, however, after marrying Mary A. Frazier [ID 3320] and having nine children with her, Doc left her and began living with Martha Ann (Matt) Keithley [ID 4007], whom he subsequently married. Because the State of Missouri claimed that Doc had neglected to obtain a divorce, he was charged with Bigamy.

Doc offered several defenses. First, he claimed that he had never actually married Mary, but the fact that he had been living with her as man and wife for many years in front of many witnesses negated this claim, even if it were true[150]. In his next effort at defense, he produced what purported to be an earlier Kentucky divorce decree. Because he had lived with Mary during their years in Missouri as man and wife however, this would unlikely have been a sufficient legal defense. Also, Doc seemed to conveniently ignore that presenting a divorce decree after denying that he and Mary had been married didn't do a whole lot for his credibility. The Court's consideration of the purported Kentucky divorce decree became moot, however, when two of Doc's own lawyers were called by the prosecution and testified that the handwriting on the decree looked remarkably like Doc's own[151].

Dr. Gonce was subsequently convicted of the charges and, after escaping for a brief time, was recaptured and sent to the Missouri State Penitentiary in August 1879 for a two-year sentence[152].

The documents transcribed in this paper come from multiple sources in the Missouri State Archives, but primarily the following:

> Stone County Circuit Court Records, Box 4, Folder 2, Case 3: Bigamy Action
> Stone County Circuit Court Records, Box 4, Folder 10, Case 6: Displaying a Weapon
> Stone County Circuit Court Records, Box 4, Folder 10, Case 26: Felonious Assault
> Stone County Circuit Court Records, Box 4, Folder 17, Case 44: Divorce Petition

The sheet number preceding the transcription of each page indicates the source and order in which the original appeared in its respective file, and will permit this transcription to be compared to the original documents if the reader is so inclined. Since many of the sheets in the archives were obviously

---

150 I've never actually found a record of Doc's first marriage, but there seems to be little doubt that he and Mary were actually married.
151 These were Mr. Patterson and Mr. Gideon. See Stone County Box 4, Folder 17, Case 44, Sheet 11 (hereafter referred to as B4F17C44-11), which is transcribed on page 97 and B4F17C44-12, which is also transcribed on page 97.
152 See record B4F17C44-20 on page 108. He was released under Missouri's ¾ time law on 28 February 1881.

out of order, I attempted to correct that in these transcriptions as best I could. Because some sheets end in the middle of a sentence that I couldn't match elsewhere, it is likely that some of the original sheets have gone missing.

In the few cases where I was unable to decipher the handwriting, the unknown portions are [*enclosed in square brackets and italicized*] like this.

Scans of some of the more interesting and/or difficult to interpret pages are provided throughout this section. A few of the easily readable sheets, usually those that are printed forms, are shown within the text rather than being transcribed.

Because each of the court actions utilized material from earlier actions as evidence, it often happens that the only extant copy from one action is in the file of another. For instance, the only surviving copy of the divorce decree from 1878 appears in the records of the 1879 bigamy trial. In this document, I have attempted to place the sheets in chronological order in order to make the proceedings easier to follow.

The documents from which these transcriptions were made appear to be notes taken by someone summarizing the proceedings and the responses of witnesses. Several notations similar to "(Here insert the affidavit …)" make it appear as if these sheets are notes from which some official record was to be assembled later. If such records exist, I haven't been able to locate them. Thus, in many instances, what are presented here are typed transcriptions of earlier handwritten notes taken by the various court clerks in Stone County.

In the original documents I transcribed, there are a number of sentences and words lined out. I assume these were struck out for legal reasons, and thus may not have made it into the "official" trial transcript (if that exists anywhere), but I've included all of them with the ~~text struck through like this~~ so the transcriptions match the originals as closely as possible.

I've printed all of the transcriptions with one and a half line spacing, not just to mimic legal documents, but for the very practical reason that the text, being legalese, is often so dense and full of run-on sentences that it would be extremely difficult to read without generous line spacing.

The Indictment for Bigamy: 5 April 1877

On April 5th of 1877, based on complaints made by Mary A. Gonce at the end of the previous month[153], a Missouri Grand Jury in Stone County returned an Indictment for Bigamy against Doc Gonce. The outside cover of this Indictment is shown below[154], followed by a transcription of the Indictment itself.

5 April 1877 [Stone County B4F02C03-25]

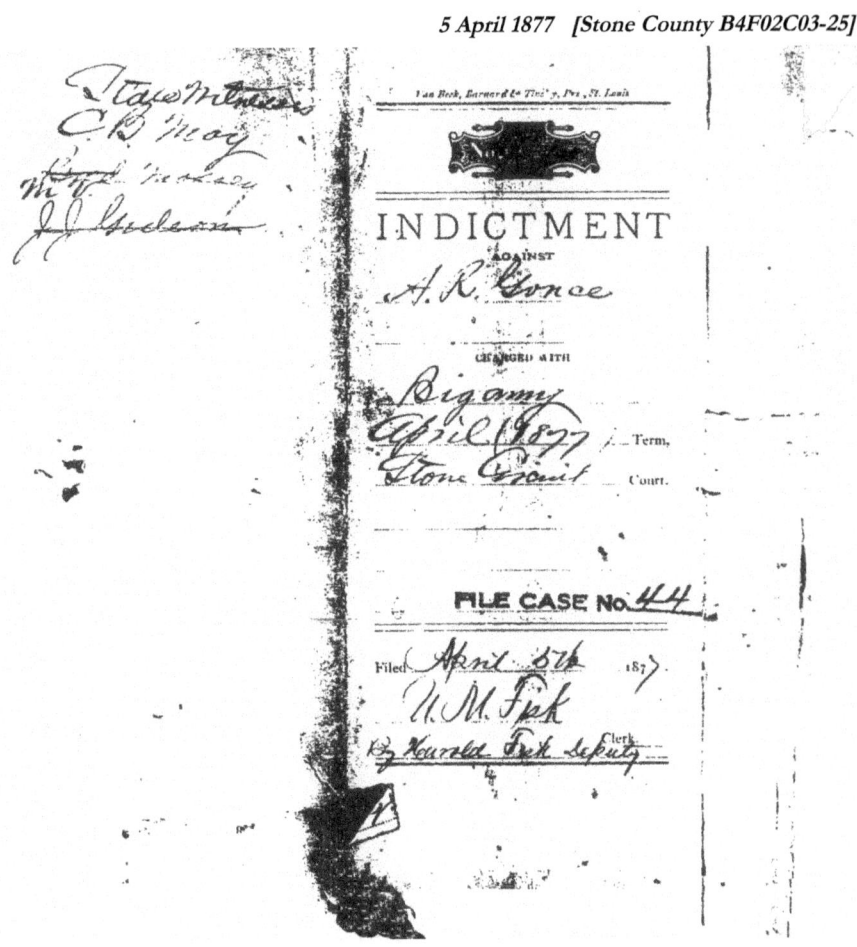

---

153 See a reference to 28 March on Mary's Divorce petition, sheet B4F17C44-35, which is transcribed on page 84. The year isn't specified, but the context makes it clear that it is March of 1877.
154 This document is marked as file case 44, and is the master from which sheet B4F17C44-41 was later copied. The marking was evidently made during that later case.

5 April 1877 [Stone County B4F02C03-26]

State of Missouri } In the Circuit Court of Stone
County of Stone } County. April Term A.D. 1877

The Grand Jurors for the State of Missouri, summoned from the body of Stone County, empanelled, charged and sworn, upon their oaths, present that A. R. Gonce late of the County aforesaid, on the 1st day of November 1876, County to the Grand Jurors unknown in the State of Arkansas, did unlawfully and feloniously marry and take to wife one Martha Ann Keithley and to her the said Martha Ann Keithley then and there was married without the State of Missouri, the said A. R. Gonce then and still having a lawful wife living to wit Mary Gonce, the said marrying and taking to wife by the said A. R. Gonce of the said Martha Ann Keithley as aforesaid being unlawful by the laws of the State of Arkansas as well as by the laws of the State of Missouri, and the jurors aforesaid upon their oath aforesaid do further present that the said A. R. Gonce afterwards to wit on the 26th day of March 1877 within the State of Missouri within the County of Stone aforesaid and from that day until the finding of this indictment unlawfully and feloniously did abide and cohabit with the said Martha Ann Keithley, and her the said Martha Ann Keithley have to wife the said former and lawful wife of the said A. R. Gonce being then and still living – against the peace and dignity of the State.

H.E. Howe (sig)
Prosecuting Attorney

A True Bill:
John H Anderson (sig),
Foreman of the Grand Jury

See the original from which this transcription was made on the facing page.

INDICTMENT.

State of Missouri, } In the Circuit Court of Stone
County of Stone   County April TERM. A. D. 1879.

THE GRAND JURORS for the State of Missouri, summoned from the body of Stone County, empannelled, charged and sworn, upon their oaths, present that A. R. Gonce late of the County aforesaid, on the 1 day of November 1876 at the State of Arkansas, County of __ to the Grand jurors unknown in State aforesaid did unlawfully and feloniously marry and take to wife one Martha Ann Keithly and to her the said Martha Ann Keithly then and there was married without the State of Missouri he the said A R Gonce then and still having a lawful wife living to wit Mary Gonce the said marrying and taking to wife by the said A R Gonce of the said Martha Ann Keithly as aforesaid being unlawful by the laws of the State of Arkansas as well as by the laws of the State of Missouri And the jurors aforesaid upon their oath aforesaid do further present that the said A R Gonce afterwards to wit on the 26th day of March 1877 within the state of Missouri to wit in the County of Stone aforesaid and from that day until the finding of this indictment unlawfully and feloniously did abide and cohabit with the said Martha Ann Keithly and her the said Martha Ann Keithly have to wife the said former and lawful wife of the said A R Gonce being then and still living against the peace and dignity of the State.

A TRUE BILL:

John H. Anderson
Foreman of the Grand Jury.

H. C. Howrie
Prosecuting Attorney.

Based on the Indictment presented on the previous page, an Arrest Warrant (Capias) was issued for Doc the following day. The body of the Arrest Warrant appears below without transcription, since it is easily readable. The cover, with the Sheriff's endorsement follows on the next page, along with a partial transcription.

6 April 1877 [Stone County B4F02C03-24]

CAPIAS.

STATE OF MISSOURI, } ss.
County of Stone

The State of Missouri,
To the Sheriff of Christian County,—GREETING:

We COMMAND you to take A. R. Gonce if he be found in your County, and him safely keep, so that you have his body before the Judge of our Circuit Court, at the Court House in the town of Galena within and for the said County of Stone on the first Monday in October next, then and there before our said Judge, to answer an indictment preferred against him by the Grand Jurors of the State of Missouri, empanneled, sworn and charged to inquire into and for the body of the County of Stone aforesaid, for

Bigamy

whereof he stands indicted. And this you shall in nowise omit. And have you then and there this Writ.

Given under my hand and the seal of our said Court. Done at office in Galena in the County aforesaid, on this 6th day of April A. D. 1877

U. M. Fisk Clerk.
By Harold Fisk Deputy

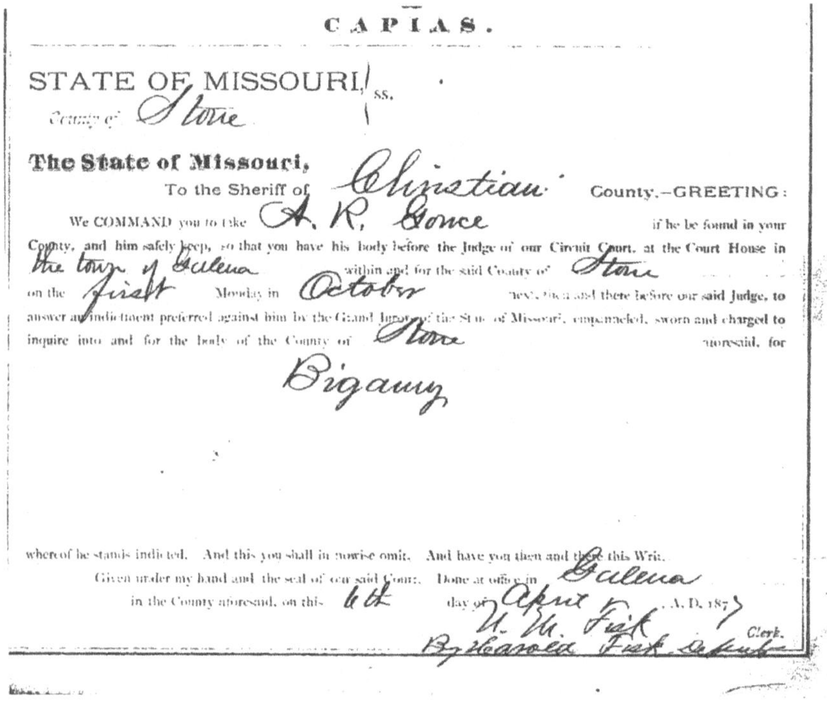

The opposite side of this Arrest Warrant showing the cover and sheriff's notes[155] is illustrated and transcribed on the next page.

155 …at least as far as I could make them out.

6 April 1877   [Stone County B4F02C03-23]

Van Beek, Barnard & Tinsley, Printers, St. Louis.

CAPIAS.

Stone County
CIRCUIT COURT.

Returnable Term. Oct 1877

State of Missouri,

A. R. Gonce

Bigamy

Sheriff will take Bond in Penalty of
Dollars.

ATTEST:

Clerk

I [...illegible] the Court [...illegible] execu[ted] the within Writ by arresting the body of A. R. Gonce and taking him before [...illegible] Judge of Circuit Court of twenty First Judicial Circuit Where [...illegible] he was [...illegible] Recognized in a Bond for his appearance to the [...illegible] of Stone County Court this May 5th 1877.

[signed] A.C.Cran's

A.C.Cran's   Fee   100
      Postage   - - - 5

The Recognizance Bond of $500.00, is shown below. Note that it took about five days for Doc to obtain this bond. Based on his later sale of land, it seems likely that he borrowed money as surety for this bond, probably from the Amos Kelly who co-signed the document.

30 April 1877   [Stone County B4F02C03-01]

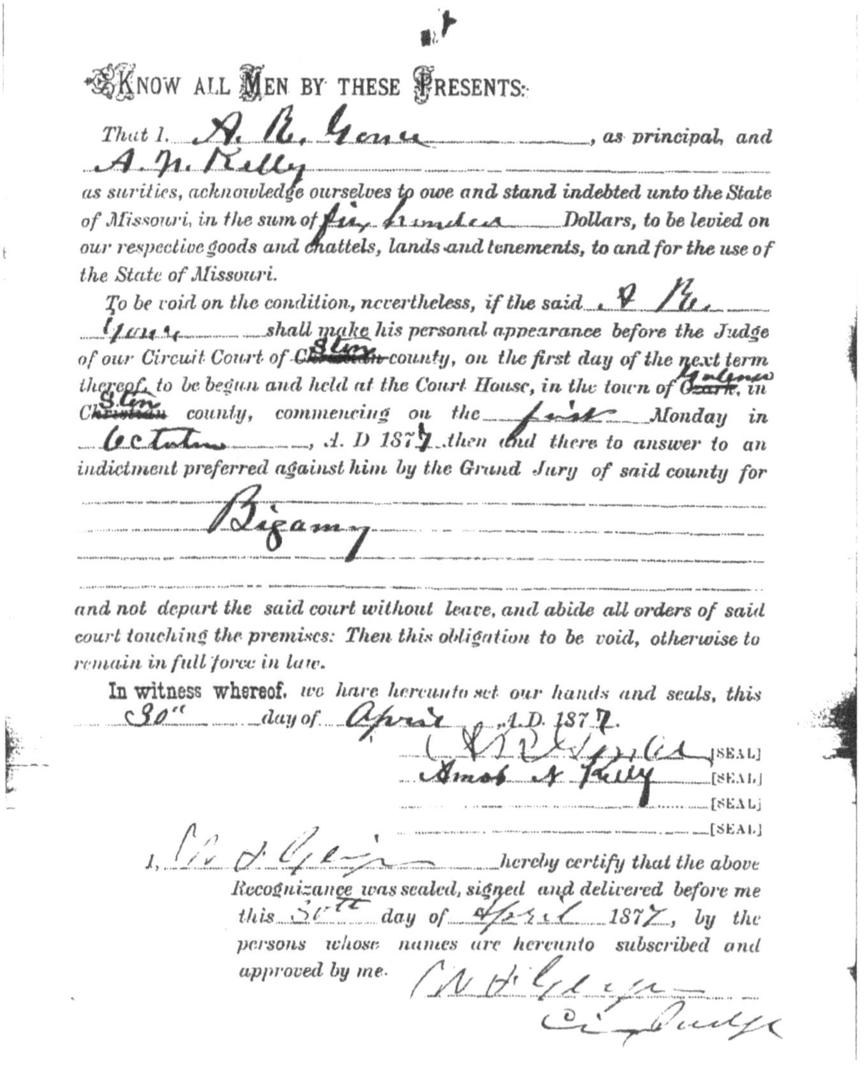

KNOW ALL MEN BY THESE PRESENTS:

That I, _A. R. Gonce_, as principal, and _A. N. Kelly_ as sureties, acknowledge ourselves to owe and stand indebted unto the State of Missouri, in the sum of _five hundred_ Dollars, to be levied on our respective goods and chattels, lands and tenements, to and for the use of the State of Missouri.

To be void on the condition, nevertheless, if the said _A. R. Gonce_ shall make his personal appearance before the Judge of our Circuit Court of _Stone_ county, on the first day of the next term thereof, to be begun and held at the Court House, in the town of _Galena_, in _Stone_ county, commencing on the _first_ Monday in _October_, A.D. 1877, then and there to answer to an indictment preferred against him by the Grand Jury of said county for

Bigamy

and not depart the said court without leave, and abide all orders of said court touching the premises: Then this obligation to be void, otherwise to remain in full force in law.

In witness whereof, we have hereunto set our hands and seals, this _30"_ day of _April_, A.D. 1877.

　　　　　A. R. Gonce [SEAL]
　　　　　Amos N. Kelly [SEAL]
　　　　　　　　　　　　　　 [SEAL]
　　　　　　　　　　　　　　 [SEAL]

I, _C. N. Gilgin_, hereby certify that the above Recognizance was sealed, signed and delivered before me this _30th_ day of _April_ 1877, by the persons whose names are hereunto subscribed and approved by me. _C. N. Gilgin_
　　　　　　　　　　　　　　C. Judge

In order to raise money to cover the anticipated cost of his legal representation, Doc Gonce sold a tract of land that he and his wife Mary owned to Charity Elizabeth Wiggins Logan, the second and much younger wife of Alexander Logan. See the biography section for further details on the very interesting history of Doc and Charity over the next eighteen years.

> *30 May 1877 [Taney County Deed Book 3; page 508]*
>
> General Warranty Deed
>
> This indenture made on the 30th day of May AD One Thousand Eight Hundred and Seventy Seven by and between A. R. Gonce and Mary A. Gonce of the County of Christian MO party of the first part and Charity E. Logan of the County of Christian in the State of Missouri party of the Second part.
>
> Witnesseth that the said party of the First Part in Consideration of the sum of One Thousand (1000) Dollars to them paid by the party of the Second Part the receipt of which is hereby acknowledged to by these presents Grant Bargain and Sell Convey and Confirm unto the said party of the second Part her heirs by A. F. Logan[156] and assigns the following described lots tracts or parcels of land lying being and situate in the County of Taney and State of Missouri to wit all that part of lot One (1) in Section Eighteen (18) and lot twelve (12) in Section Seven (7) that lies South West of the following described line beginning at a corner South Thirty Six and a half degrees West thirteen chains and sixty eight and a half links (13 68c/l) from the fraclineal quarter Section Corner left bank of White River known as County field Notes as corner & thence North forty three degrees West to the mid line of lot to Twelve (12) in the above described Section Seven (7) also all of lot two (2) in Section eighteen (18) All in Township to twenty two of Range to twenty one West of Fifth P.M. Containing Fifty and eighty five hundredths 56.85[157] acres more or less To Have and To Hold the premises aforesaid with all and Singular the rights privileges appurtenances and amenities thereto belonging or in any wise appertaining unto the said party of the second Part and unto her heirs by A. F. Logan and assigns Forever the said A. R. Gonce and Mary A. Gonce hereby covenanting that they are lawfully [leized?] of an indefensible Estate in fee in the premises herein conveyed that they

---

[156] Alexander F. Logan is ID 4108 in my Genealogical Database. Although Charity wasn't yet a widow at the time of this land transaction, the sale was to her alone. Charity's husband Alexander lived at least until the time of the 1880 census (LDS Series 1254738 Page 242). Charity also had a child (Luther E. Logan) in about 1879. My assumption is that, because Alexander had other adult heirs, he may have been attempting to insure that his second wife Charity was provided for in the event of his death.

[157] Yes, the text appears to say "Fifty and eighty five hundredths" followed by the numeric "56.85," which doesn't match. I assume "Fifty" is correct and that the "6" is a very sloppy "0."

have good right to convey the same, that the said premises are free and clear of any encumbrances done or suffered by them or those under whose they Claim and that they will Warrant And Defend the title to the said premises unto the said party of the second part and unto her heirs and assigns Forever against the lawful claims and demands of all persons whosoever. In Witness Whereof the said party of the first part have hereinto set their hands and seals the day and year first above written.

A. R. Gonce
Mary A. Gonce

State of Missouri } ss
County of Christian

Be it remembered that on this 30 day of May AD 1877 before me the undersigned a Notary Public within and for the County of Christian and State of Missouri personally came

30 May 1877 [Taney County Deed Book 3; page 509]

A. R. Gonce and Mary A. Gonce, who are personally known to me to be the same persons whose names are subscribed to the foregoing instrument of writing as parties thereto and acknowledged the same to be their act and deed for the purposes therein mentioned and the said Mary A. Gonce being by me first made acquainted with the contents of said instrument upon an examination separate and apart from her husband[158] acknowledged that she executed the same and relinquishes her dower in the Real Estate therein transferred freely and without fear Compulsion or undue influence of her said husband. I was qualified May 5, 1875. My term expires March 17 1879. In Witness Whereof I have hereto set my hand and affixed My Official Seal at my office in Ozark the day and year first above written.

W. H. Pollard
Notary Public

Recorder's Certificate

State of Missouri } ss
County of Taney

In the Recorder's Office I, Thomas F. Layton Clerk of the Circuit Court and Ex-Officio Recorder in and for the County aforesaid do hereby Certify that the instrument in writing hereto attached with the Certificate

---

[158] Note that Mary was questioned separately to determine if she was coerced in any way to sign over the property to Charity Logan. Since the essential purpose of this sale was to raise money for Doc's defense against the Bigamy charges, it likely seemed odd to the court (as it does to me) that she would willingly agree to what amounted to a loss of property.

hereon was filed for record on the 21 day of July 1877 And that the same is duly recorded in Book ? for recording deeds at page 39 and 40. In Witness Whereof I have hereto set my hand and affixed the Seal of said Court. Done at office at Forsyth this 7th day of August 1877.

Thomas F. Layton, Clerk

The above and foregoing instrument of writing with the Certificate thereon was on the 14 day of April 1888[159] duly filed in the office for the record.

R. S. Branson, Recorder
Per Wm. L. Peck, Deputy

In the midst of these proceedings, Doc's first child with Martha Keithley, their son Rolyn, was born on 23 September of 1877.

After being released from custody and arranging for the sale of his parcel of land on the White River, Doc apparently fled Stone County. When he didn't appear for his trial in October of 1877[160], the Court issued another warrant for his arrest. For reasons that are unclear to me, they must have gotten information that he was in Barry County, and on 17 December 1877 a Scire Facias[161] was issued to the authorities there to search for and apprehend him.

The Scire Facias was returned by the Barry County Sheriff over a year later, in January 1879, attesting that Doc could not be found in that County. He had already (been?) returned by September 1878, however, and was able to file a response to Mary's request for a divorce, since he was once again in Jail.

---

159 The original clearly says 1888 here, although that doesn't seem reasonable; perhaps government bureaucracies were as lethargic back then as they are now. The date is most likely 14 April 1878.
160 See Sheet B4F02C03 24 on page 78. The arrest warrant set his trial for the circuit court session beginning on the first Monday in October.
161 Stone County B4F02C03-14 and B4F02C03-15, neither of which is transcribed here.

Mary A. Gonce's Petition for Divorce: 26 September 1878

26 September 1878   *[Stone County B4F17C44-35]*

Mary A. Gonce	Pltf	}	State of Mo
vs			County of Christian
A. R. Gonce	Deft		In Christian Co Court

Plff states that she on the 28th day of March 185_[162] in the State of Tennessee lawfully maried (sic) to Deft that she continued to live with Deft until about 17 day October 1876 that during that time she faithfully demeaned herself and discharged all her duties as wife of Deft and treated her[163] with kindness and affection but Deft wholly degraded his duties as her husband did absent himself from Pltf and did abandon Pltf and go away with one Martha A. Keithley into the State of ArKansas did subsequently in said state cohabit with said Keithley that afterwards Deft returned to the State of Missouri and has since his return which was about __ day of February 1877 has continued to live and cohabit with said Keithley in Counties of Taney, Christian, Stone and Barry this State and is now living in adultery with the said Keithley in the County of ___ in the State of ArKansas

[Stone County B4F17C44-34]

Mary A. Gonce	Pltf	}	September 1878
vs			Christian County
A. R. Gonce	Deft		Mo.

Now at this day comes the Defendant and enters his appearance to this action and asks that this cause be tried at this term of the court and for answer to Plaintiff petition denies each and every allegation therein contained.

                                        Gideon + Patterson

                                             Attys for Deft.

On the back of which is the following endorsements to wit

M. A. Gonce	Pltf	}	
v			Ans of Deft
A. R. Gonce	Deft		

                                                  Filed Sept A.D. 1878

                                                  Jas. R. Bell, Clk

---

162 The document has no specific year, just the decade as shown. As far as I am aware, this is the only source available that gives the month and day of Doc and Mary's original marriage. The year is known from the 1850 U.S. Census (see page 5), on which the box labeled "Married within the Year" is checked.

163 Presumably this was supposed to be "him."

Divorce granted to Mary A. Gonce: 26 September 1878

26 September 1878 [Stone County B4F17C44-32]

Mary A. Gonce   Plaintiff
vs
A. R. Gonce   Defendant

} Divorce Decree

Now at this day comes on to be heard the above entitled cause and the said plaintiff and Defendant appearing by attorney, the said Defendant having been duly notified by publication and having also answered in the said cause the court after having the testimony in the cause doth find that the Plaintiff and Defendant were united in matrimony in the year 1850 in the State of Tennessee, that they have lived in the State of Missouri as husband and wife for about twelve years and that the Defendant now is the lawful husband of the Plaintiff that the facts stated in the petition are true; that as the lawful wife of the Defendant – the Plaintiff has been aggrieved and injured by the misconduct and mistreatment of the Defendant; that about the 17th day of October 1876 the Defendant abandoned the Plaintiff and has since been living in adultry (sic) and unlawful criminal intercourse with Martha A. Keethley *(sic)*; that there was born of the said marriage children as follows:

26 September 1878 [Stone County B4F17C44-33]

Wm M, Arthur, Martha E. Ella, Olive, Thomas, Alice, and Benjamin F.

Whereon it is by the Court Ordered that the bonds of Matrimony contracted as aforesaid be and the same are hereby dissolved and that the said Plaintiff have and retain the custody and control of the said children and that she have and recover of and from the Defendant her costs in the said cause laid out and expended and that execution issues therefor (sic)

~~J. Frank Seaman~~
~~By Henry Bronson~~
~~clerk S.C.~~

The original of the page from which the above transcription was made is shown on the next page, and gives a list of all eight of Doc's surviving children[164] with Mary A. Frazier.

---

164 One of their twin daughters, Nancy, had died before 1870.

W^m. M. Arthur, Martha E., Ella Olive, Thomas, Alice, and Benjaman H.

Whereon it is by the court Ordered that the bonds of matrimony contracted as aforesaid be and the same are hereby dissolved and that the said ~~Plaintiff~~ have and retain the custody and control of the said children and that she have and recover of and from the Defendant her costs in the said cause laid out and expended and that execution issue. Therefor

~~Frank Jerman~~ clerk
By Henry ~~Jimson~~

Once again, Doc managed to obtain several guarantors for a $500 recognizance bond and, after an altercation in the courtroom that resulted in additional indictments, was released on 15 March 1879 as documented below.

25 February 1879   [Stone County B4F02C-18]

DR. ABRAHAM RUDOLPH GONCE

[Stone County B4F02C03-19]
[Stone County B4F02C03-20]

NO TRANSCRIPTION:

The two sheets B4F02C03-19 and B4F02C03-20 contain the court clerk's completely handwritten copy of the Recognizance Bond presented above. Sheet 19 contains the transcription down to Doc Gonce's signature. Sheet 20 contains the remainder of the transcription, plus the Sheriff's response (which is transcribed on page 92 below). This handwritten copy seems to have been made specifically for the Sheriff's use in processing Doc's release after posting his bond.

In an article[165] dated 16 August 1973, A. F. St. Claire wrote: "They were trying Doc Gonce at the old log cabin on Bull Creek… They paneled the jury, got set for the trial. Mr. (Ike) Cupp (Justice of the Peace) gave the court a coffee break for fifteen minutes before they started. The doctor and the constable (Babe Weatherman) had a few words. It ended with a shootout, though no one was injured."

As can be seen from the whole article referenced above, Mr. St. Claire was relatively weak and less than accurate as far as specific details go in his summary of Doc's life. In this case as well, unless the passage above is describing some other trial, it would seem that his identification of Babe Weatherman must be incorrect. The Indictments below indicate that Doc's assault was on Alexander Osborn.

Elmer (sometimes known as Earl) L. "Babe" Weatherman spent his entire life in and around Walnut Shade, Spokane, and Pleasant Shade, but I could find no record (other than Mr. Derry's article) of him having served as Constable. In any case, since he lived from 24 April 1877 to 15 April 1972, it seems quite doubtful that he was a constable in February of 1879. His father was William P. Weatherman; and I could find no record of him being called "Babe" or being a constable either. Mr. St. Claire's anecdote, therefore, may not be correct in its particulars.

---

165 Pioneer Doctor: The True Story of Pioneer, Dr. Abraham R. Gonce The Ozark Headliner; 16 August 1973, page 1. The complete text of this article, along with some notes, is provided in the earlier biography of Doc Gonce on page 52.

Felonious Assault & Display of Weapon: 26 February 1879

On 26 February 1879, an Indictment was handed down for displaying a deadly weapon.

26 February 1879   [Stone County B4F10C26-08]

INDICTMENT

State of Missouri   } In the Circuit Court of Stone
County of Stone   } County. February Term A.D. 1879

THE GRAND JURORS for the State of Missouri, summoned from the body of Stone County, empanelled, charged and sworn, upon their oaths, present that A. R. Gonce late of the County aforesaid, on or about the 1st day of February 1879, at the town of Galena, County of Stone, State aforesaid, did unlawfully and willfully exhibit and display in the presence of Alexander Osborn A fire arm being a pistol it being then and there alegally [...illegible...] in a rude angry and threatening manner and not in the necessary defence of his person family or property.

contrary to the statutes in such cases made and provided and against the peace and dignity of the State.

Thomas J. Gideon[166]
Prosecuting Attorney Pro Tem

A True Bill
J. L. Hight
Foreman of the Grand Jury

---

166 I haven't been able to determine if he is related to J. J. Gideon, one of Doc's attorneys.

Dr. Abraham Rudolph Gonce

On the same day, and based on the Indictment above, the Arrest Warrant shown below was issued for Doc Gonce.

26 February 1879   [Stone County B4F10C26-06]

On the same day (26 February 1879), a second, related, Indictment was handed down based on the felonious assault charge.

26 February 1879   [Stone County B4F10C26-16]

INDICTMENT[167]

State of Missouri } In the Circuit Court of Stone
County of Stone   } County. February Term A.D. 1879

THE GRAND JURORS for the State of Missouri, summoned from the body of Stone County, empanelled, charged and sworn, upon their oaths, present that A. R. Gonce late of the County aforesaid, on or about the 1st day of February 1879, at the town of Galena, County of Stone, State aforesaid, did then and there unlawfully, willfully and feloniously make an assault upon the body of one Alexander Osborn and did then and there on purpose unlawfully, willfully and feloniously with a deadly weapon to wit a pistol which [...illegible...] he the said A. R. Gonce in his right hand had and held charged and loaded with gunpowder and leaden balls did then and there unlawfully, willfully and feloniously, on purpose make an assault with the intent him the said Alexander Osborn then and there to kill.

Contrary to the form of the statutes in such cases made and provided[168] against the peace and dignity of the State.

Thomas J. Gideon[169]

Prosecuting Attorney pro tem

A True Bill

J. L. Hight

Foreman of the Grand Jury

---

167 A reproduction of the original of this indictment is shown on page 22.
168 In all other uses of this form I have seen, the word "and" is always present at this location but was not written here.
169 As with the previous indictment, I haven't been able to determine if Thomas Gideon is related to Doc's attorney J. J. Gideon.

The Arrest Warrant stemming from the second indictment (for felonious assault) is shown below:

26 February 1879   *[Stone County B4F10C26-14]*

> **STATE OF MISSOURI,** County of *Stone*, ss. **The State of Missouri,**
>
> To the Sheriff of *Stone* County Greeting:
>
> WE COMMAND you to take *A. R. Gonce* if he be found in your County, and him safely keep, so that you have his body before the Judge of our Circuit Court, at the Court House in *Galena* within and for the said County of *Stone* on the *forthwith Monday* then and there before our said Judge, to answer an indictment preferred against him by the Grand Jurors of the State of Missouri, empaneled, sworn and charged to inquire into and for the body of the County of *Stone* aforesaid, for *felonious assault* whereof he stands indicted. And this you shall in no wise omit. And have you then and there this writ GIVEN under my hand and the Seal of our said Court. Done at office in *Galena* in the County aforesaid, on this *26th* day of *Feb* A. D. 1879.
>
> *Frank Leandr[?]* [signature], CLERK.

A Motion to Quash (Stone County B4F10C26-10) the less serious of these charges was presented and approved on 28 February 1879 and is illustrated on page 23.

15 March 1879 (part of 25 February 1879 Form)   *[Stone County B4F02C03-20]*

...

I, Thomas L. Giles sheriff of Stone do hereby certify that C..B. May one of the former Bondsmen of A. R. Gonce who was held to answer an indictment of Bigamy did on the 14th day of March 1879 deliver to me the body of the Said A. R. Gonce with this copy of Recognizance and the Said A. R. Gonce did on the 15th day of March 1879 [entered?] a Bond as required by Law & the Said A. R. Gonce was thereupon released from custody this the 15th day of March 1879. Sheriff's [*.is Ame..tory..ss*] to Jail $8.00

T. L. Giles, Sheriff

Abraham Rudolph Gonce's Trial for Bigamy: beginning 26 August 1879

26 AUG 1879 [Stone County B4F17C44-41]

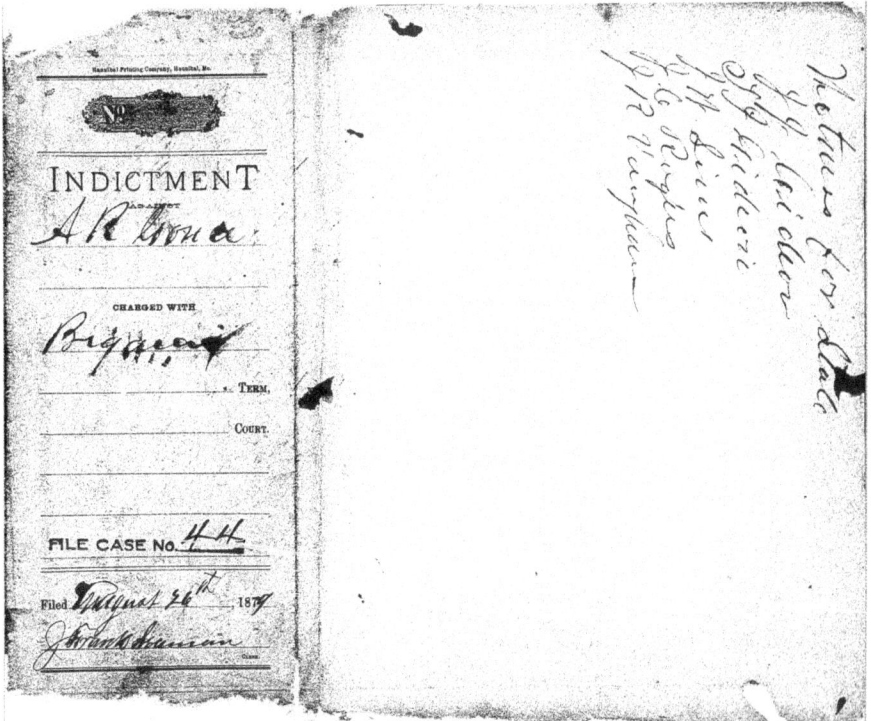

With the August Term of the Circuit Court in session, a new Indictment (above) was filed, and a new arrest warrant[170] and subpoenas were issued; Doc's trial was finally under way.

[Stone County B4F17C44-03]

State of Missouri } In the Circuit
vs } Court of Stone
A. R. Gonce } Co. Mo.
                      Aug Term 1879

   Be it remembered that on the 26th day of Aug 1879, the same being the 3d day of the ~~Stone County~~ August term 1879 of the Stone County Circuit Court where and when the following proceedings were had to wit in the above entitled case to wit the State to sustain its case so introduced the following witness to wit.

---

170 Stone County B4F17C44-16, issued 26 August 1879; this and other repetitious documents are not repeated in this paper.

[Stone County B4F17C44-04]

~~State of Missouri, Pltf~~
~~against~~   } ~~Testimony on~~
~~A. R. Gonce, Deft~~   ~~Part of the State~~

J. W. Sims[171] for the State on oath says: I live in Christian County Mo. I have been acquainted with the defendant A. R. Gonce for the term of twelve or fifteen years. I am also acquainted with a woman who was formerly called Mary A. Gonce. She is now living in Christian County Missouri. I have been intimately acquainted with defendant for several years. His son married my daughter[172]. Defendant and Mary A. Gonce have staid all night at my house and slept together. Defendant called her his wife and treated her as his wife. The last time I saw them living together was in Ozark four or five years ago.

Cross examined –

I think I have heard Dr. Gonce call Mary A. Gonce his wife. He has practiced medicine in my family. Gonce and I are on tolerably friendly terms now. We did have some difficulties once. I do not know that defendant and the woman called Mary A. Gonce were ever married.

[Stone County B4F17C44-05]

Jas. M. Patterson[173] for the State on oath says: I have known the defendant for about two years. I have been about the house of defendant several times. He always recognized Mary A. Gonce as his wife and I have heard him say that he had the best wife in the world. He also treated the children as his own and so did Mary A. Gonce (or the person known as Mary A. Gonce).

I have been his attorney nearly ever since I first got acquainted with him and have transacted a great deal of business for him.

On cross examination the witness stated: I do not know that the children are his or hers either – I have been counsel in this particular case with which he is now charged and a great deal of this information came to my knowledge ~~while~~ and in fact all of it while I was acting as his counsel.

---

171 J. W. Sims is Martha Sims' father and, thus, William McClellan (Mac) Gonce's father-in-law.
172 This refers to Doc's oldest son William McClellan (Mac) Gonce [ID 3480] and Mac's wife Martha Ann Sims [ID 3481].
173 James M. Patterson was one of Doc's attorneys. He was recalled later; see sheet B4F17C44-11, which is transcribed on page 97.

[Stone County B4F17C44-06]

J. J. Gideon[174] for the state on oath says:

I am an attorney at Law and live in Christian County Mo. I have known the defendant for ten or twelve years and have known a woman by the name of Mary A. Gonce or whom people called Mary A. Gonce for about six or seven years. They lived in the same house together in Ozark for some time. There were several children about that I think were recognized as theirs. I taught school on near (sic) Taney Creek and [*some?*] of their children came their (sic). Dr. Gonce inquired as to whether they were learning or not. I lived ~~as~~ close to deft in ~~the~~ Ozark + passed their House ~~Night + too~~ morning noon + night + I frequently saw them eating at the same table.

[Stone County B4F17C44-07]

J. C. Rogers sworn says:

I am the clerk of the circuit court of Christian County.

Here the defendant objected for the reason that there are better evidence. [~~of the ....~~] to which objection the court overruled which the deft at that time ~~objected~~ excepted.

I am custodian of the records of the Christian County Circuit Court + then produced the files in cause of Mary A. Gonce and A. R. Gonce together with the judge of the court in the cause and identified as the records of Christian County Circuit Court. The State then offered in evidence a petition & decree of divorce & said cause read to the [....] to the reading of which deft by atty then and there objected which objt was by the court overruled, deft at the time duly excepted. (Here the clerk will insert the copy of the petition [*a...*] + decree of divorce[175] from Christian Circuit Court in the suit of Mary A. Gonce vs. A. R. Gonce)

---

174 J. J. Gideon was one of Doc's attorneys. He was recalled later; see sheet B4F17C44-12, which is transcribed on page 97.
175 A transcription of this petition and decree is given on sheets B4F17C44-32 and B4F17C44-33, which are transcribed beginning on page 85.

[Stone County B4F17C44-08]

Westley Henry testimony

My name is Westley Henry. I live in Lawrance Co Mo. I am a minister in the Greeneville Baptist Church. On the night of the 10th day of April 1877 A. R. Gonce came to S. W. Mathew's where I was ~~and asked~~ with a young woman he called Martha Ann Keithley + wanted me to marry them which I did at that time. I did not at the time return to the Clerk for record a certificate of the marriage but I did afterward. Deft object to the testimony of Henry because it was not the best evidence which objt was by the Court overruled to which ruling of the Court the deft then and there excepted.

[Stone County B4F17C44-09]

Cross Examination

I am a licensed minister. I have not got my license with me but have at home. I ~~was~~ married them on Goff Creek in Stone County. I got my license from the presbytery of the free will Baptist of the Goff Creek Association of the free will Baptist.

[Stone County B4F17C44-10]

Half a dozen or so of them got together and gave ~~to~~ me the license. I [*follow?*] farming. I live in Lancaster County now.

J. Frank Seaman sworn says that

I am Clerk of the Circuit Court of Stone County Missouri and have charge of its records.

Here the deft objected for the reason that there is better evidence to which objection the court overruled and the deft at that time excepted. I have the records of marriage. Here he produced what purported to be the "Marriage Records" of Stone County.

Whereupon the Prosecuting against the objections of the Defnt read the following [*Sectry?*]

(Here the Clerk will copy the [*Sectry?*] of Marriage certificate of A. R. Gonce + Martha Ann Keithley)[176]

to which objection the court overruled and the deft at the time duly

---

176 I have been unable to locate a copy of this marriage certificate,

[Possible Missing Page(s) would be in this location]

Copies of the two original sheets from which the transcriptions on this page were made are shown on the following two pages.

[Stone County B4F17C44-11]

the witness the certified copy deft divorce. I think the hand write of the decree is in the hand writing of the deft to the best of my knowledge it looks like it. To this deft objected + court overruled + permitted [*to show?*] to the jury. Deft at the time excepted.

Cross Ex

I don't think I ever was used as a witness before to prove writings. ~~To this all the deft~~

J. M. Patterson recalled[177], says I am acquainted with the handwriting of A. R. Gonce – the writing on the decree of divorce I believe to be in the hand write of the deft. I am acquainted with his handwrite have known it for a long time – has been his atty for several years. The clerk's certificate + signature I believe to be in the same handwriting.

The deft objected to this mode of impeaching the validity of a duly certified record, the court overruled the same and permitted the same to go to jury, the deft at the time excepted.

[Stone County B4F17C44-12]

J. J. Gideon[178] for the State in rebuttal on oath says: I am an atty at law. I am acquainted with the handwriting of defendant. The copy of the decree resembles the hand writing of the defendant. ~~I am no expert and was never interested as such before I am an attorney at law~~. The deft objects, Crt ~~ovr~~ overruled + deft excepts.

Cross examined

I do not mean to swear that this copy of decree is a forgery or that the seal hereto is not genuine.

Here the ~~deft~~ State closes and

---

177 J. M. Patterson's original testimony is on sheet B4F17C44-05, which is transcribed on page 94.
178 J. J. Gideon's original testimony is on sheet B4F17C44-06, which is transcribed on page 94..

The original of Stone County Box 4, Folder 17, Case 44, Sheet 11 is shown below; my transcription is on page 97.

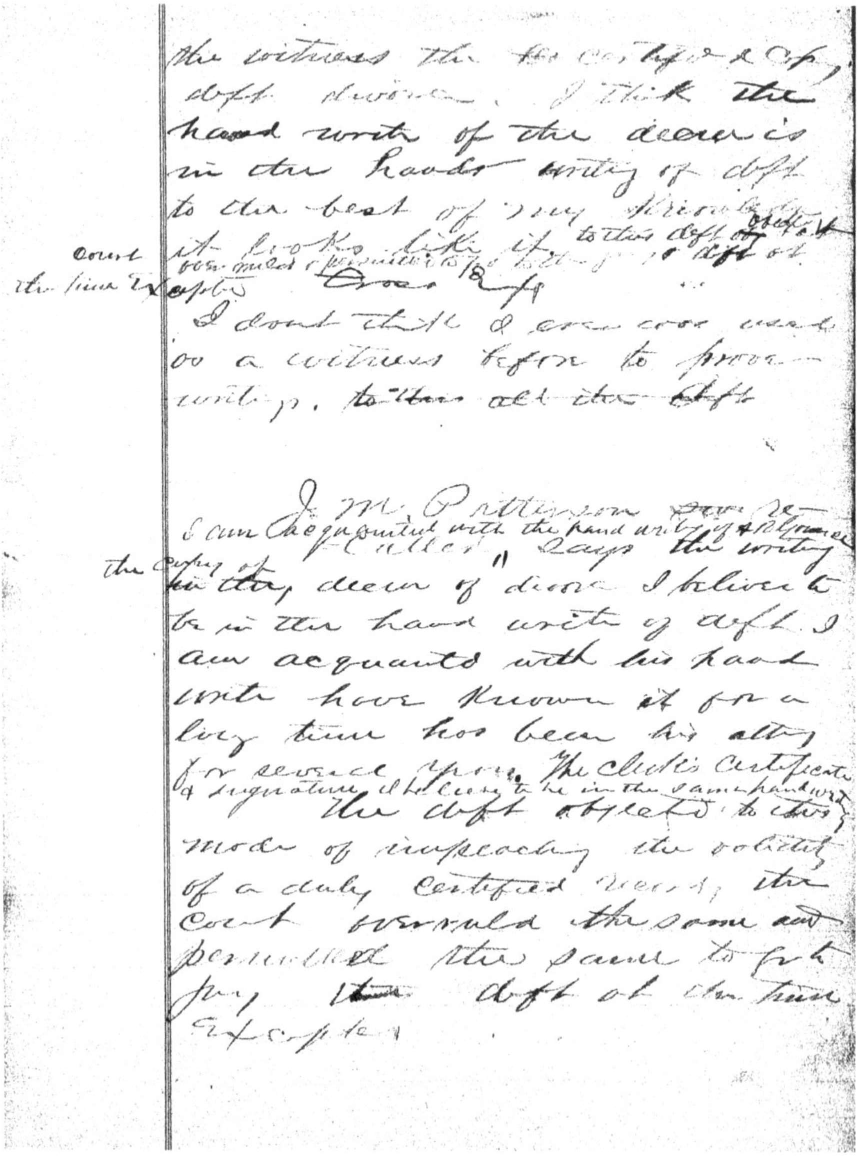

The original of Stone County Box 4, Folder 17, Case 44, Sheet 12 is shown below; my transcription is on page 97.

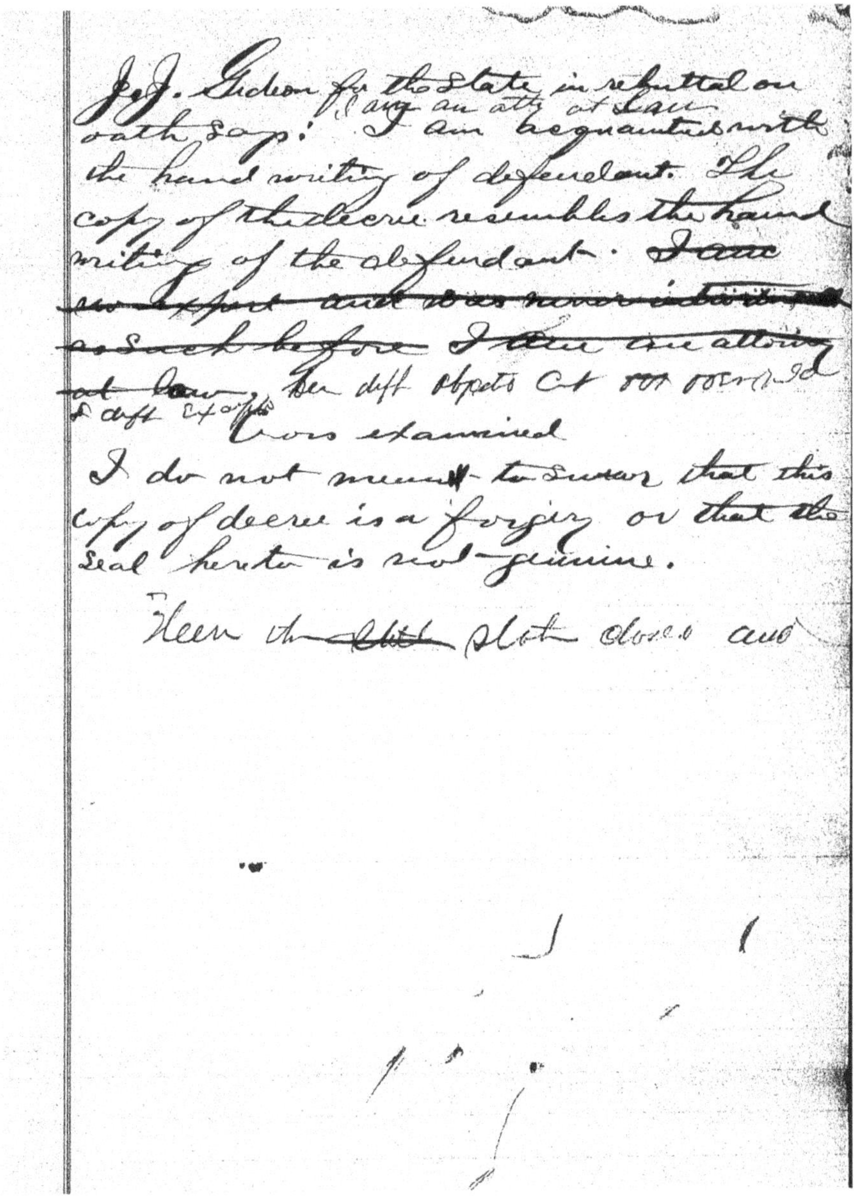

[Stone County B4F17C44-14]

the court then gave the following instructions for the State to the jury of which the deft at the time duly excepted.

(Here the clerk will copy all of the instructions given by the court as asked for by the State)[179]

The deft then asked the Court to give here the following instructions and declarations of law ~~but~~ which the court refused and the deft at the time duly excepted.

(Here clerk will copy [*ak….?*]) (also instructions [*gir?*] for deft.)[180]

Upon the instructions given by the court the jury rendered the ~~follog~~ following verdict. (Clk here copy same)[181]

Whereupon the deft filed the his following motion for new trial in words as follows to wit:

(Here Clk [*wit?*] same)[182]

which the court at said time overruled to which the deft at that time objected.

The deft then filed his motion in arrest in [*aff..le?*] judgment.[183]

The original sheet from which the above transcription was made is shown on the facing page.

---

179 The instructions asked for by the State are on sheets B4F17C44-25, B4F17C44-23, B4F17C44-24, B4F17C44-26 to B4F17C44-30, and B4F17C44-31; transcriptions of this series of sheets begins on page 102.
180 The instructions asked for by the Defense are on sheets B4F17C44-39, B4F17C44-36 to B4F17C44-38, B4F17C44-21 and B4F17C44-40; transcriptions of this series of sheets begins on page 106.
181 The Jury's verdict is on sheet B4F17C44-20; my transcription of this sheet is on page 108.
182 The request for a new trial is on sheets B4F17C44-01 and B4F17C44-02; my transcription of the motion begins on page 108.
183 This motion is on sheet B4F17C44-22; my transcription of the motion begins on page 105.

The Court then gave the following instructions for the state to the giving of which the deft at the time duly excepted.

(Here the clk will copy all of the instructions given by the court as asked for by the state)

The deft then asked the Court to give him the following instructions & declarations of law. & which the Court refused and the deft at the time duly excepted

(Here Clk will copy ones) (also instruction giv for deft) Upon the instructions given by the Court the jury rendered the following verdict

(Clk Here copy same)

Whereupon the deft filed his following motion for new trial in words as follows to wit

(Here Clk inst said)

which the Court at said time over ruled to which the deft at the time excepted

The deft then filed his motion in arrest

[Stone County B4F17C44-25]

State

vs

A. R. Gonce

Inst on part
of State

Filed August 27th 1879

J. Frank Seamon, Clerk

[Stone County B4F17C44-23]

Given If you find the deft guilty you will say in your verdict "we the jury find the deft guilty as charged in the indictment" + you will assess his punishment at imprisonment in the State penitentiary for any term not more than five or less than two years or by imprisonment in the county jail not more than twelve or less than six months or by a fine not less than five hundred dollars or by both a fine of not less than one hundred dollars + imprisonment in the county jail not more than 12 months or less than three months + one of you will sign the verdict as foreman.

[Stone County B4F17C44-24]

GivenObj If the Jury believe from the evidence that the defendant A. R. Gonce did at any time within three years [arept?] before the finding of the indictment in this case Marry Martha Ann Keithley ~~his present wife~~ in Stone County and at the time of said marriage had a wife then living they will find the defendant guilty as charged in the indictment and will assess his Punishment at imprisonment in the Penitentiary for a period of not less than two nor more than five years or imprisonment in the County Jail not less than six nor more than twelve months or by fine of not less than five hundred dollars or by both a fine ~~and~~ of not less than one hundred dollars and imprisonment in the county Jail not[184] ~~less~~ more than twelve nor less than three month

---

184 The word "not" was probably struck out unintentionally in the original. It should read "no more than…"

[Stone County B4F17C44-26]

GivenObj — The Court instructs the jury that although you may believe from the evidence that in the year 1857 the defendant was divorced from Mary A. Gonce, yet if you further find from the evidence that afterwards he continued to live and cohabit with the said Mary A. Gonce and ~~trea~~ lived with her as man and wife – held out to the world that she was his wife in that event the law presumes that she was his wife, and that it is upon him to show that she was not.

[Stone County B4F17C44-27]

Given — If the Jury believe from the evidence that Wesley Henry was at the time he solemnized the rites of matrimony between the defendant and Martha Ann Keithley a Minister of the Gospel or was acting as such, said Marriage was legally Solemnized and it makes no difference whether or not he had license from any particular denomination to Preach or Perform the function of a Minister of the gospel.

[Stone County B4F17C44-28]

Given — If after you have considered all facts and circumstances in evidence in the case, it appears to you that any other reasonable hypothesis or theory may be true except that the defendant is guilty, you will find the defendant not guilty.

[Stone County B4F17C44-29]

Given — The court declares the law to be that there is a distinction between civil and criminal cases in respect to the degree or quantity of evidence necessary to justify a jury in finding their verdict. In civil cases it is the duty of the jury to weigh the evidence carefully and find for the party in whose favor the evidence preponderates, although it be not free from reasonable doubt, but in criminal trials the party indicted is entitled to the legal presumption in favor of his innocence and that his guilt must be fully proven not by a ~~nes~~ mere preponderance or weight of evidence as in civil cases but his guilt must be proven beyond a reasonable doubt.

[Stone County B4F17C44-30]

Given — The court declares the law to be that the burden of proof to establish the guilt of defendant devolves upon the State, and that the law clothes the defendant with a presumption of innocence which attends and protects him until it is overcome by testimony which proves his guilt beyond a reasonable doubt. By "a reasonable doubt" is meant a substantial doubt based upon the evidence in the case + not a mere possibility of deft ~~innosence~~ innocence.

[Stone County B4F17C44-31]

GivenObj — The court instructs the jury that in arriving at a verdict you will not take into consideration the testimony of J. R. Vaughan, Jas. M. Patterson, J. J. Gideon and T. J. Gideon in relation to the identification of defendant's handwriting and the impeachment of the record evidence offered by defendant.

Given — If you find the deft not guilty, you will say in your verdict that the jury find the deft not Guilty as charged in the indictment + one of you will sign the verdict as foreman.

27 August 1879   [Stone County B4F17C44-19]

State

v

Gonce

Motion to Exclude[185]

Filed August 27th 1879

J. Frank Seamon, Clerk

---

185 Only the cover seems to be extant; I haven't located the actual Motion to Exclude.

27 August 1879 *[Stone County B4F17C44-22]*

State of Missouri } Stone County
vs   } Circuit Court
A. R. Gonce   } Aug Term 1879

} Motion ~~for to~~
} in arrest of
} Judgt

Comes the defendant and moves the court to arrest the judgment and assigns the following reasons therefor.

<u>1</u>st Because the court erred in refusing to sustain the defendant's motion for new trial.

<u>II</u> Because the court erred in permitting improper and incompetent testimony to go to the jury.

<u>III</u> Because the court erred in permitting the state to prove the records of Christian County Clerk by J. C. Rogers [*or til he was clerk in manner til it was down?*]

<u>IV</u> Because the ~~court + same~~ indictment states no facts

---

27 August 1878 *[Stone County B4F17C44-13.1]* [186]

State

v

<u>A. R. Gonce</u>

Bill of Exception[187]

Filed August 28th 1879

J. Frank Seamon, Clerk

FILE CASE No <u>44</u>

---

186 A decimal point is used to distinguish sides of sheets that have content on both sides.
187 Only the cover seems to be extant; I haven't located a formal list of Exceptions filed in this case.

27 August 1878 *[Stone County B4F17C44-13.2]*

The court having examined the above and foregoing bill of exceptions and finds the same true and court signs the same and made them a part of this record.

Witness my hand and seal this 27th day of Aug 1879.

W. J. Gerkin [*Cy berly?*] (seal)

[Stone County B4F17C44-39]

State

v

Gonce

Refused

Inst[188]

Filed August 28th 1879

J. Frank Seamon,

Clerk

[Stone County B4F17C44-36]

[189] The Court declares the law to be that the burden of proof is on the prosecution throughout to establish the defendant's guilt by evidence, and that defendant is not required to show his innocence until the prosecution, by the evidence it actually produces, Establishes the defendant's guilt beyond a reasonable doubt; and that to establish the defendant's guilt, the evidence must be clear and certain, satisfying the minds of the jury beyond a reasonable doubt of deft's guilt. That it is not sufficient to justify a verdict of guilty that there may be strong suspicions or probabilities of his guilt, or that the weight of evidence is in favor of the truth of the charge against the defendant, but the law requires proof by legal and creditable evidence of such a ~~character~~ nature that when it is all considered by you, you feel a clear and satisfactory conviction beyond a reasonable doubt ~~that~~ of the defendant's guilt

---

188 This next set of sheets contains the instructions that the defense recommended be given to the jury. Although some instructions appear reasonable, the court refused to adopt any of them.

189 This is requested jury instruction number 1, although the number isn't written on the sheet.

[Stone County B4F17C44-37]

Refused

[190] The Court instructs the Jury that the State did not prove, that the defendant married Mary A. Gonce

[Stone County B4F17C44-38]

Refused

3. That if you find from the evidence that the defendant was divorced from Mary A. Gonce in the State of Kentucky before he was married to Martha A. Keithley if you should find that if he was ever married to the said Martha A. Keithley you will find the defendant not guilty.

Refused

4. That even though you should find that ~~Deft~~ defendant did live with Mary A. Gonce after he was divorced from her, if you find he was divorced from her, and even raised children by her, such of it self, is not sufficient to constitute them husband and wife and would not legally prevent ~~them~~ him from legally marrying an other woman.

[Stone County B4F17C44-21]

Refused

5. It is not sufficient to authorize you to convict defendant that you should believe from the evidence that he lived with ~~a~~ Mary A. Gaunce as husband and wife but before you can convict him, the evidence must ~~pas~~ be so conclusive of the Guilt of the defendant as to exclude ~~any [xxxx] of~~ every reasonable hypothesis of ~~that~~ the defendant's innocence.

[Stone County B4F17C44-40]

Refused

6. That before you can convict the defendant you must believe from the evidence that he was actually married to Mary A. Gonce as charged in the indictment and that such marriage was a valid marriage and celebrated according to the laws of state in which such marriage was solemnized, and that during the existence of such marriage the defendant Unlawfully and Feloniously married and took to wife   Keithley as charged in the indictment.

---

[190] This is requested jury instruction number 2, although the number isn't written on the sheet.

The Jury's Verdict

[Stone County B4F17C44-20]

> We the Jury find the Defendant Guilty of the charges set forth in the Indictment and ~~fix the time~~ assess his punishment at two years ~~in the penitentiary~~ imprisonment in the state penitentiary.
>
> Thomas W. Peterson fourman (sic)

Denial of Appeal and Doc's Escape

The appeal was denied and Doc, who apparently disagreed with the idea of spending time in the Penitentiary, escaped from his handlers and disappeared.

28 AUG 1879 [Stone County B4F17C44-01]

> State of Missouri
>
> vs
>
> **A. R. Gonce**
>
> Affidavit for
>
> Appeal
>
> Filed August 28th 1879
>
> J. Frank Seaman, Clerk

[Stone County B4F17C44-02]

> State of Missouri } Stone County Circuit Ct
> vs
> A. R. Gonce   Aug Term 1879
>
> Comes the deft + by leave of the Court files herein his affidavit for an appeal to the supreme Court and assigns the following reasons therefor.
>
> Because he has been injured and aggrieved by this the judgment of this Court that this appeal is not taken for vexation or delay but in fact for that justice be done.
>
> Whereupon he prays the court that an appeal be granted to the Supreme Court.
>
> A. R. Gonce
>
> Subscribed and sworn before me this August 28th 1879.
>
> J. Frank Seaman
>
> Clerk

Since Doc was now a convicted felon, he qualified for the honor of having Governor Phelps issue a reward of $150, transcribed below, for his capture and return.

15 September 1879 [State of Missouri: Register of Civil Proceedings 1879-1882

Reward for Doc Gonce's Capture
The Messages and Proclamations of the Governors of the State of Missouri Compiled and Edited by Grace Gilmore Avery, A.B. and Floyd C. Shoemaker, A.M.; Volume VI; Published by the State Historical Society of Missouri, Columbia, Missouri, 1924. From Pages 222 and 223 (S151)
OFFERING A REWARD SEPTEMBER 15, 1879 *From the Register of Civil Proceedings 1879-1882, p. 89* STATE OF MISSOURI, EXECUTIVE DEPARTMENT WHEREAS, A. R. Gonce was convicted and sentenced by the circuit court of Stone county to two years in the penitentiary for the crime of bigamy; and afterwards broke jail, and has fled from justice and cannot be arrested by ordinary process of law, NOW THEREFORE, I John S. Phelps Governor of the State of Missouri, by virtue of authority in me vested and for good and sufficient reasons appearing, do hereby offer a reward of One hundred and fifty dollars for the arrest and delivery of said fugitive to the sheriff of said county of Stone, at the county seat thereof, at any time within one year from the date of these presents. John S. Phelps (Seal)   In Testimony Whereof I have hereunto set my hand and caused to be affixed the Great Seal of the State of Missouri. Done at the City of Jefferson, this fifteenth day of September Ad 1879. By the Governor   MICH'L K. MCGRATH, Secretary of State.

Doc was captured in less than two months, although I've been unable to determine where he was captured or who, if anyone, received the reward. The escape didn't seem to affect the length of his sentence, however. In fact, although he didn't begin serving his sentence until 24 October 1879, he was still paroled under Missouri's ¾ rule, and that was calculated from his original reporting date – not from his actual reporting date.

Doc's story from October 1879 on continues on page 28.

SECTION III:
MURDER TRIAL TRANSCRIPTIONS

27 August 1844 – 15 June 1885

Murder Trial Transcriptions

Preface

On Friday afternoon June 27, 1884, at about 4:30 pm, Doctor Abraham Rudolph Gonce [ID 2883] shot and killed his patient Charles Keysser [ID 4111], a neighbor, farmer and local Postmaster[191]. This incident is described more fully beginning on page 29. An indictment for murder was returned in Christian County, Missouri, where the murder took place, but due to a change in venue, the trial itself took place in Greene County. This section presents transcripts of the legal proceedings resulting from the murder.

In the Greene County Archives and Records Center in Springfield Missouri[192] is a collection of more than two hundred sheets related to this trial, which I have arbitrarily numbered in the order in which I encountered them. Where there is writing on both sides of a sheet, I have numbered each separately. I have transcribed most of these sheets in this document. These sheets include subpoenas, summonses, affidavits, expense reports and, of most interest, reports of the trial proceedings. The pages, unfortunately, were not in sequence or chronological order. For purposes of this paper, therefore, I've tried to place everything in chronological order. The sheet number preceding the transcription of each page indicates the order in which the original appeared, and will allow this transcription to be compared to the original documents if the reader is so inclined. Scans of some of the more interesting and/or difficult to interpret pages are provided for comparison purposes.

As with my earlier transcripts of Doc's bigamy trial, the documents from which these transcriptions were made appear to be notes taken by someone summarizing the proceedings and the responses of witnesses. Several notations similar to "(Here insert the affidavit ...)" make it appear as if these sheets are notes from which some official record was to be assembled later. If such a record exists, I haven't been able to locate it.

These records appear to be incomplete. There are, for example, summonses for witnesses for whom no testimony is shown. A few pages

---

191 Throughout these documents, the surname of the victim Charles (Charlie) Keysser was variously spelled "Kaiser," "Keiser," "Keyser," and "Kiser." I have tried to retain the spelling in each location as it appears on the original but this turned out to be more difficult to do than I had imagined. I have also attempted to retain spellings, grammar (or lack thereof) and capitalization as they appear in the original. For the most part, those sections that I cannot decipher I've enclosed in [square brackets]. Anyone reviewing this document to get a better understanding of what went on in the trial probably isn't that concerned with the spelling, but I simply wish to make it clear that my transcriptions may not be as perfect as I would like them. Corrections based on examination of the originals are welcome.

192 Located at 1126 Boonville in Springfield Missouri – Zip Code 65802.

begin or end in the middle of a sentence for which I could find no corresponding partner. There is reference to pre-trial testimony before an examining magistrate that isn't present. Nonetheless, the record gives a fairly good overview of the proceedings and is thus, at least for those interested in Dr. Gonce's murder trial, quite useful.

In the original documents I transcribed, there are a number of sentences, words, and entire paragraphs lined out. I assume these were struck out for legal reasons, and thus may not have made it into the "official" trial transcript (if that exists anywhere), but I've included all of them with the ~~text struck through like this~~ to match the originals as closely as possible.

Again, following the earlier transcriptions of the bigamy trial, I've printed all these transcriptions with one and a half line spacing, not just to mimic legal documents, but for the very practical reason that the text, being legalese, is so dense and full of run-on sentences that it would be extremely difficult to read without generous line spacing.

COURT PROCEEDINGS – 21st Judicial Court Of Christian County

Although I have not been able to obtain any records from Christian County for the indictment and change of venue, the Greene County Circuit Court issued a subpoena, shown in reduced size below, to the Christian County Court Clerk for his records, and the records provided were included in the Greene County Archives. The transcriptions of these are given first in order to preserve a chronological order.

[Greene County Archive Sheets 18 & 19]

Front (reduced size) *Back (reduced size)*

Subpoena Duces Tecum requesting that the Clerk of the Circuit Court of Christian County provide the Court of Greene County with "the original files in case of the State of Mo. vs A. R. Gonce for murder.

AUGUST 1884

S	M	T	W	T	F	S
					1	2
3	4	5	11	12	8	9
10	11	12	18	19	15	16
17	18	19	20	21	22	23
24	25	26	27	28	29	30
31	*1*	*2*	*3*	*4*	*5*	*6*

SEPTEMBER 1884

August 1884 Term – Key Dates and Characters

25 1st Day: August Court Term begins session

27 3rd Day: Indictment for Murder Found and Served

30 6th Day: Plea of Not Guilty Entered by A. R. Gonce

2   8th Day: Continuance granted to February Court Term

W. F. Geiger: Judge

Almus Harrington: Prosecuting Attorney

P. H. Travers: Defense Attorney

DR. ABRAHAM RUDOLPH GONCE

Grand Jury Indictment, Plea, and Continuance: beginning 25 August 1884

[Greene County Archive Sheet 54]

State of Missouri } ss
County of Christian }

Be it remembered that at a regular term of the Circuit Court in and for the County and State aforesaid, begun and held at the Court House in the Town of Ozark on Monday the 25th day of August, AD 1884, there were present Hon. W. F. Geiger, Judge of 21st Judicial Circuit Court of Mo, Almus Harrington, Prosecuting Attorney for Christian Co., William Gardiner, Sheriff of Christian County, Jno. C. Rogers, Clerk of said Court:

When and where the following proceedings were had to wit:

<u>Sheriff and Deputies Sworn</u>,

Now at this day comes Wm. Gardiner, Sheriff of Christian County and James J. Bruton and Joseph J. Pearce his deputies in open Court and are sworn by the Clerk as required by law touching their duties in summoning and returning Grand and [*illegible/faded*][193].

<u>Grand Jury Returned and Sworn</u>:

Now at this day comes Wm. Gardiner Sheriff of Christian County, County Missouri and returns unto open Court a list of names of twelve good and lawful men of the body of the County of Christian aforesaid to serve as Grand Jurors, viz. Joseph Ash, G..W. Taylor, H. W. Stuart, B. A. Stone, B. F. Plummer,

---

193 Text marked [*like this*] is illegible (at least to me) or faded in the original. Corrections are welcome.

[Greene County Archive Sheet 55]

Andrew McHaffie, Job Cash, Joel Hall, Abe Payne, D. F. Thompson, A. L. Turner and A. M. Laney, they having been duly selected by the County Court of said County at its regular May Term 1884, and now for good cause shown the Court doth excuse from said Jury B. A. Stone, Andrew McHaffie and A. L. Turner and doth order that the sheriff proceed to summon three other men from the body of the County of Christian to serve in lieu and stead of the said excused persons. Whereupon the said Sheriff returns the names of Wm. Park, A. Green and C. G. Neal, said Grand Jury being now composed of the following named persons to wit. Joseph Ash[1], G. W. Taylor[2], H. W. Stuart[3], Wm Park[4], B. F. Plummer[5], A. Green[6], Job Cash[7], Joel Hall[8], A. Payne[9], D. F. Thompson[10], C. G. Neal[11], and A. M. Laney[12], twelve good and lawful men of the body of the County of Christian and the said G.W.Taylor being by the Court appointed foreman, said Grand Jurors being duly empowered, sworn, and charged as the law directs retire to consider of their indictments and presentments.

And afterwards to wit on the 27th day of August 1884, being the 3 Judicial day[194] said August Term of the Court the following among other proceedings were had, to wit:

---

194 The "Judicial Days" are numbered from the opening of each session of the circuit court and include Monday through Saturday; The 3rd Judicial Day of this session was therefore was 27 August 1884.

[Greene County Archive Sheet 56]

Indictment Returned

Now at this day comes the Grand Jury and through the foreman thereof return into open Court two true bills of indictment and having further business retire to consider their indictments and presentments.

One of which said indictments was the words and figures following to wit:

State of Missouri } In the Circuit Court of
County of Christian   Christian County
                         Missouri August Term, AD 1884

The Grand Jurors for the State of Missouri within and for the County of Christian upon their oaths present that A.R. Gonce, on the 27th day of June, AD 1884, at the County of Christian aforesaid in and upon one Charles Keysser in the peace of the State of Missouri, then and there being feloniously wilfully deliberately, premeditatedly, and of his malice aforethought did make an assault and with a certain shotgun, loaded with powder and leaden balls, which said shot gun he the said A.R. Gonce in his hands then and there had and heed? him the said Charles Keysser feloniously willfully deliberately premeditatedly and of his malice aforethought by means

The original of Greene County Archive Sheet 56, from which this transcript was made, is shown at the right on the facing page.

Indictment Returned

Now at this day comes the Grand Jury through the Foreman thereof, return to open Court two true bills of indictment and having further business return to consider their indictments and presentments

One of which said indictments was in the words and figures following to wit:

State of Missouri } In the Circuit Court
County of Christian } of Christian County
Missouri August [term]
A.D. 1884.

The Grand Jurors for the State of Missouri, within and for the County of Christian upon their oaths present That A. R. Gonce on the 27th day of June A.D. 1884, at the County of Christian aforesaid, in and upon one Charles Kyser, in the peace of the State of Missouri, then and there being, feloniously willfully deliberately, premeditatedly and of his malice aforethought, did make an assault and with a shot gun, loaded with powder and leaden balls, which said shot gun he the said A. R. Gonce in his hands then and there had and held him the said Charles Kyser feloniously willfully deliberately, premeditatedly and of his malice aforethought by most

[Greene County Archive Sheet 57]

of the powder and balls aforesaid did shoot penetrate and wound and [*clearly?*] then and there did give to him the said Charles Keysser five mortal wounds of the width of One inch and of the depth of Six inches in and upon the right side of the said Charles Keysser, of which said mortal wounds the said Charles Keysser then and there died. And the Grand Jurors aforesaid, upon their oaths aforesaid do say, that the said A.R. Gonce him the said Charles Keisser, in the manner and by the means aforesaid feloniously willfully deliberately premeditatedly and of his malice aforethought did Kill and Murder; contrary to the form of the Statute in such cases made and provided against the Peace and dignity of the State of Missouri.

Almus Harrington
Prosecuting Attorney Christian Co Mo

This is a true bill

G.W. Taylor, Foreman of the Grand Jury

Filed August 27th 1884

Jno C. Rogers, Clerk

State Witnesses

J. M. Gideon, Wm. Webber[195], A. E. Kysser, Minnie Kysser, J. A. Johnson, E. T. Phillips, W. M. Gonce, M. C. Phillips, Francis Hall, Newton Cox,

The original of Greene County Archive Sheet 57, from which this transcript was made, is shown at the right on the facing page.

---

195 No summons was present in the sheets I reviewed for any of the following witnesses on this list: Wm. Webber, A. E. Keysser, Minnie Keysser, W. M. Gonce, M. C. Phillips, G. W. Flood, Milton Forbes, G. W. Clevenger, Judge Larkins, Wm. Larkins, and W. A. Aven.

of the powder and balls aforesaid did shoot penetrate and wound and there then and there give to him the said Charles Kysser five mortal wounds of the width of One inch and of the depth of Six inches, in and upon the right side of the said Charles Kysser, of which said mortal wounds the said Charles Kysser then and there died, And the Grand Jurors aforesaid upon their oaths aforesaid do say, that the said A R Gonce him the said Charles Keyser, in the manner and by the means aforesaid feloniously, willfully, deliberately, premeditatedly, and of his malice afore thought did Kill and Murder, Contrary to the form of the Statute in such cases made and provided and against the Peace and dignity of the State of Missouri.

Almus Harrington
Prosecuting Attorney Christian Co

This is a true bill
G W Taylor Forman of the Grand Jury

Filed August 27th 1884
Jno C Rogers Clerk
State of Missouri.

J M Gideon, Wm Arthur, S E Kysser Mamie Lynn
J A Johnson, E T Phillips W H Gonce.
M C Phillips, Francis Hall Newton

[Greene County Archive Sheet 58]

G. W. Flood, J. Winn, Milton Forbes, G. W. Clevinger, Judge Larkins, Wm. Larkins, J. M?. Hawkins, A. C. Gideon, W.A. Aven?, J. D. Collins, W. E. Smith, Squire Norman, and Joseph Wilson.

And afterwards to wit on the 27th day of August a certificate of service of Copy of said indictment was filed in the office of the Clerk of the Circuit Court of said County in words and figures following,

State of Missouri }
County of Christian }

I Wm Gardner Sheriff of Christian County Mo, do hereby certify that I delivered to A.R. Gonce, in Christian County MO a certified copy of an indictment against him, Charging him with the Murder of Charles Keysser, and said Indictment being found at the present August Term of Court 1884 of Christian County Circuit Court. Done this August 27th 1884 at 10 OClock AM

        Wm Gardiner
        Sheriff Christian Co MO

And afterwards to wit on the 30th day of August 1884 being the 6th Judicial day of said Aug Term of Court the following among other proceedings

[Greene County Archive Sheet 59]

were had to wit		
State of Missouri Pltf	}	Indictment
vs		Murder 1st degree
A.R. Gonce Deft		Plea of Not Guilty

    Now at this day comes Almus Harrington, Prosecuting Attorney of Christian County, who prosecutes for the State of Missouri in this behalf, and also defendant A. R. Gonce in his own proper person and by his attorney and council in open Court and being duly arraigned on said Indictment for plea thereto says he is not guilty in manner and form as charged in the indictment.

    And afterwards to wit on the 2nd day of September 1884 It being the 8th Judicial day of said August Term of Court the following proceedings were had to wit

State of Missouri Pltf	}	Indictment Murder 1st degree
vs		Affidavit for Continuance
A.R. Gonce Deft		filed by Defendant

    Now at this day comes the defendant A. R. Gonce in his own proper person and by his attorney and council into open Court and be leave of the Court files his affidavit for a continuance of this case to the next regular term of this Court.

[Greene County Archive Sheet 60]

Which said Affidavit in words and figures following to wit:

		In the Circuit Court of
The State of Missouri	}	Christian County Missouri
vs		August Term, 1884
A.R. Gonce		Affidavit for Continuance

A.R. Gonce, being sworn states, that he is defendant, and that he now stands indicted in the above mentioned Court for Murder in the first degree, that he has been indicted at this term of this Court; and that previous thereto he has been and still is confined in jail upon such charge, which imprisonment has been for over two months, that during that time he has had but little opportunity to prepare his defense, That on last Saturday was the first time that he was arraigned and required to answer said indictment, That immediately thereafter he prepared a partial list of his witnesses and ordered subpoenas, to be issued for them, and affiant is informed that only a portion of them has been served, That said list was not complete, that there are other witnesses who are material to affiants defense, that defendant does not at this time know where they live, That their names and testimony are hereinafter given,

[Greene County Archive Sheet 61]
Affiant states that said witnesses reside in different Counties and are absent without any fault upon his part, That if a continuance be granted him until next term of this Court he can procure the testimony of said absent witnesses, That the time has been so short that defendant has been unable to prepare his defense, That his attorneys has but recently been employed: The Names of the parties, who are absent and whose attendance is desired as witnesses for the defendant, are credible persons and that defendant believes that their testimony is true and that he so believes because he has been so informed by them and others That One Spenser Smith[196] if present would testify that he saw the difficulty which resulted in the death of the said Keysser, That at the time the defendant came along the road and passed Keysser's house on the way to the defendant's home that when opposite a point where the deceased was plowing in a field the deceased stopped and threw his plow lines on the plow handles and abused and threatened the defendant and said to the defendant are you ready or you are ready are you, and turning to the defendant

---

196 In the eventual trial, Spenser Smith was actually summoned as a Prosecution Witness. See Greene County Archive Sheets 32 and 33. His testimony begins on Archive Sheet 177, transcribed on page 148.

[Greene County Archive Sheet 62]

in a defiant and threatening manner shoved his hand in his pocket and drew a weapon on Defendant and that thereupon the deft shot him: That he Smith saw someone go to the body of the deceased soon after he was shot and take up a pistol or something looking like one[197] and took the same to Kaisser's house.

That Martha Brown[198] if present would swear that in a conversation with Mrs. Lizzie Keisser[199] a Witness in this case on the part of the State, on the next day after the said Charle Keysser was killed said to her the said Martha Brown that she knew and saw that either Gonce or her husband had to be killed, that Gonce had passed their house that morning and that her husband was in a great rage, and that as it was she would rather have had Keysser killed, than for her husband to have been guilty of killing the defendant, and that she saw a gun sitting in Keysser's house on the morning after the killing, the same being Keysser's gun and the only one he had.

That Ambrose Keithley[200] would, if present, testify on the day and at the house and at the time at which Mrs. M. C. Phillips[201] will testify in behalf of the State that the Defendant said that the Dutch around Highlandville ought to be killed and if he

[Greene County Archive Sheet 63]

lived long enough he lived to kill some of them, he was present and that ___ Defendant Gonce did not make any such statement as that sworn to by the said M. C. Phillips on defendant's preliminary examination and which she is intending again to swear to on the trial of the Defendant in this case.

That the defendant can prove by Dick Logan[202], James B. Wilhite and John T. Nelson[203], that they knew the deceased Keysser and that he was a quarrelsome dangerous and vindictive man and that they knew his reputation in this respect and that he had the reputation of being a dangerous and quarrelsome man and of a

---

197 In Smith's testimony he said nothing of the sort.
198 There was no summons for Martha Brown in the records I examined, nor did I find any testimony by her.
199 This is Sarah Elizabeth Logan ID 4110, daughter of Alexander A. Logan ID 4108 and wife of the victim in this case, Charles G. Keysser ID 4111.
200 Ambrose Keithley was summoned by the defense (see Archive Sheets 48 and 49), but I found no testimony of his recorded.
201 Mrs. Phillips' testimony is given beginning on page 137. Interestingly enough, she had earlier written to Doc Gonce's wife (see letter on page 158) asking for fifty dollars in order to "get out of the way" and not testify.
202 The records contain a Prosecution summons for a G. W. Logan, but no summons for Dick Logan.
203 John T. Nelson was another person summoned by both the Prosecution and the Defense.

violent disposition.

That defendant can prove by Wash Huff[204], John T. Nelson and Mrs. Mary Brown that on the day of the killing and at that time the defendant was apprehensive of great danger of bodily harm about to be inflicted upon him at the hands of the deceased.

That the defendant can prove by one John T. Jones[205] that as he the defendant has today learned but who has not been subpoenaed in this cause for the reason that the defendant has not had an opportunity to have him subpoenaed and did not know what he would testify until the defendant

[Greene County Archive Sheet 64]

began the preparation of this affidavit that the deceased Keysser was a violent and dangerous man and was in the habit of going about the Country armed and with a pistol in his pocket by day and under his head at night.

That said Ambrose Keithley lives in Taney County, Smith in Stone County but is at work in Greene County that Martha Brown, Wilhite, Mrs. Mack Gonce, Dick Logan + Jones live in Christian County that the said Sigle Evans[206] lives in Greene County and the remainder of said witnesses in Stone County.

That Mrs. Mack Gonce will swear that at the time of the difficulty she heard loud talking and a difficulty in and about Keysser's field and [*some one say all right?*]

That there are no other witnesses by whom these facts can be so fully proven present and that this application is not made for vexation or delay merely but to obtain substantial Justice in the trial of [*my?*] cause.

    A R Gonce

Subscribed and sworn to before me this 2nd day of Sept AD 1884

    Jno C. Rogers

    Cir Clerk

---

204 I could find no summons, deposition, or testimony for Wash Huff in the records I reviewed.
205 There is a Defense summons in the records for John T. Jones, but I have found no record of his testifying.
206 I haven't been able to identify this person.

DR. ABRAHAM RUDOLPH GONCE

[Greene County Archive Sheet 65.1]

and afterwards to wit on the 2nd day of September 1884 It being the 8th Judicial day of said August Term of Court the following proceedings were had to wit

State of Missouri   }   Murder 1st degree
vs   Continued on Affidavit of
A.R. Gonce Deft   the defendant

Now at this day comes Almus Harrington Prosecuting Attorney of Christian County who prosecutes for the State of Missouri in this behalf and the defendant A. R. Gonce in his own proper person and by his Attorney and Council in open Court and this cause is by the Court continued on the affidavit of the defendant until the next regular term of this Court.

FEBRUARY 1885

S	M	T	W	T	F	S
1	2	3	4	5	6	7
8	9	10	11	12	13	14
10	11	12	18	19	20	21
22	23	24	25	26	27	28

February 1885 Term – Key Dates and Characters

23   February Court Term Session Begins
23   1st Day: Change of Venue Filed and Granted

       W. F. Geiger: Judge
       G. A. Watson: Prosecuting Attorney
       P. H. Travers: Defense Attorney

Change of Venue requested and granted: 23 February 1885

[Greene County Archive Sheet 65.2]

State of Missouri   }
Christian County

     Be it remembered that a regular term of the Circuit Court within and for said County of Christian was begun and held at the Court House in the Town of Ozark on Monday the 23d day of February AD 1885 at which were present Hon W. F. Geiger Judge of the 21st Judicial Circuit of Missouri, G. A. Watson, Prosecuting Attorney of Christian County, and Wm Gardner Sheriff of Christian County and Jno C. Rogers Clerk of said Court

[Greene County Archive Sheet 66]

When and where on the 23d day of February AD 1885 It being the 1st Judicial day of said February Term of Circuit, the following proceedings were had to wit

State of Missouri Pltf 　} 　Indictment Murder 1st deg
vs. 　　　　　　　　　　　Petition and affidavit for a
A.R. Gonce Deft 　　　　　Change of venue filed

Now at this day comes G. A. Watson Prosecuting Attorney of Christian County who prosecutes for the State of Missouri in this [xxxx] as well also the defendant A. R. Gonce in person and his attorneys into open Court and by by leave of the Court files his Petition and affidavit for a change of venue in this cause to some other County in this judicial circuit.
Which said Petition and affidavit is words and figures following to wit:

State of Missouri
vs. 　　　}
A.R. Gonce

To the Honorable Circuit Court of Christian County Mo now in session Your Petitioner A. R. Gonce would most respectfully state to this honorable Court that he now stands indicted in this Court for murder and that the minds of the inhabitants of the County of Christian

[Greene County Archive Sheet 67]

are so prejudiced against him that he cannot have a fair trial in Christian County Mo and that the knowledge of the facts of such prejudice has first come to his knowledge since the last term of this Court.

　A. R. Gonce

State of Mo 　　　　}
County of Christian

A.R Gonce being duly sworn says that the above and foregoing petition and allegations therein set forth he believes to be true.

　A. R. Gonce

Sworn and Subscribed to before me the 23d day of Feby 1885.

   Jno. C. Rogers, Clerk

   By Jno. P. Collins, Dep

and afterwards to wit on the 23d day of February 1885 the f[207] same being the first judicial day of said February Term AD 1885 the following proceedings were had to wit:

State of Missouri Pltf   } Indictment Murder 1st degree
vs.   Venue to Greene County
A.R. Gonce Deft

Now at this day comes as well G. A. Watson Prosecuting Attorney of

[Greene County Archive Sheet 68]

Christian County who prosecutes for the State of Missouri in this behalf and the said Defendant in his own proper person and by attorney and application for a change of Venue in this cause made by the defendant herein and heretofore filed coming on to be heard and from an examination of said application It appearing to the Court that defendant alleges that the inhabitants of Christian County are so prejudiced that he cannot have a fair trial and the said application being verified by the defendant and the premises all and singular being seen and fully understood by the Court it is ordered that the Venue of this cause be changed to the Circuit Court of Greene County in the 21st Judicial Circuit of Missouri and the Clerk of this Court is ordered to make out and certify a Transcript of the record and proceedings had in said cause had in the Christian Circuit Court as required by law.

State of Missouri   }
County of Christian   } ss

   I, Jno C. Rogers Clerk of the Circuit Court within and for the said County do hereby certify that this and foregoing transcript of the record

---

[207] This is not a typo – it is clearly a very neat "f" separated by spaces, but I have no idea what it means.

[Greene County Archive Sheet 69]

of and proceedings in the cause where the State of Missouri is Plaintiff and A. R. Gonce is defendant including the opening orders of Court swearing of sheriff, empannelling of the Grand Jury and return of the Indictment in said cause as fully as the same remains of record in my Office.

(SEAL)

Witness my hand as Clerk and the seal of said Court thereto Affixed. Done at Office in Ozark this 1st day of April 1885.

Jno C. Rogers
Clerk

INDEX

Open Order of Court Aug 1 1884	1	(Archive Sheet 54)
Sheriff and Deputies Sworn	1	(Archive Sheet 54)
Grand Jury Empanelled	1	(Archive Sheet 54)
Indictment Returned	3-4	(Archive Sheets 56 and 57)
Indictment	3-4	(Archive Sheets 56 and 57)
Certificate of Sheriff service of Copy	5	(Archive Sheet 58)
Arraignment of Defendant	6	(Archive Sheet 59)
Affidavit for Continuance	7-11	(Archive Sheets 60 – 64)
Continuance	12	(Archive Sheet 65)
Opening Order Court Feb 1 1885	12	(Archive Sheet 65)
Petition and Affidavit for Change of Venue	13	(Archive Sheet 66)
Order Granting Change of Venue	14-15	(Archive Sheets 67 and 68)
Certificate of Clerk	15-16	(Archive Sheets 68 and 69)

This ends the transcription of the Christian County Records subpoenaed by Greene County.

> Comments on the Change of Venue
> *The Change of Venue to the Greene County Courthouse in Springfield seems to be a token change at best. Springfield was not that far away relative to the areas in which Doc Gonce practiced, and the Springfield Daily Herald was the only newspaper available in that area. Their arguably biased 29 June 1884 reporting of the murder (transcribed on page 29 and reproduced on the following page) was probably seen by more Greene County residents than Christian County residents.*

DR. ABRAHAM RUDOLPH GONCE

COURT PROCEEDINGS – Circuit Court Of Greene County

JUNE 1885

S	M	T	W	T	F	S
	1	2	3	4	5	6
	8	9	10	11	12	13
14	15	16	17	18	19	20
21	22	23	24	25	26	27
28	29	30				

May 1885 Term – Key Dates and Characters

1 May Court Term in Session at beginning of June
1 Defendant's Motion for Continuance
4 Trial Begins
10 Instructions to Jury
10 Guilty Verdict Returned (2nd Degree Murder: 30 years)
13 Motion for New Trial (denied)
15 Bill of Exceptions and Final Motions

M. G. McGregor: Judge
J. J. Gideon: Prosecuting Attorney
P. H. Travers: Defense Attorney

Defendant's Motion for Continuance: 1 June 1885

[Greene County Archive Sheet 85]

State of Missouri

vs

A. R. Gonce

Motion and Affidavit

for Continuance

Filed June 1st 1885

John R. Ferguson, Clk

[Greene County Archive Sheet 79]

The State of Missouri   } In Circuit Court of
vs.   Greene County, MO
A.R. Gonce   May Term 1885

Now comes the defendant A. R. Gonce and his attorneys and files this motion for a continuance of this cause for the following reasons to wit: on the account of the absence of a material witness by the name of Wiley Cloud, which will more fully appear from and by the affidavit the said defendant herewith filed.

Vaughn, Travis, Payne & Patterson
Attorneys for Deft

[Greene County Archive Sheet 80]

State of Missouri } ss
County of Greene }

A. R. Gonce, being sworn - makes oath and says that he now stands indicted for murder in 1st degree, that he is confined in the jail of Greene County Missouri, and desires a trial for his case at this term of the Circuit Court of said County, but is unable to have his trial at this time for the want of material witness who is absent without his knowledge, consent of for [*curement?*]

That the testimony of absent witness is material to affiant's defense and that he cannot safely proceed to trial without said testimony - that affiant knows of no other person present that he can prove the same facts by - That the name of said absent witness is Wiley Cloud and lives in Stone County Missouri a distance of about thirty miles from this place.

That if said witness was present he would testify as set forth in his testimony hereto attached and made a part of this affidavit.

That affiant caused a subpoena to be issued for said Wiley Cloud some two weeks ago[208] and had the same placed in the hands of the Sheriff of Stone County with full instructions to have it served upon said absent witness together with other witnesses.

That said subpoena has been served upon all the other witnesses but as to said Cloud the same

---

208 This was on 13 May 1885; a copy of this summons, from Archive Sheet 46, is presented on page 206.

(signed) J. R. Ferguson Jun(Start)85 FILED

[Greene County Archive Sheet 81]

was returned endorsed not served, that immediately defendant procured another subpoena for said Wiley Cloud[209] and gave it to another person with full instructions to go and serve the same upon said Wiley Cloud - that Affiant fully believes that he can [pr---?] the presence and personal attendance of said absent witness within ten days from this date

That said listing is material as will appear from a statement of his testimony hereto attached, and he believes that he will so testify because the said witness did so testify in the case before Judge Geiger on an application for bail. That affiant has been informed today that on yesterday the said Wiley Cloud was at his home in Stone County as [afiisda?]

That said testimony is true, and that this application is not made for [execution?] or delay, but to obtain substantive justice upon the trial of the Cause.

                    A. R. Gonce (signed)

Sworn to before me this 1st day of June 1885

                    John R. Ferguson, Clerk

[Greene County Archive Sheet 82]

My name is Wiley Cloud. I live in Stone County MO about 30 miles from Springfield and I have lived there about all my life. I am now about 24 years old. On the morning of the 27 day of June 1884, the day that Kaisser was killed I was going from my House in Stone County MO to Hylandville Christian County MO and I went by Charles Keyser's and called for a bottle of German Syrup and asked Mrs. Keiser the price. I told her I could Get it for less in Hylandville and She said I could ask Mr. Kaiser. I turned and commenced to talk to Mr. Keyser who was in his field and we saw someone coming towards us down the road from towards Hylandville, and Kaiser asked who is that I said it is Dr. Gonce. Kaiser said "God damn him I said I would kill him and I will do so."

---

209 This was on 3 June 1885; a copy of this summons, from Archive Sheet 20, is presented on page 206.

[Greene County Archive Sheet 83]

Dr. Gonce came up and spoke and asked me how is George Wilson and I said "he is very bad and is looking for you this morning" and Gonce and I was talking. Kaiser Got over the field fence just behind Gonce and he was Swearing all the time we were talking and said God damn you Gonce I intend to kill you. Gonce then road (sic) off. Going towards Wilsons and Keiser walked on towards the House + got over the yard fence and went in the direction of his store house Swearing? and his wife met him and caught hold of him and said to him "don't do that Charley you will ruin yourself," he tried to push her out of his way and went to the porch of his dwelling house - and said to Gonce who had got some distance away "God damn you I said I would kill you and God Damn you if you ever pass this road

[Greene County Archive Sheet 84]

again I will do it." I then went on to Hylandville and I saw no more of Kaiser but as I went back a [House?] I went by Kaiser's House and did not see him. I saw Dr. said Gonce that evening in Stone County, MO and I told him not to go home by Kaiser's for he was in the Brush watching for him Gonce, and if he went that way he would be killed by Kaiser and I told Gonce that I had been to Hylandville and came back by Kaiser's and did not see Keyser, but did see where the brush was broken down as though a man had been standing there over the road and told Gonce that Kiser was in the brush watching for him.

Greene County Archive Sheet 84, transcribed above.

State of Missouri vs A. R. Gonce: Case for the Prosecution:

[Greene County Archive Sheet 197]

The State to sustain the issues on its part introduced the following testimony:

Dr. Collins sworn:

I live in Christian County. I remember the circumstances of Kaiser being killed. It was on the 26th[210] of June 1884 in Christian Co. Missouri. About 2 weeks before this I had a conversation with the defendant. In this conversation the defendant told me that the Sunday previous Kaiser had come to his - Gonce's - house, and requested him to come out. that he went out and Kaiser accused him of telling that he (Kiser) had had the "clap", said he wanted to settle it, that defendant put his hand in his pocket on his pistol and cocked it, that Kaiser heard him cock it and went off; that he (deft) was sorry he had not killed Kaiser that Sunday, and if he came around again he would kill him. This was in Highlandville and within two weeks of the killing.

On cross examination:

I don't know what day of the month or week it was. Gonce said Kaiser had come to his house on Sunday morning and demanded why he had told that so malicious tale on him, called him [...*faded/illegible*...] to settle it

[Greene County Archive Sheet 198]

th[...*illegible*...] settle it any way Gonce would say; that Gonce then cocked his pistol and Kaiser went off. In the conversation, Gonce said that what he had said of Kaiser was true, Kaiser said it was not, and from this the quarrel arose. This conversation Gonce had with me was in front of [*Ganett's?*] store and lasted about half an hour. In the conversation Gonce told me that Kaiser said he would shoot it out or settle it any way. Gonce did not say in that conversation that he was sorry if he had had anything to do with Kaiser, & didn't tell me that Kaiser had come with a pistol, but said that Kaiser said he was willing to settle it then or anywhere or in any way that Gonce wanted to - Gonce said all right, cocked his pistol and Kaiser left. Kaiser was a German and had lived there ten years.

---

210 Actually, it was on the 27th of June. Contrary to "Christian County – Its First 100 Years" reports, Doctor John D. Collins began practicing in Ozark in the late 1870s. He did not move into the area after Dr. Gonce was sent to prison, as that history reports, but had already established himself in the area and knew Gonce.

I testified before the examining magistrate ~~I said that Gonce told me he didn't want any thing to do with Kaiser~~. I don't remember just what I said then.

[Greene County Archive Sheet 196]

Thomas S. Norman, sworn:

I lived in June 1884, within 1/2 mile of Ponce de Leon. I saw Gonce the day Kaiser was killed about 27th June 1884. I met him as I was going to dinner. He seemed to be in trouble and told me that Kaiser had threatened to kill him; that Kaiser had told him he should never pass that road again alive and had tried to get his gun to kill him, Gonce, but was prevented by his family; he said that he, Gonce, was not afraid; and Gonce asked me what I would do under the circumstances. I believe he asked me if I had a revolver and I told him no & said if I had I wouldn't loan it to you for you're a man that would use it. Says I, I will tell you what I would do, I would [*find?*] him over to keep the peace. Gonce replied I can't well do that for I can't [sw...] I am afraid of him, but I believe he will [*brush?*][211] me. I said, Doc, you had better go back

[Greene County Archive Sheet 192]

2^{212}

some other way, Christian County don't like you much anyway. He said he believed he would get some arms and go back that way. He seemed to be in a deep study and made off towards Winn's, and I saw him no more that day. After he left I heard 6 shots[213] that seemed to be at or near Kaiser's house. This was June 27th 1884, and Kaiser was killed about 4 or 5 O'Clock that afternoon.

On Cross Examination:

Gonce was horseback when I saw him. He had a good practice and had not been drinking. He said Kaiser had tried to kill him that morning while he was quietly riding along the road, and said he was afraid Kaiser would shoot him from the bush. I inferred that he intended to arm and take care of himself. He seemed determined and his face was red.

---

211 It seems like "ambush" would be appropriate here, but there is definitely no "am" at the beginning of this illegible word. This original of this sheet is reproduced on the facing page.
212 The numbers at the top of various pages seem to be mostly sequential/chronological, but they don't represent page numbers or court days. I haven't been able to determine their significance, if any.
213 The shotgun Doc used could not have fired six shots without reloading several times.

Thomas S. Norman, sworn:

I lived in June, 1884, within ½ mile of Paul D'Lera. I saw Gonce the day about 27th June 1884 Kaiser was killed. I met him and was going to dinner. He seemed to be in trouble and told me that Kaiser had threatened to kill him; that Kaiser had told him that he should never pass that road again alive, and had tried to get his gun to kill him, Gonce, but was prevented by his family. He said that he, Gonce, was not armed, and asked me what I would do under the circumstances. + said if I had would n't loan it to you, for you're a man that would use it revolver and I told him no. Says he, I will tell you what I would do, I would bind him over to keep the peace. Gonce replied, I can't well do that for I can't prove it. I am afraid of him, but I believe he will brush me. I said, Doc, you had better go back

Greene County Archive Sheet 196, transcribed on the previous page.

[Greene County Archive Sheet 195]

Mrs. M. C. Phillips, sworn:

Gonce and a man by the name of Keithley[214] came to my father's to get dinner. This was before Kaiser was killed.

    I heard Gonce say at that time to Keithley that the Dutch around Highlandville ought to be killed and if he lived long enough he would kill some of them. (Objected to by the defendant for the reason that it is incompetent, irrelevant, and has no reference to the deceased.)

    The court overruled defendant's objection, and permitted the statement to go to the jury. To which ruling of the court the defendant then and there at the time excepted.

    They (Gonce and Keithley) were sitting at the table at the time of the conversation, and it was about 2 o'clock in the afternoon two weeks before the killing. Gonce was talking [/. ....] to the people of Highlandville. He called no names.

Here the letter afterwards introduced by the defendant is shown witness, and she says:

"I wrote the letter, that is my signature."[215]

[Greene County Archive Sheet unk]

[216]

[Greene County Archive Sheet 191 (page 193 is identical)]

about 2 weeks ago about what Gonce had said about him; that he would have killed the damn son of a bitch then if he had not [*wilted?*]. The next day I heard of Kaiser being killed. He was killed on Friday. Deft said he wasn't armed this morning but now I am. Said they had had a fuss about two weeks before, because he had doctored Kiser + told what was the matter with him + Kiser tried to make him take it back. I saw Kiser next day in his coffin.

    On Cross Examination:

---

214 This was Ambrose Keithley, Doc's brother-in-law; see Archive Sheet 62 on page 124.
215 This letter, written on 15 May 1885 to Doctor Gonce's wife, and in which Mrs. Phillips offers not to testify against Doc Gonce if she is paid fifty dollars, is introduced by the defense later. It appears on Greene County Archive Sheet 160, which is transcribed on page 159.
216 It appears there is a missing page or pages here.

Gonce was on the public road when I met him. He seemed to be excited or mad or frightened. He said Kaiser had told him that he should not pass that road again alive; and said he had nothing against Kaiser.

When I saw Kiser that day was at his table + I thought was eating his dinner.

[Greene County Archive Sheet 194]

Newton Cox sworn:

I saw Gonce at my yard fence the day Kaiser was killed. This was ½ mile from Ponce. Gonce asked me to bring him a match to light his pipe. I took him some fire. Gonce had a gun at that time. Saw the same gun afterwards at Highlandville. Winn[217] had it afterwards. I live in the main road from Highlandville to Ponce D'Leon.

It was a breech loading shot gun – examined it. Saw Winn have it afterwards at Ponce de Leon. Kiser was killed same day Gonce passed my house – 27th June 1884.

Martha Gonce[218] sworn:

Defendant is my father in law, and was at my house between 3 + 4 O'Clock of the day Kaiser was killed. He had a gun and stayed about an hour. My husband was at home. We lived about 100 yards from the Highlandville and Ponce De Leon

[Greene County Archive Sheet 190]

<u>3</u>

road and half mile south of Kaiser's. Gonce said he was sick and I said what's the matter and he said he was troubled more than anything that Wiley Cloud had told him that Kaiser was waylaying him in the road; that as he was going to Ponce that morning Kaiser and Cloud were talking at the road, and when Kaiser saw him coming he broke and ran in the house to get his gun, but was prevented by his wife, who said to him "hold on Charlie, don't do that" and that Kaiser said to his wife "I intend to kill the damned old rascal - I said I would kill him and I will do it," and when he got nearly out of hearing Gonce said Kaiser bellowed at him and told him, if he ever passed that road again he would be a dead man. Gonce said he believed it was Kaiser's intention to kill him, that he didn't want to kill Kaiser or hurt him and

---

217 This is presumably Joshua Winn, who was summoned as a prosecution witness (see Greene County Archive Sheets 26 and 27); I haven't located any testimony from him in the records, however.

218 This is Martha Ann Sims [ID 3481], wife of William McClellan "Mack" Gonce [ID 3480], who was Doctor Abraham Rudolph Gonce's oldest child.

Dr. Abraham Rudolph Gonce

wouldn't unless he had to. He said he wanted to find out if Kaiser was waylaying him, and I told him I would send the children[219] to see. The children came back and said Kaiser was plowing in his field. Gonce said all right that he wasn't afraid if Kaiser was not in the

[Greene County Archive Sheet 189]

bush. Gonce then stated he had a gun and a revolver. He took the revolver from his coat pocket and put it in his pants pocket and said it was a good one. I heard one shot in the direction of Kaiser's about 1/4 hour after Gonce left. I saw Gonce when he passed Kaiser's house. He was riding slowly and it was from 5 to 10 minutes after he passed till I heard the report of the gun. I heard some talk between Kaiser and Gonce. I knew the voice of Kaiser but could not tell what he said about the time the gun fired I heard Gonce say "all right."

On Cross Examination:

Gonce seemed to be much worried and troubled - said he was afraid

[Greene County Archive Sheet 188]

Kaiser would kill him, that Wiley Cloud had told him Kaiser would kill him. I sent my son[220] to see if Kaiser was in the bush. Gonce told my husband that something had to be done; that if he met Kaiser on open ground he would not be afraid of him. I couldn't see either Gonce or Kaiser at the time of the shooting + Kaiser was talking loud like he was in anger. I heard Gonce say "all right." I lived by Keiser two years.

---

219 Note the plural here; compare to the testimony on sheet 188 below and 156 (on page 164).
220 This most likely refers to their oldest son James McClellan Gonce [ID 3680], who would have been almost thirteen years old at the time of the shooting. Earlier testimony from Martha Sims Gonce (see page 139), Doc's daughter-in-law, suggests that James' younger brother Carl Abraham [ID 3682] may also have gone to see where Keyser was as well. She refers to "sending the children."

[Greene County Archive Sheet 6]

> **OATH OF WITNESS.**
>
> **STATE OF MISSOURI,** } ss.
> COUNTY OF GREENE.
>
> I, the undersigned, do solemnly swear that I was duly subpœnaed as Witness in the case wherein *State of Mo* is Plaintiff, and *A. R. Gonce* is Defendant, on the part of said *State of Mo* and that I have served *one* days and traveled *50* miles in obedience to said subpœna, *and have withdrawn myself from business during the full time for which pay is claimed.
>
> *Wm Larkins*
>
> Subscribed and sworn to before me this *5th* day of *May* 188*5*.
> *John R. Ferguson* CLERK.
> °Revised Statutes, Chapter 103, Section 5630.

There are seven oath sheets in the Archives; the one shown above is for William Larkins, whose testimony is given on the next transcribed sheet. These oaths appear to be made for the purposes of reimbursement of expenses, rather than as a prelude to giving testimony.

A complete list of the oath sheets found in the archives is given below.

Oath Sheets in Greene County Archives for Gonce Murder Trial

Name	Date	Archive Sheet Number	Note
Clevinger, G. W.	5 MAY 1885	1	
Phillips, E. F.	4 MAY 1885	2	
Phillips, E. F.	4 MAY 1885	3 (outside cover)	
Thrissimond, Jesse	4 MAY 1885	4	
Thrissimond, Jesse	4 MAY 1885	5 (outside cover)	
Larkins, Wm.	5 MAY 1885	6	Shown above
Larkins, Wm.	5 MAY 1885	7 (outside cover)	
Tirbon, J. M.	5 MAY 1885	8	
Larkins, Judg	5 MAY 1885	9	
Nelson, John T.	7 JUL 1885	199	
Nelson, John T.	7 JUL 1885	200 (outside cover)	

[Greene County Archive Sheet 187]

William Larkins[221]:

I was at Kaiser's plowing, about 200 yards from the house the day Kaiser was killed 27th June. Went to plowing at 8'Oclock in the morning. Kaiser was plowing in another field. I was in the field. Keiser's horse is [in al?] North West from the house. Kaiser was South East of me. I saw Gonce that day between 9 + 10 O'clock, going south from Kaiser's house. ~~We~~ I turned out about 11½ O'Clock. ~~We~~ I passed Kaiser's house going home. I was plowing far? faster?. ~~We~~ I saw Kaiser sitting on his porch with his family. ~~We~~ I went back about 2 O'clock and Kaiser was in the field plowing then. ~~We~~ I stopped a few minutes when Kaiser was at work. He had a shirt and cotton pants. Between 3 + 4 Oclock I heard a gun fire south east from where I was + screaming. ~~We~~ I then stopped work and ~~we~~ I went in a run to where Kaiser was and found him lying there. His wife was turning him on his side when I got there. The plow was 8 feet from where Kaiser was killed, and the ground was fresh plowed. From the tracks Kaiser made a circle to the left.

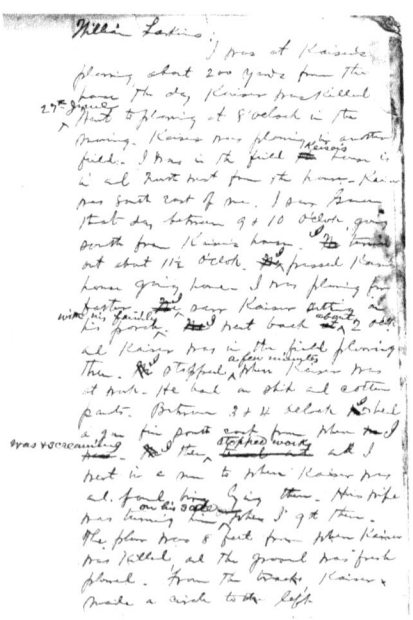

Greene County Archive Sheet 187 showing the beginning of William Larkin's testimony from which the above transcription was made.

---

221 Larkins was a farm hand working at Charlie Keysser's, although he did not live with the Keyssers.

[Greene County Archive Sheet 185]

3½

I saw blood and saw where shot struck the corn 10 or 12 feet about 15 feet from the plow. He was plowing corn[222] with one horse and was going west + plow where he was shot was 30 feet from the fence along the lane. Blood from plow, circling around with his tracks to south to where laid. He gasped twice after I got there. When I got where he was nobody there but Mrs. Kiser + children.

On Cross Examination:

The road passing Kaiser's house was east and west. The lane is about 200 yards long. Kaiser's plow was standing 30 yards from fence facing west, the lines hanging on the plow fastened together at the ends. I didn't see Gonce that evening. I was just 200 steps from where Kaiser was killed. I stepped the ground I expected to be a witness. Heard no talk before or at the time of plowing. There was no noise where I was. There were hand holds in the lines; they were not fastened together. I don't know whether I was certain of anything.

Re X[223] – I noticed horse tracks along fence, in the road + south of traveled track of road nearest where Kiser was shot to where shot had been fired for distance

[Greene County Archive Sheet 186]

of 30 yards. The travel was in center of road + road 30 feet wide + these tracks about 4 feet from the fence next to where Kiser was killed + 5 or 6 feet from traveled part of road – I examined these tracks about one hour after Kiser was killed. I didn't notice any fire arms on Kiser's person or about there when I went down – I took his horse + went after Mr. Carter + Mr. Flood – gone 5 or 10 minutes. Kiser had shirt + pants on when he was killed – The road was torn up at side where tracks were.

---

222 Since the corn was already growing at the time, we can only assume that he was actually clearing out weeds from between the rows. On June 27th, the corn would not have been very high ("knee high by the fourth of July" being the traditional farmer's maxim.)

223 I assume this means "re-direct," not "re-cross."

[Greene County Archive Sheet 181]

4

Judge Larkin[224] sworn:

I saw Kaiser the day he was killed. After he was killed Geo. Clevenger, William Forbes, Flood and Smith went with me. When I got there his wife and children were there. When I heard of killing went down on 26th or 27th of June 1884. Saw him dead in his field same day he was shot. Was dead when I got there. In Christian County, Missouri - nobody there when we got there but Mrs. Kiser + her children. (makes plat showing tracks and position of plow - 16 tracks to where he fell starting from between plow handles. Saw horse tracks in lane outside. Lane about 30 feet wide. Wagon track in center about 8 or 10 feet wide. A gap in fence where Kiser had driven in + horse tracks along fence from outside from there nearer field. Corn was shot up and bloody. He had on thin cotton shirt + [*thur?*] cotton pants. Had two pockets in front. That was all he had on - except hat and shoes. - no socks - noticed wounds. Shot with small shot - Keiser was dead when I got there. I saw Gonce bet 3 + 4 o'clock one mile from Kisers' talking to Smith. Didn't hear what he said.

William Forbes sworn:

I found plow wrench on Kaiser's person, in his right pants pocket, just after he was killed. He had 2 pockets in his pants. I was there 2 or 3 hours before his body was examined. The body was 10 or 12

---

224 "Judge" was his name, not his profession. On the oath card he signed, it appears that his name may actually be "Judg," rather than "Judge". He was called to testify again – see page 155.

Dr. Abraham Rudolph Gonce

[Greene County Archive Sheet 184]

feet from the plow. Some 40 or 50 shots in his right side and arm. From the tracks he must have turned to the left nearly east in a circle. His first tracks were? south east of plow and then went north east. The tracks of horse in the road 5 or 6 feet from main track in road and facing where Kaiser was. I found the same tracks between Kaiser's fence and the road about 20 steps. I was at Flood's harvesting + as soon as we heard it Clevinger, Judge Larkins, Flood, Smith and myself went there together. Nobody there but deceased's family. Searched deceased + found an iron plow wrench or clovis pin with wrench in end in right pocket + tobacco in left. Mr. Carter + I searched. That was all we found. Plow was 10 or 12 steps from fence. Horse tracks in road near fence, between travelled track + field fence nearest deceased.

Dr. E. B. Brown: Am Physician + Surgeon - I examined the body, found 44 holes on right side, ranging inward, downward, and backward. The holes were made with No.2 [*Tarpee?*]

Greene County Archive Sheet 184, transcribed above.

[Greene County Archive Sheet 182]

shot. I probed four particularly. One in the left arm and behind the elbow right backward, one in front and above the hip in same direction. I found some difficulty in [*broking? the hip?*] Couldn't probe wounds in breast without raising his right arm - no shot rounds in his right arm[225]. ~~If the right arm was hanging by the side from the [xxxx] of the shot, some of them would have struck the arm~~. I have had experience in surgery.

Ques: From the examination of the wounds and from the probing and the direction of the shot ~~[illegible] or they went through the body~~ and the position you had to place the body in to probe the wounds what position was the body in at the time the wounds were inflicted?

To this question the defendant objected, because the answer involved a matter of opinion of the witness; [*al?*] the position of the body was a question of fact to be found by the jury.

But the court overruled the objection of defendant and permitted the witness to answer the question, to which ruling of the court the defendant then and there at the

---

225 It seems to me that this testimony that there were no shot rounds in the victim's right arm would have been viewed by the Defense as convincing proof that Kaiser was reaching behind him at the time he was shot, particularly since subsequent testimony indicated that the shots had come from the victim's front side. Doctor Brown seemed to reach that same conclusion, but it was struck out in the record as shown. The original from which this transcript was made is shown on the next page.

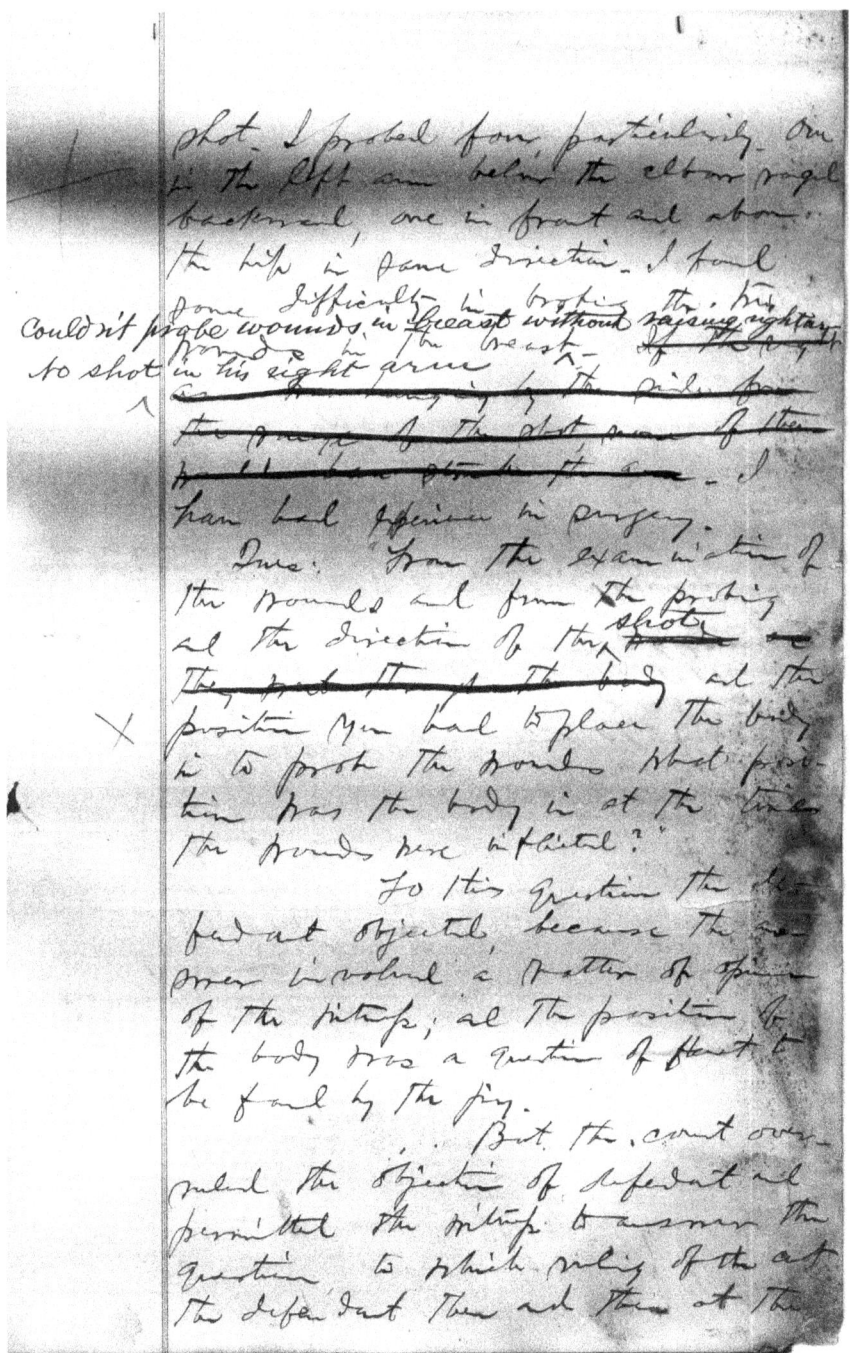

Greene County Archive Sheet 182, transcribed on the previous page.

[Greene County Archive Sheet 183]

time excepted.

Ans: I can't tell what position he was in. The reason why the probe wouldn't enter is because the muscle was below the hole. We had to raise the right arm to probe the wound. ~~I supposed~~ the wounds caused his death. In my opinion the shot that extended below the third rib I believed entered the heart and killed him. Raising shoulder alone or throwing arm back would not raise muscle sufficiently. To put the arm on a level with the shoulder would raise the muscle from 1/2 to 2/4 inch and we so raised it before probe entered. I thought from the probing that shot at nipple entered heart + would cause almost instant death. Other shots entered lungs + abdomen.

Dr. Fulbright[226] sworn: Physician + surgeon. Examined deceased after death. Probed wounds had to elevate right arm to do so -

Question: Was the position you had to place the body in to probe the wounds and from the range of the wounds, in your opinion what position was the body in when the wounds were inflicted?

Objected to by defendant because it is not a matter of skill or science. But the court overruled the objection of defendant and permitted the witness to answer the question, to which action

---

226 This is assumed to be J. H. Fulbright, for whom there is a Summons (Archive Records Sheet 26 and 27).

[Greene County Archive Sheet 177]

5

of the court the defendant then and there at the time excepted.

Answer: I don't know what position. The man that did the shooting must have stood to the right[227] and in front of the man shot. Kaiser came to his death from the effects of the wounds.

Cross ex – You could raise that muscle raising the arm to a level with the shoulder. We couldn't raise the muscle by raising the shoulder.

Spencer Smith[228] sworn:

Saw Gonce on the day Kaiser was killed – first at Ponce, then beyond Flood's, near the sign board between ¼ and ½ mile from Kaiser's. I was coming to Springfield. He was traveling same direction. I heard the report of a gun and in about 10 minutes afterwards Gonce overtook me in the road. He said he had killed Kaiser and seemed to be cool about it + had gun. I said that looked bad + he said Kaiser had run on to him and

[Greene County Archive Sheet 178]

he had to kill him. He had a gun across his saddle in front of him. This was about 3 O'clock. I viewed the ground, saw where Kaiser had circled around and fell but saw no plow. When I saw Clevenger, Larkins, Flood + Forbes harvesting + went + told them + we went down together. Found him dead + no one but Mrs. Kiser + little ones there. Saw shots in corn + blood. I left in about ten minutes. Carter came before I left.

On cross examination:

About 11:30 O'Clock that morning I asked Mrs. Kaiser if I could water my team at their well[229]. I drove on 75 yards from the Well after watering and I stopped and stayed there til 2 O'Clock. I saw nothing of Kaiser. Gonce told me that Kaiser had run on to him. ~~When I got to where Kaiser's body was there were 3 or 4 persons there, I saw [illegible] looking for tracks.~~ The well is 25 or 30 steps from the [*st..?*] and right across the road from where Kaiser was killed 45 or 50 steps. I was in plain view of the field where I stopped. From the time I started

---

227 Based on the previous testimony of Dr. E. B. Brown, this must mean to Kaiser's right from Kaiser's perspective, not Gonce's – i.e. "to the victim's right."
228 There is a Prosecution Summons for Spenser Smith on Archive sheets 32 and 33.
229 Mrs. Kaiser testified that she didn't remember his coming there that morning. See Sheet 174 on page 151.

[Greene County Archive Sheet 179]
to when Gonce overtook me was about 8 or 10 minutes. I had my wife along who was an invalid in a covered wagon.

George Clevenger[230] sworn:
When I got there Kaiser was dead + Mrs. Kaiser was holding his head in her lap. I was the 1st one to get there with Flood, Smith, Larkins + Forbes. Carter came next. I found plow and gear, assisted in examining the ground, found blood and gun wadding and corn shot off. The plow was pointing west and in front of tracks. The tracks turned off to left of plow and circled south. There were horse tracks on outside of fence, between fence and traveled road. ~~I never examined between fence and wall.~~ It seemed as though the horse's head had been turned towards the field, then he had turned and gone angling across the ~~field~~ road

[Greene County Archive Sheet 180]
like he was scared. It seemed like the other tracks on the outside of fence turned around and gone [*illegible*] of the road
Don't know how far the tracks were apart. It looked like horse had been jumping. I saw some wadding in a little wash that was between the plow and fence. The tracks at the fence were in position with the wadding and plow, the tracks outside of the fence, the wadding, the plow and the corn about where Kaiser was shot were in a line. Kaiser must have been standing between plow handles when shot + line of wadding.

Mrs Kaiser[231]:
I am the widow of the deceased. I first saw Gonce in the afternoon between 4 + 5 o'clock of the day my husband was killed.

---

230 Although testifying here for the State, George Clevenger was issued a Summons by the Defense; this is on Archive Sheets 44 and 45. George was harvesting at the time of the shooting.
231 This is Sarah Elizabeth Logan [ID 4110], daughter of Alexander A. Logan [ID 4108] and wife of Charles G. Keysser [ID 4111]. Her younger step-mother Charity Logan later married her husband's killer.

[Greene County Archive Sheet 173]

<u>6</u>

He had passed our gate horseback going towards Highlandville + had a gun. I was at the house and Kaiser was in the field plowing at the time.

Husband killed by deft 27th June 1884 in Christian Co. Mo. (points out deft). Was on porch when deft passed with gun - I went into road + followed deft, Deft turned his horse to fence.

I went out to the gate in the road, Gonce stopped and turned his horse around and asked my husband "are you ready." My husband said "no." and then Gonce raised up his gun and shot him, as quick as he could get his gun up. Kaiser was plowing at the time + did not stop until spoken to. He held to the plow handle with his left hand and raised his right. When Gonce shot him he went backward, then forwards and fell on his face. When Gonce shot he went off as fast as his horse could go in the direction of Highlandville. Will Larkins got to Kaiser first - Kaiser had been plowing that afternoon about 1 1/2 hours when he was killed. He had on cotton shirt and [*cottonade?*] pants with 2 pockets in front. Wiley Cloud stopped at our fence that

[Greene County Archive Sheet 175]

morning when Kaiser was in the field plowing. I found out that Kaiser was mad. I thought he was mad at Cloud. I heard them talk, heard Kaiser's voice and went on the porch and Kaiser was in the yard coming to the house and I asked him what was the matter and he replied he knew what he was doing and went back to the field to work. You can't see much past the gate from our house going towards Ponce from the shrubbery is in the yard. I first turned around and went back in the house. I didn't see Gonce there that morning[232]; but had heard of his making threats against my husband before that day -

My husband was not armed in the field. Gonce asked him if he was ready. He said no. Kaiser did nothing. ~~I can't say whether [xxxx] right hand was]~~

---

232 This is contradicted by Wiley Cloud's testimony; Cloud indicated that she not only saw Doc that morning, but intervened to keep Charlie from going after him. See Cloud's deposition on sheet 83 (page 134) and his testimony on sheet 162 (page 156). Doc Gonce mentioned her involvement that morning as well on sheet 155 (page 163).

[Greene County Archive Sheet 174]

On cross examination:

Kaiser did not quarrel with Gonce in the field. He just said no. I don't know where his right hand was when he was shot. He went ~~about~~ 7 steps, then forward in a circle and fell and Gonce started off fast as his horse could run down the side of the road. I was on the porch when Gonce went by. I heard short words by Kaiser ~~after I started from the house~~, but don't know what they were, in the morning when Cloud was there. I asked him, what was the matter. He said that he knew what he was doing. I thought he and Wiley Cloud were quarreling. Kaiser was in the field plowing when Cloud came and asked for German syrup. I did not see Wiley any more. I did not testify before that when I went out I saw Wiley Cloud going off up the road. When I last saw Cloud he was in the lane in front of the store, then I went back in the house. I don't remember of Smith's passing the

[Greene County Archive Sheet 176]

house and watering his horses[233] that morning. I don't remember that I swore before the [*pinter?*] that I saw Wiley Cloud ride off up the road in a gallop and couldn't see him but for a short distance. It is 40 or 50 yards from the house to where Kaiser was plowing. When Gonce passed by I said to Minnie I was afraid Gonce would hurt her pa. I got about half the distance to where they were when Gonce stopped. I started from the house as soon as Gonce passed the gate. I was kind of running when I heard the conversation between Gonce and Kaiser. I hollered but don't know what I said. Gonce had passed the house frequently and I was never alarmed at him before. Gonce was gone when I got over the fence. He didn't have a gun when he passed other times

---

233 Compare to Smith's testimony on sheet 178 (page 149).

[Greene County Archive Sheet 169]

7

Mr. D. J. White[234], sworn:

I saw Gonce on the day of the killing. Met him in the road ¾ mile this side of Kaiser's house. He was traveling the road when I first saw him, and riding fast. When he came up to me he said you will find a dead man down the road. I asked who. He said Kaiser. I asked him if he killed him. He said yes he had killed the damn son of a bitch. I asked Gonce if Kaiser had tried to go in the house that morning to get a gun. He said no that Kaiser got between the porch and gate and turned round and told Gonce not to pass that way again. I left Highlandville about 4 O'Clock and had ridden about a mile when I first saw him. I heard the horse

[Greene County Archive Sheet 170]

coming in a run before I saw Gonce.

On Cross Examination:

I live a mile N.W. of Kaiser. I was going to Carter's my father in law. I met Flood ¼ mile from his house. I had heard in Highlandville that Kaiser had tried to kill Gonce that morning. Gonce didn't tell me that Kaiser had said anything to him that morning.

Minnie Kaiser[235], sworn:

Dr. Gonce killed father. The first I saw of Gonce he was passing the house, horseback and had a gun. Pa was in

---

234 I can't determine who this is. There were Prosecution summonses issued for Thomas White, Sen. (Archive Sheets 28 and 29) and W. D. White (Archive Sheets 34 and 35), but the initials don't match either of these.
235 This is Minnie H. Keisser, oldest of the five children of Charles and Sarah Keisser. She was about 12 years old at the time of the murder and 13 at the time of the trial.

[Greene County Archive Sheet 171]

the field plowing at the time. I was sitting in the door when Gonce passed. He was going east[236]. When he passed Ma started down to where Pa was and I followed her and got about 1/3 of the way when the gun fired. Gonce asked Pa if he was ready and Pa said no. Then Gonce shot and started toward Highlandville in a run. Pa walked 16 steps and fell. The children[237] were in the orchard when it started. Gonce was close to the fence when he fired. Pa lived about 1½ minutes.

Cross Examination:
Mother and I were standing in the door when Gonce passed, and she said there goes Gonce, He might kill Pa and she started. I followed. I

[Greene County Archive Sheet 172]

climbed over the fence first. Gonce was gone then. I was about in the gate when I heard the ~~shot~~ talk. When Gonce spoke Pa stopped and turned round facing Gonce and held the plow with his left hand.

I saw Wiley Cloud at the house that morning. I heard loud talk and supposed it was Wiley Cloud and Pa talking. I didn't see Gonce there in the morning. I went to the house about ½ hour before Pa turned out in the morning. He turned out between 10 + 11 Oclock. When I heard the talk in the morning Pa was talking like he was mad. The talk lasted between 5 + 10 minutes. I saw Wiley Cloud on his horse while the talk was going on. I heard Cloud say something about German syrup. Pa was still in the field when the talk was going on. I didn't see Cloud when he rode off. I didn't tell

---

236 That is, he was heading toward Highlandville. The road going to Highlandville goes east at this point, but mostly runs north.
237 The "children" (Minnie herself was only 12) were probably Alma (b. 1876), Herman (b. 1878), and Olga (b. Mar 1882); the last child Clara (b. Feb 1884) was still a baby and probably would have been in the house.

[Greene County Archive Sheet 166]

8

Squire McDonald[238] that I heard Pa use awful rough language. I didn't tell him I didn't know how long Pa slept. I didn't tell him that Ma told me that Pa had hold of the plow handle when he was shot. Ma hollered after Gonce shot but I don't know what she said. Pa was 15 steps from the fence when he was shot.

Here the testimony of witness taken at preliminary examination was shown her. She admitted her signature and said she had sworn as therein stated.

Sarah E. Kaiser, recalled[239], sworn:

My brother's wife took the clothing. The children were in the orchard when Gonce passed. Minnie was standing on the porch. It is ½ mile from our house to Flood's. I don't remember that I said anything to Minnie except I was afraid Gonce would hurt her Pa. I don't know when Gonce was there in the morning. I made pants and shirt husband wore at time + same were shown witnesses + identified by her.

[Greene County Archive Sheet 167]

Judge Larkins[240] sworn:

The clothing exhibited is the same Kaiser had on when killed. I got them at Logans. The shirt was cut and torn off. Wounds corresponded with holes pointed out in shirt.

This was all the testimony on the part of the State and the State here rested its case.

---

238 I found no other references to Squire McDonald, nor do I have any idea who he is, but assume he must have been the original "examining magistrate" mentioned in a few other places. There was evidently some conflict between what Minnie stated during the original investigation and this testimony. See archive sheet 147 transcribed on page 171.
239 Mrs. Kaisser's previous testimony was transcribed beginning on page 150; she had three brothers, but this likely refers to her brother George W. Logan, since he was only one summoned by the Prosecution. The Summons is on Archive Sheets 14 and 15.
240 Judge Larkins' previous testimony was transcribed beginning on page 143.

State of Missouri vs A. R. Gonce: Case for the Defense:

[Greene County Archive Sheet 168]

The defendant to sustain the issues on his part introduced the following testimony:

Wiley Cloud[241], sworn:

    I was born in Stone County, am   years[242] old, knew Kaiser, knew Gonce. I was at Kaisers about 10 o'clock in the morning of the day Kaiser was killed. I had started from home to Highlandville. I live 3 ½ miles from the line between Stone + Christian Counties. Kaiser was in the field plowing when I rode up and I asked Mrs. Kaiser where Kaiser was the price of the medicine I wanted. She held it up and hollered to Kaiser and asked him the price of it. He was about 50 yards off and he hollered back 75 cents. I said I could get it at Highlandville from Keithley for 60 cents. Just then Gonce rode in sight at bend in the road going south toward

[Greene County Archive Sheet 162]

9

Ponce DiLeon. When Gonce came in sight Kaiser asked me who it was. I said Gonce. Kaiser then let loose of plow and lines and started towards the house and said God damn his old soul. I will kill the God damned old son of a bitch. I said I will kill him and I will do it. By that time he got astride the field fence, and when he got to his yard fence he did not take time to open the gate but climbed over the fence and ran into the store – just in the store and right out again – and started towards his house, saying all the time he was going to kill Gonce; and Kaiser's wife caught hold of him and told him not to kill Gonce, and [*bothered?*] him till Gonce got about yards below the house. Kaiser looked after Gonce and said if he should never pass that road again alive. Gonce was then riding pretty [*pertly?*] down the road towards Ponce. Mrs. Kaiser had hold of Kaiser two or three minutes. Kaiser was trying to go

---

241 Wiley Cloud was summoned by both the Prosecution and Defense, these summonses are reproduced on page 206.
242 In the original, a space was left for Wiley Cloud's age, but nothing was filled in.

[Greene County Archive Sheet 163]

into the house and was making the threats I have stated. I was as close to Kaiser as from here to the court house door. Kaiser was a loud spoken man. Gonce never said anything to Kaiser during all this time. I went back by there between 11 + 12 o'clock that day and saw Kaiser's plow in the field. It looked as if it had not been touched since I saw Kaiser in the morning first. It was about 50 corn rows from me. I saw Gonce at Ponce as I went back. He asked me if I had seen Kaiser. I told him if I was in his place I would not – not – go back that road. I saw some bushes parted as I went along the road and told Gonce that I believed Kaiser was in the bush. I saw this bush shaking like a bug or something was there + heard grunting like a hog. This was 200 yards from Kaiser's house towards Ponce. I told Gonce this. Where I saw the bushes parted was on the main traveled

[Greene County Archive Sheet 164]

road.

On Cross Examination:

When I passed Kaiser's in the morning about 10 o'clock, I stopped there 10 or 12 minutes and about even with his store and was 50 yards from his while I was talking to him. I was a better friend to Gonce than any other common man[243]. I was gone to Highlandville 1½ or 2 hours. I saw Kaiser's wife and some of his children that morning when I went by to Highlandville and Kaiser was plowing in the field. Kaiser started in [illegible] when I told him it was Gonce coming. I met his wife pretty near corner of store. The whole time I was there was not over 10 minutes. From the store

---

243 The use of the term "common man" seems to indicate that Cloud considered Doc Gonce to be of a somewhat higher class.

[Greene County Archive Sheet 165]

to house is 8 or 10 steps.

John Nelson[244], sworn:

    Heard Gonce and Kaiser had a quarrel at Gonce's house on Sunday about 2 weeks before Kaiser was killed. Kaiser went to Gonce's went into the yard. I was there at Hay's 60 or so yards away. I went from there to Garretts. I didn't understand any thing either of them said. They quarreled about 10 minutes. They were standing between the building and smoke house.

[Greene County Archive Sheet 158]

<u>10</u>

Pleasant Maples sworn:

    I lived in Christian County near Highlandville, 3 years and 1¼ from Kaiser + saw him 3 days before he was killed. I met him hunting horses and he asked me if I had heard the scandalous tale that Gonce had told about him and his wife having the bad disorder[245], and said that he or Gonce one had to die inside of a month from that day. He told me he meant just what he said. The reputation of Kaiser in the neighborhood where he lived was that of a quarrelsome man.

On Cross Examination:

    I told this to no one till after Kaiser was killed. I kept it still 8 or 10 days.

---

244 Like the earlier witness Wiley Cloud, John T. Nelson was summoned to testify by both the Prosecution (Archive Sheets 22 and 23) and Defense (Archive Sheets 46 and 47).
245 Based on Dr. Collins' earlier testimony on page 135, this "bad disorder" was Gonnorhea.

[Greene County Archive Sheet 159]

F. P. Berry[246] sworn:

I was born April 3rd 1817 – have lived in Stone County 50 years. I live 7 or 8 miles from Highlandville. Kaiser fell in with me one day a week or ten days before he was killed. I was going to Highlandville horseback. All at once I heard a gun fire. This scared my mare and she threw me off the saddle to the ground. The [*polter/poltes?*] reins was hitched to the front of the saddle and when I fell my foot caught in the stirrup. This kept the mare from getting away. Immediately a man came dashing up with a pistol pointed at me and I said don't shoot. He says then, "is this you Mr. Berry. I was watching for Dr. Gonce and thought you were Gonce." This man was Kaiser the same man Gonce killed. Says he, "Where did I hit you. I made sure it hit you; but I am glad it didn't. I wouldn't hurt you for $10,000 – no not for the world. I thought you were Gonce." He pulled off my blouse to see if I was hurt. When he

[Greene County Archive Sheet 160]

found I wasn't hurt, he told me he intended to waylay Gonce till he killed him, and that if I ever told it he would shoot me to pieces, + I didn't tell it till he was killed. It was a dark cloudy day about a week or 10 days before the killing of Kaiser at 10 o'clock in the morning. He said Gonce had business somewhere and had to go one or the other of the roads.

Letter of Mrs. M. C. Phillips[247]

Read as follows: "Reno, Mo. May 15 1885.

Mrs. Gonce, I drop off a few lines in regard to me appearing against Mr. Gonce in Court. I am not under any bond or anything now, and if you will give me fifty dollars I will get out of the way where they will not get me. Answer immediately.

Your Truly

M. C. Phillips"

---

246 One of the first acts of the prosecution upon the conclusion of the defense's case was to present witnesses (including Dr. Collins) attacking Mr. Berry's general credibility; this begins on page 172. Originals of the two transcribed pages with Mr. Berry's odd testimony are reproduced on the following pages.

247 This letter was referenced earlier on page 124; the original can be seen on page 161.

Greene County Archive Sheet 159, transcribed on the previous page.

fuss I wasn't hurt, he told me he intended to any way. Gonce told he killed him, and that if I ever told it he would blow me to pieces, & I didn't tell it till he was killed. It was a dark cloudy day about a week or six days before the killing of Roins at 10 o'clock in the morning. He said Gonce had business somewhere and had to go one or the other of them roads.

Letter of Mrs. M. C. Phillips read as follows:" Reno, Md. May 15th (~~Clerk reading~~) Mrs. Gonce, I drop you a few lines in regard to my appearing against Mr. Gonce in court, I am not under any bond nor anything now, and if you will give me fifty dollars I will get out of the way where they will not get my. Answer immediately. Yours Truly
M. C. Phillips"

Greene County Archive Sheet 160, transcribed on page 159.

Greene County Archive Sheet 154, transcribed on the following page, with Doc's own testimony.

[Greene County Archive Sheet 161]

A. R. Gonce sworn[248]:

[Greene County Archive Sheet 154]

A.R. Gonce, sworn[249]:

I am the defendant, am 52 years old. Known Kaiser. He came to my home in Highlandville on Sunday morning between 10 + 11 O'Clock. I had a lock at the gate. He then got off his horse and came around by the smoke house. I said "What is the matter Charlie?" He replied that he had come to settle that matter. He said "I want you to take back what you have said[250]" and put his hand to his pocket and said "You take it back or I'll shoot it out." He came at me [*rough?*] with his left hand. I told him I guessed he had heard more than I had said. He said we would shoot it out 5 or 10 steps any distance. I said "I don't want any trouble with you. We both have young families and you mustn't pay attention to what you hear." He said "You must take it back." I said "I never took back a thing that was true." He said "let us go to the back and shoot it out." My wife then came out and tried to pacify him. He said "When anybody asks you about this you say no." I said, I will never say it,

---

248 This page is otherwise blank, and apparently restarted on the following page.
249 The original of this page is reproduced on the previous page.
250 "What Doctor Gonce had said" was apparently that Charlie Keysser and his wife Sarah had contracted Gonorrhea.

[Greene County Archive Sheet 155]

but I will not make a practice of telling it[251].

The next time I saw him was when he was talking to Wiley Cloud at Kaiser's place. Kaiser seemed to be mad. He was in the field close to the fence talking to Cloud. He broke for the house, saying as he went, he would kill him, he said he was going to kill the damned son of a bitch and he would do it. His wife caught him and told him not to kill me[252]. I was getting away. He said as I was going away, "if you ever pass this way again I will kill you, you damned son of a bitch."

I saw Wiley Cloud again that day at 1 or 2 O'Clock at Ponce. I asked him if he had seen Kaiser. He told me not to go back that way, that Kaiser was in the bush and he thought he intended to kill me. Before that, I had got a pistol from Winn and then went and got a shot gun[253], also, and started home. I went to Brown's 3 miles before I stopped. This was 3/4 mile from Kaiser's. I went to get Brown[254] to pilot me by Kaiser's. I next went

[Greene County Archive Sheet 156]

to my son's Mack[255] Gonce and told his wife I wanted him to go with me that I was afraid to go by Kaiser's. I said to him, if you are afraid to go send one[256] of the children. One of them next came back and said Kaiser was in the field plowing. I then got on my horse and rode till I got to being on the public road on my home, to where Kaiser was [*him?*]. When I rode up he was coming angling toward me. He looked up and saw me. When he saw me he stopped his plow and threw his lines on the plow. I asked him what he meant if he was going to kill me. He said "I am by God or by damn it." When he stopped his plow and threw down his lines he put his right foot out and his hand behind him like putting it at his hip pocket and said I'll show you and when he did this I just threw over my gun and shot him, and went on to Ozark and gave myself up. When he put his hand behind him I knew I must act promptly, as from his actions I thought he was going to do something unusual[257].

---

251 I interpret this odd sentence to mean something like "I'll never deny it, but won't volunteer it."
252 Contrast this to Mrs. Kaiser's earlier testimony that she hadn't seen Doc that morning.
253 He must have gotten the shotgun from Winn as well based on the earlier testimony of Newton Cox; see page 139.
254 This was William F. Brown who, in the event, apparently didn't accompany Doc past Kaiser's.
255 "Mack" was what everyone called Doc's son William McClellan Gonce.
256 Compare this singular to archive sheets 190 (page 139) and 188 (page 140).
257 Compare this clear statement to the fuzzy one on archive sheet 141 (page 174).

Question : From Kaiser's action in putting his hand behind him at his hip did it or not appear to you that he was going to draw a pistol or other weapon?[258]

To this question the State objected. The court sustained the objection and

[Greene County Archive Sheet 157]

ruled that the witness could not answer the question. To which ruling of the court the defendant there and then at the time excepted.

Question : Did you believe that Kaiser was trying to get a pistol or other weapon to shoot you when he put his hand behind him?

The State objected to this question. The court sustained the objection and ruled that the witness could not answer the question. To which ruling of the court the defendant there and then at the time excepted.

Question : When Kaiser put his hand behind him what did it appear or seem to you that he was going to do?

To this question the State objected. The court sustained the objection and ruled that the witness could not answer the question. To which ruling of the court the defendant there and then at the time excepted.

[Greene County Archive Sheet 150]

12

Question : What did you believe or think Kaiser was going to do when he put his hand behind him?

The State objects to this question. The court sustained the objection and ruled that the witness could not answer the question. To which ruling of the court the defendant then and there at the time excepted.

---

258 This is the first in a series of eight questions by the defense trying to introduce a motive of self-defense. Whether this indicates bias or some legal nicety isn't known, but the court obviously didn't want to hear it.

Question : From the appearance of things, including Kaiser's past actions, and his actions at that time and any threat which you had heard of him making against you, what did you believe he intended to do at the time he put his hand behind him?

    The State objected to this question. The court sustained the objection and ruled that the witness could not answer the question. To which ruling of the court the defendant then and there at the time excepted.

[Greene County Archive Sheet 151]

Question : When Kaiser put his hand behind him what belief, if any, did you have as to what he was going to do?

    To this question the State objected. The court sustained the objection and ruled that the witness could not answer the question. To which ruling of the court the defendant then and there at the time excepted.

Question : What apprehensions, if any, had you at the time Kaiser put his hand behind him in the manner stated by you?

    The State objected to this question. The court sustained the objection and ruled that the witness could not answer the question. To which ruling of the court the defendant then and there at the time excepted.

Question : I will ask you to state Dr. Gonce why you shot Charles Kaiser on that day.[259]

---

259 This was the defense attorney's last-ditch effort (of 8 tries) to suggest an immediate motive for the shooting. Since the previous medical testimony seemed to support the notion that the victim (Kaiser) had his right arm at least slightly behind him at the time he was shot, it seems strange to me that the judge never permitted these questions to be answered.

[Greene County Archive Sheet 152]

To this the State objected. The court sustained the objection and ruled that the witness could not answer the question. To which ruling of the court the defendant then and there at the time excepted.

During the examination of the Defendant, Juror Dickerson[260] ~~against the~~ without objection of the Deft asked questions as follows:
How far was Mrs. Keiser behind you when you shot Keiser?
How far was it from Keiser's house down to where Keiser was plowing in the field?
And these questions were answered as in his examination in [*Auff?*]
I did not know any other road

Having the words "against the" crossed out and substituted with the word "without" seems suspiciously revisionist, since the meaning of the resulting phrase then becomes quite different. The original archive sheet reporting these questions can be seen on the next page.

[Greene County Archive Sheet 153]

to go home except the one I traveled by Kaiser's house. I did not leave the road when Keiser was shot by[261] I jerked my horse to the right just as Keiser threw down the lines + began the movement to put his hand behind him or as he put his hand behind him and when I shot my horse jumped forward which threw him off the road.
Cross X – I spoke to Keiser first + asked him what he meant. I testified before Judge Geiger on application for habeas corpus. I was moving in a walk.

---

260 This was P. Dickerson, Juror number 12.
261 I assume Doc actually said "but," but the original clearly says "by."

To this the State objected. The Court sustained the objection and ruled that the witness could not — from the question, to which ruling of the court, the defendant then and there at the time excepted.

During the examination of the ~~the~~ Defendant, Juror Dickinson ~~against the~~ ^without objection of the Deft asked questions as follows:

How far was Mrs Kiser behind you when you shot Kiser?

How far was it from Kiser's House down to where Kiser was plowing in the field?

and these questions were answered as in his Examination in Chief

I did not know any other road

Greene County Archive Sheet 152, transcribed on the previous page, with the interesting revision.

[Greene County Archive Sheet 148]

14²⁶²

Wm F. Brown²⁶³

    I knew Keiser – lived a mile from him. His reputation as an overbearing high tempered man was bad.

Cross Examined –

The most I knew of him was while I was active as a Justice of the Peace in dealing with him in several scrapes.

Frank Kentling²⁶⁴ –

    Have known Keiser for several years + his reputation as a quarrelsome high tempered man was

[Greene County Archive Sheet 149]

bad.

    Cross examined –

He threatened to kill me and we were not on good terms. He was not considered a dangerous man by me but was by others.

    He was a blustering man – made more noise than anything else.

M. Blyen²⁶⁵

    He knew Keiser and lived near him. Keiser's reputation was bad as a quarrelsome dangerous man.

    Cross Examined –

He named ten men with whom Keiser had had trouble and said he Kaiser was prevented from hurting Dick Logan²⁶⁶ with a rock.

---

262 I found no sheet with the number 13 on it, but there doesn't seem to be an obvious break in continuity between the sheet marked 12 (see Archive Sheet 150, transcribed on page 165) and this one.

263 William F. Brown, a sometime Justice of the Peace, was summoned by the Defense; this is on Archive sheets 44 and 45.

264 Frank Kentling was summoned by the Defense; this is on Archive sheets 44 and 45. Kentling was an early pioneer of the area, and had founded the town of Highlandville as a stopover on the old Wilderness Road from Springfield Missouri to Harrison Arkansas. Frank Kentling was the first postmaster of Highlandville, and was succeeded by Charles Keyser. Charles Keyser had purchased his land from Frank Kentling when Keyser first came to the area.

265 Martin Blyen was summoned by the Defense; this is on Archive sheets 36 and 37.

[Greene County Archive Sheet 145]

15

[Testimony of] Mrs. Martha Gonce[267]

I am the defendant's wife - On Sunday about two weeks, before Keiser was Killed he came to our house in Highlandville - The First thing I heard Keiser was hollering for the Doctor.

He Keiser came into the yard and said "Yes you come and go with me - I want to talk with you."

The Defendant went with him and he Keiser began telling Deft that he was going to kill him if he did not take back certain things which Keiser said that Deft had stated. Deft said that he did not want did not want to have any trouble with him, that he had already had enough and would Almost run from a man before he would have any trouble with him - Keiser wanted Deft to

[Greene County Archive Sheet 146]

take something back. And Deft finally said he would not. Keiser then said "I will shoot it out with you at 6, 8, or 10 steps," or something like that, but Deft said he would not fuss with him.

He then said he wanted the Deft to go to the brush with him, but Deft would not do that.

He said he had cause to shoot it out with him and he would if Gonce did not take back what he had said - the Doctor asked him if he meant it and he said, Yes he did and that he had a pistol in his jacket - Keiser was knocking his fists together all the time and saying what he would do with him - My husband

---

266 Keiser's wife was Sarah Logan, but none of her relatives I'm aware of was named Richard or Dick. She had brothers George W., John, and Anthony, and half-brothers Robert S., Benjamin R., and Americus C.

267 This is Martha Ann (Matt) Keithley [ID 4007], whom Doc had married in 1877. His marriage to Matt was what resulted in his earlier conviction and prison term for Bigamy.

[Greene County Archive Sheet 147]

had no pistol and did not run his hand in his pocket so far as I saw - I believe he would have killed my husband if I had not have interfered between them.

The defense here read portions of the testimony of Minnie Keyser given before the examining magistrate as follows:

(Clerk will copy) [268]

[Greene County Archive Sheet 143]

15

G. W. Masters[269], sworn:

I saw Kaiser a short time before he was killed. He said he had been watching the road with his shot gun for some damn rascal or rascals.

~~J. W. Kirk, sworn:~~

~~I am acquainted with Kaiser's reputation. It was bad as a quarrelsome man. He and Jim Gideon and Lewis Hendrix say so.~~

~~(Juror Mitchell here asks witness if Kaiser didn't always treat him well. To which witness answered yes. And the juror then said to witness "If Kaiser always treated you well, you can't say he was anything but a good man)~~

J. W. Kirk[270] testifies that he knew Keiser and had lived in a few miles of him for many years + knew his reputation as to being quarrelsome and dangerous and that it was ~~bad~~ that

[Greene County Archive Sheet 144]

of being rather quarrelsome.

---

268 I could not locate this previous testimony of the victim's daughter Minnie Keyser to the examining Magistrate, but her trial testimony begins on page 153.
269 Reverend Masters was summoned by the Defense; this is on Archive sheets 40 and 41.
270 J. W. Kirk was summoned by the Defense; this is on Archive sheets 52 and 53. His earlier testimony begins on page 158.

Pleasant Maples[271] testified likewise that he lived near Kiser + that his reputation as an overbearing and quarrelsome man was bad.

On his cross examination he said that Keiser was dangerous and had that reputation. Knew deceased well + had dealings with him + knew nothing against him except from reputation.

A Juror (~~Mitchell~~) here ~~against Defendant's~~ without objection[272] asked the witness these questions.

Ques. : Did Keiser always deal fair ~~and square~~ with you?
Ans. : Witness answered - Yes.
Ques. : ~~If he treated you well, how can you say that he was anything else but a good man?~~[273]
Ans. : ~~I cannot.~~

Greene County Archive Sheet 144, transcribed above.

State of Missouri vs A. R. Gonce: Prosecution Rebuttals:

---

271 Pleasant Maples was summoned by the Defense; this is on Archive sheets 44 and 45.
272 This would have been J. C. Mitchell, who was Juror Number 6, and obviously not a friend of Doc's. As earlier, the original writing suggesting the defense objected has been crossed out to indicate that they did not object.
273 This particularly egregious non-sequitor (by a member of the jury no less) was mentioned by the defense in its requests to have the verdict thrown out and for a new trial, but the apparent general acceptance of this illogical conclusion didn't seem to bother anyone, and the judge overruled it.

[Greene County Archive Sheet 139]

The defendant here rested his case.

The Prosecuting Attorney for the State introduced Charles Galloway, Wm Vaughn, T. J. Hawkins[274], Thomas White, John Collins, C. B. Owen + Richard Cox who testified that the reputation of the witness F. P. Berry was not good for truth and veracity.

John C. Rogers sworn – Clerk Circuit Court Christian County – produces affidavit for continuance sworn to by deft[275] –
State here offered part of deft's affidavit for a continuance referred to above to contradict deft. Commencing with words "said witnesses are credible persons &c, + continuing through statement of what Spencer Smith if present would swear to – and deft objected as not contradictory[276], no foundation laid, incompetent, irrelevant + immaterial – tending to prejudice deft with Jury + deft had not been examined with reference thereto – thereupon
A. R. Gonce, the Defendant was recalled by the State + questioned as follows:

Ques. : Who was present when you shot Kaiser?
Ans. : I did not see anyone present but Mrs. Kiser + her daughter near

---

[274] The State issued a summons to a J. M. Hawkins (on Archive Sheets 22 and 23), but I don't know who T. J. Hawkins is.
[275] This affidavit was presented beginning on page 132.
[276] Strictly speaking, it wasn't contradictory to what the defense suggested he would say (see page 124), but it certainly wasn't at all similar. See Mr. Smith's testimony on page 148.

[Greene County Archive Sheet 140]

Ques. Did you see any revolver there?
Ans. I did not.
Ques. Did you see anyone pick up a revolver there?
Ans. I did not.
Ques. What was it Keiser said there Dr.?
Ans. I asked him what he meant or what if he intended to kill me! He said Yes by God or by Damn I do.

All of the above questions and answers were objected to because the State had no right to recall the Deft after the Deft had rested his case + because the matter had been gone over before + that recalling the Deft in this way tended to prejudice his case + the Jury against him but

[Greene County Archive Sheet 141]

the Court overruled these objections and compelled the Deft to answer.

Ques. Did Keyser say are you ready or you are ready are you.
Ans. I think not. I was excited and did not have much time to think about the matter.
Ques. Did he put his hand in his pocket and draw a weapon.
Ans. He put his hand behind him but I can't say that he drew a weapon. I had to go to work at once[277] or at least I thought so. I didn't see Spencer Smith there; I overtook him afterwards. I signed and swore to that application for continuance.

All these questions + answers were objected to for the reasons above set forth but overruled and Deft excepted.

Here an affidavit for a continuance was shown the Deft + he said in answer to an inquiry by

---

277 From the context it seems like this probably means "I had to make a decision and act on it at once," because I can't see the sense of "I had to go to work, so I shot him." This sheet is reproduced on the next page. This interpretation is supported by his earlier testimony on archive sheet 156 (transcribed on page 164).

the Court overruled these
objections & compelled the
Deft to answer —

Ques. Did ~~say~~ ^Keyser say are you ready
~~or you are ready are you~~
Ans. ^I think not — I was
excited and did not have
much time to think about
~~the~~ matter

Ques. Did he put his hand
in his pocket & draw
a weapon —

Ans. He put his hand behind
him but I can't say ~~that~~
he drew a weapon. I
had to work at
once or at least I thought
so. ^I didn't see Spencer Smith there. I even took
continuance ^afterwards. I ~~signed~~ swore to that application for

All these questions & an-
swers were objected to for
the reasons above set
forth but overruled and
Deft excepted — ⨁

Here an affidavit for
a continuance was shown
the Deft & he said in
answer to an inquiry by

Greene County Archive Sheet 141, transcribed on the previous page, with the interesting revision.

[Greene County Archive Sheet 142]

the State which was objected to by the Deft + overruled + exception taken, that the signature to the affidavit was his and that he swore to the affidavit.

This affidavit was as follows:

(Clerk will here copy)[278]

The State then offered in evidence all that part of the above affidavit beginning with the words[279]

and ending with the words

& which was as follows:

(Clerk will copy)[280]

The Deft objected to this for reasons as follows: Because the same was irrelevant incompetent and immaterial, because

[Greene County Archive Sheet 136]

17

no proper foundation had been laid for the introduction of this testimony and because the same was not in rebuttal.

But these objections were overruled + the same was read to the Jury which ruling of the Court the Deft then and there at the time objected + excepted.

The Court ruled that if deft wished it State would have to read all of application – or deft might read balance not offered.

This was all the evidence.

---

278 This affidavit for continuance, submitted in Christian County, was presented earlier, on page 122.
279 Neither set of words appears; the archive sheet is blank in those areas. See the reproduction on the facing page.
280 The portion of the affidavit was not specified on the sheet I transcribed, but I am assuming it is the portion of archive sheet 61 related to what Spenser Smith would say if called to testify. See page 124.

the State which was objected
to by the Defd & over-ruled
Exceptions taken, that the
signature to the affidavit
was his own & that he
swore to the affidavit —

This affidavit was
as follows;
(Clerk will here copy)
The State then offered in
Evidence all that part of
the above affidavit beginning with the words

and ending with the words
& which was as follows;
(Clerk will copy)
The Defd objected to this
for reasons as follows
Because the same was
irrelevant incompetent
and immaterial, because

Greene County Archive Sheet 142, transcribed on the previous page.

[Greene County Archive Sheet 137]

During the progress of the trial at least one half of the Jurors Joined in the Cross Examination or Examination of the witnesses these questions at times being leading and irrelevant.[281]

During the closing argument by the Prosecuting Attorney the shirt and pants worn by Keiser at the time of his death and which had been offered in evidence, were brought in and spread out and displayed xxxxx on the Counsel's table in the immediate front of the Jury + during his closing the

[Greene County Archive Sheet unk]

[282]

[Greene County Archive Sheet 138]

all of which the Deft objected and excepted to this action of the Court in presenting the xxxx to xxxxx.

In the opening argument[283] by J. J. Gideon for the State he alluded to Gonce having been Kaiser's physician to which allusion the defendant objected for the reason there is no testimony in the case that Gonce was Kaiser's physician and ex xxxx xxx to the Court permitting said allxxxxx + Court said he could not then remember whether evidence showed Gonce had been Kaiser's physician or not + he must confine himself to testimony. And the prosecuting attorney in closing the case, remarked to the jury that Gonce had been the physician of Kaiser – that Esau Smith[284] swore Gonce had said so the State with confidence that was in testimony. To which [penxxxx] defendant objected for the reason that there was no evidence that Gonce had been Kaiser's physician, and then and there [xxxxxx] excepted to the action of the court in permitting such remarks by the prosecuting attorney.

[Greene County Archive Sheet 132]

---

281 It would certainly be interesting to know why the clerk of the court struck this out.
282 It is difficult to be certain, but it appears there may be a missing page or pages here.
283 I saw nothing in the Archive Sheets that appeared to be an opening argument or a summary of one. It also isn't clear to me why the Defense didn't want any testimony on the record that Abraham Rudolph Gonce was Charles Kaiser's physician.
284 The original very clearly says "Esau," but there is no summons, nor is there any testimony, for any Esau Smith.

This was all the testimony in the case[285].

The court of its own motion instructed the jury as follows against the objections of the defendant.

(Here insert the instructions given by the Court)[286].

The defendant then and there at the time excepted to the ruling of the court in giving said instructions against his objection.

The defendant then requested the court to instruct the jury as follows:

(Here insert all the instructions asked for by defendant and refused by the court.)[287]

But the court refused all of said instructions to which action of the court in refusing said instructions the defendant then and there at the time excepted.

And on the 13th day June, the same being within four days from the time of the rendition of the verdict[288] herein, the defendant filed his motion for a new trial in words and

Greene County Archive Sheet 132, transcribed above.

[Greene County Archive Sheet 133]

figures following to wit:

(Here insert defendant's motion for a new trial)[290]

---

285 Based on subsequent motions and affidavits, this must have taken place on Wednesday June 10, 1885.
286 I was unable to locate these instructions in any of the extant material.
287 My transcription of the instructions presented and requested by the defense team begins on page 183.
288 My transcription of the Verdict sheet returned by the Jury begins on page 189.

..x and
the
affidavit
of deft
Gonce[289]

Which said motion the court on the said 13th day of June 1885 overruled. To which action of the court in overruling defendant's motion for a new trial the defendant then and there at the time excepted.

In support of his motion for a new trial the defendant filed first the following affidavit of J. P. Simpson + [*neff?*] filed affidavit of Juror Bryant, then filed affidavit of George Porter + State then filed additional affidavit of Juror Bryant as follows: (Here insert the affidavit of J. P. Simpson and George Porter + affidavits of Juror Bryant)[291].

And in further support of his motion for new trial the defendant introduced the following testimony:

M. C. Roberts:

I am a deputy sheriff and remember taking Gonce out during the trial as many as two times + I probably took him out at other times than two – At one time I

[Greene County Archive Sheet 134]

went out through the Clerk's office with the Deft and we went to the Jail or the privy – At the time I wxxx and returned there was a witness named Cox on the stand testifying – I remember that Mr. Traverse[292] attorney for the Deft came to me and told me to remember the circumstances + said that the name of the witness was Cox[293] who was testifying. I saw the witness' face. He had a [*Samely?*] mustache + whiskers. I got permission of the Court to take the Deft out above times but do not know whether I got permission at the time I have referred to or not. In taking deft out went past Judge's stand + deft requested it. I don't remember taking him out without Court's permission. When I came back a witness was in the chair didn't know his name or whether he had been testifying. I took him down

[Greene County Archive Sheet 135]

I only know what Travers told me afterwards – except fact that I took witness deft down at his request a short time before Travers spoke to me + was gone 3 or 4

---

289 I don't know what this is, but the affidavit referred to is on Archive Sheet 114, beginning on page 195.
290 The defendant's motion for a new trial is transcribed beginning on page 193.
291 The affidavits are transcribed on the following pages: Simpson's on page 200, Porter's on page 195, and Bryant's on page 197. Bryant made another similar affidavit on the same date that is shown on page 198.
292 This is P. H. Travers, Doc Gonce's lead defense attorney.
293 Richard Cox is mentioned as testifying on Archive Sheet 139, which is transcribed on page 172. Newton Cox's testimony begins on Archive Sheet 194, which is transcribed on page 139. Deputy Sheriff Roberts is most likely referring to the testimony of Newton Cox.

minutes.

P. H. Travers, one of the defendant's attorneys, being sworn, said:

When Newton Cox, a witness for the State, was testifying in the [*forinwon?*] of the first day he being the 5th witness examined in the case – I was engaged in taking down his testimony + after he had been testifying 2, 3 or probably four minutes I looked up and saw Gonce and the Deputy Sheriff Mr. Roberts coming through the Clerk's office into the Courtroom. I had not before then noticed that Dr. Gonce the Deft was absent being busy taking down Cox's testimony. As soon as Gonce came and I took

[Greene County Archive Sheet 128]

7

his seat I got up and went to Mr. Roberts and asked if he had held the Deft out and he replied that he had + saw then resumed my seat by Mr. Vaughan an Attorney for the Deft + called his attention to it. The Court was not made aware of it to my knowledge.

Jas R. Wayburn

Swore that about the time Gonce came in and took his seat Mr. Travers spoke to him and called his attention to the fact that Gonce the Deft had been out of the Court room during part of the Examination of the witness Cox.

[Greene County Archive Sheet 131]

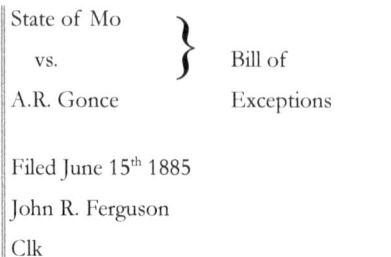

State of Mo
vs.   } Bill of
A.R. Gonce   Exceptions

Filed June 15th 1885
John R. Ferguson
Clk

[Greene County Archive Sheet 129]

The Court knew nothing of def't leaving Court Room at any time when any proceedings were being had. Several times def't, in charge of deputy Sheriff passed by Court's Stand into Clerk's Office + proceedings were immediately stopped + Court does not believe any proceedings were had of that def't could pass out that way without Court noticing it, after Wm Larkins had gone off stand + before Judge Larkins came on, Sheriff took def't out through the audience + front door, + court noticed deft come inside bar after 4 or 5 preliminary questions had been asked witness + Court required Attorneys to ask same questions again + instructed Sheriff to notify the Court when deft went out, and at no time was Court's attention led to any other there til motion for new trial had been filed.

On the 15th day of June 1885 the Deft filed his motion in arrest of the judgment in words + figures as follows:

(Clerk will copy)[294]

Which Motion was the same day overruled by the Court and to which ruling + action of the Court the Deft at the time excepted.

[Greene County Archive Sheet 130]

Wherefore the Defendant prayed the Court [*illegible*] and seal this bill of Exceptions which is done on this the day of June 1885 and the same thereby made a part of the record.

M. G. McGregor (Seal)
Circuit Judge

---

[294] The defendant's motion is on Archive Sheets 124 and 125; they are transcribed beginning on page 201.

State of Missouri vs A. R. Gonce: Defendant's Requested Instructions to the Jury:

[Greene County Archive Sheet 95.2]

STAMP:

Filed

Jun 10th 1885,

J. R. Ferguson, Clerk

[Greene County Archive Sheet 91]

REFUSED

You are instructed that if Keiser had recently threatened Gonce, that he had gone to Gonce's house armed and had offered to shoot it out with him and had asked Gonce to go to the woods for that purpose, that prior to the killing: Kaiser had shot at F. P. Berry believing that he was Gonce and Said to the witness Berry that he intended to kill Gonce and to lie in the Woods if necessary until he did kill him; and that when the defendant was passing along the road engaged in his business as a physician by the House of Keiser and Keiser reiterated such threats and tried to enter his house for the purpose of obtaining a weapon or for some other purpose in the attempted execution of such threats but is restrained by his wife and declares that he will kill the defendant if he ever travels that road again; that the defendant had the right under such circumstances to

[Greene County Archive Sheet 92]

REFUSED

arm himself to resist such threatened attack and had the right in the transaction of his business to go along the public highway and if in so doing he the defendant met Keiser and believed he was armed and ready to execute such intention to kill, and that he had the right to believe from the threats, the previous conduct of the deceased, and at the time of the killing and the character of the man, and the circumstances attending the meeting that the presence of Keiser put his life in immediate peril and that for his personal safety it was necessary to shoot him then he was not oblige (sic) to wait until Keiser actually assaulted him but had the right to attact (sic) and even kill Keiser if necessary or apparently necessary in these instances stated for his own self defense.

[Greene County Archive Sheet 93]

REFUSED

3. The Court instructs the Jury that although the defendant A. R. Gonce was indicted and is now on Trial for the killing of Charles Keiser yet the Law presumes him innocent of the crimes charged and that the presumption of innocence continues to secure and protect him until the State proves his guilt beyond a reasonable doubt,

[Greene County Archive Sheet 94]

REFUSED

4. If the Jury find from the evidence that the testimony can reasonably be reconciled either with the theory of Guilt or Innocence then the Law requires you to give Defendant the benefit of the Theory of innocence and acquit him.

[Greene County Archive Sheet 96]

REFUSED

5. The right of self defense does not impose the duty of retreat, and is a right which the law not only concedes but guarantees to all men. When the danger is not of their own seeking the defendant therefore may have killed Charles Kaiser and still be not guilty of any offense against the law; and if you believe from the evidence that at the time Gonce shot Kaiser he had reasonable cause to believe and did believe from the appearance of things as they presented themselves to his mind at the time he had the conversation with Kaiser – Gonce being on his horse in the road and Kaiser at his plow in the field – that he was in danger of receiving great personal injury at the hands of Kaiser, and there was reasonable cause for Gonce to apprehend immediate danger of such personal injury being inflicted upon him by Kaiser, and to avert such apparent danger he shot Kaiser and at the time he shot had reasonable cause to believe and did believe it necessary to shoot Kaiser to protect himself from such apprehended danger, then and in that case you will acquit the

[Greene County Archive Sheet 95.1]

defendant on the ground of necessary self defense.

6. And it is not necessary to the defense that the danger was actual or real or that the danger was really impending and about to fall upon Gonce. All that the law requires is that Gonce had reasonable grounds to believe and did believe that great personal injury was about to be inflicted upon him by Kaiser, and that he had reasonable cause to believe that it was necessary for him to fire the shot to avert the danger; and whether the defendant had reasonable cause to apprehend such danger and whether defendant actually believed or had reasonable cause to believe that at the time he shot, Kaiser was about to inflict great personal injury upon him, the jury are to determine from all the facts and circumstances in the case.

REFUSED

[Greene County Archive Sheet 97]

7. The burden of proof to establish the guilt of the defendant devolves upon the State throughout, and the law clothes the defendant with the presumption of innocence which attends and protects him until it is overcome by evidence which shows his guilt beyond a reasonable doubt. It is not sufficient in this case to justify a verdict of guilty – that there may be strong suspicions of defendant's guilt, but the testimony must be of such a nature that when you have considered it all you feel a clear conviction of defendant's guilt. This much the law requires, and if this much has not been proved you will acquit.

REFUSED

[Greene County Archive Sheet 98]

8. All and any threats made by Kaiser against Gonce, if any were made, which were not communicated to Gonce are to be considered by the jury in determining the animus of Kaiser towards Gonce at the time of the shooting. If Kaiser apparently manifested to Gonce any design to put such threats into execution.

9. If the reputation of Kaiser was that of a quarrelsome, dangerous and high tempered man, then you will take such fact into consideration in determining the reasonableness or unreasonableness of defendant's apprehension of great personal injury at the time he did the shooting.

REFUSED

[Greene County Archive Sheet 99]

REFUSED

10. If Kaiser had threatened to kill Gonce, and Gonce had been apprised of such threat, then the jury will take this fact into consideration in determining the reasonableness or unreasonableness of defendant's apprehension of great personal injury at the time he did the shooting.

[Greene County Archive Sheet 100]

REFUSED

11. If Kaiser had threatened to take the life of Gonce, and this fact had been made known to Gonce, then Gonce had the right under the laws of the State of Missouri to arm himself with whatever and what number of weapons he saw fit, in order that he might defend himself, if necessary or apparently necessary, from the execution of such threats by Kaiser, and being so armed, he had the right to travel on horseback along the road between Highlandville and Ponce de Leon or any other public road in the State of Missouri, and if while traveling along a public road he came in sight of Kaiser, he had reason to believe and did believe from the words or actions of Kaiser that Kaiser intended to put his threat to kill him into execution, then he had the right to act upon appearances and kill Kaiser, if it was apparently necessary to do so to prevent Kaiser from killing him, or inflicting great personal injury upon him.

[Greene County Archive Sheet 101]
[Greene County Archive Sheet 102 duplicates Sheet 101]

REFUSED

12. If Kaiser had made threats against the life of the defendant, and the threats were communicated to defendant, defendant then had the right under the law to have the deceased [*bond?*] over to keep the peace if he was afraid Kaiser would put such threats into execution, but it was not obligating upon the defendant to have said Kaiser bond? Over to keep the peace, and his failure to have the said Kaiser so bond? over dispenses the defendant of none of his rights under the plea of self defense.

[Greene County Archive Sheet 103]

REFUSED

13. If the jury believes that Kaiser placed his right hand in such a position as to cause Gonce reasonably to believe that he, Kaiser, was about to draw and use upon him, Gonce, a pistol or other deadly weapon, then Gonce had the right to act upon appearances and shoot Kaiser, if necessary or apparently necessary, to prevent great personal injury, although it should afterwards turn out that Kaiser did not in fact have a deadly weapon and was not in fact attempting to draw one.

[Greene County Archive Sheet 104]

REFUSED

14. You are instructed that you are the sole Judge of the credibility of all the witnesses who have testified in this case, that you are not to disbelieve the testimony of F. P. Berry because the witness Cox and others have testified that his reputation for truth and veracity was bad, but taking into consideration his age, manner upon the witness stand, personal conduct as a witness, his interest or want of interest in the trial with all other facts and circumstances in evidence in the case you believe or disbelieve him like any other witness who may have testified before you.

[Greene County Archive Sheet 105]

REFUSED

15. If Kaiser had threatened to kill Gonce and this threat had been communicated to Gonce, and Kaiser had told Gonce that he should not pass the road again, alive, then Gonce had the right to arm himself in order to defend himself, if Kaiser attempted to put his threat in execution, and being so armed, Gonce had the right in the prosecution of his business, to ride along the road by Kaiser's house and fields, and, if so riding along said road, he met Kaiser he was not bound to flee from him, but had the right , if he had reasonable cause to believe that Kaiser intended to inflict great personal injury upon him to protect himself from the infliction of such personal injury, and even to kill Kaiser if it was necessary or apparently necessary to prevent the infliction of such personal injury and in determining this apparent necessity, Gonce had a right to take into consideration the threats that Kaiser had previously made against him, if any.

[Greene County Archive Sheet 106]

REFUSED

16. If Kaiser had threatened to kill Gonce and had said he would waylay him on the road and Gonce was made aware of these threats by Kaiser; and if Kaiser had told Gonce that he should not pass that road again alive meaning the road by Kaiser's house and fields on the public road between Ponce De Leon and Highlandville, then Gonce might naturally and reasonably infer that Kaiser meant what he said and intended to do what he said he would do. Gonce then had the right to arm himself in anticipation of any attempted execution by Kaiser of his threats, and for the purpose of defending himself against the same if apparently necessary for him to do so, and being so armed he was not bound to avoid Kaiser or flee from him but had the right in the prosecution of his business to travel along the said road by Kaiser's house and fields, and if while passing along said road he came upon Kaiser, he was not bound to wait till Kaiser attacked him or advanced upon him, but if from any manifestation or demonstration on

[Greene County Archive Sheet 107]

REFUSED

Kaiser's part [xxxten?] by word or action he had reasonable cause to apprehend immediate personal injury at the hands of Kaiser; then he had the right to act in self defense and to kill Kaiser if apparently necessary to protect himself from such personal injury; and in determining the reasonableness of his apprehension and the necessity for his action he had the right to take into consideration Kaiser's reputation as a threatening, quarrelsome and dangerous man, and also the threats Kaiser had previously made against him.

State of Missouri vs A. R. Gonce: Verdict of the Jury:

[Greene County Archive Sheet 88]

State of Missouri

vs

A. R. Gonce

Jury Decision

Filed June 1885

[Greene County Archive Sheet 87]

Sworn[295] on Thursday June 4th

State of Missouri vs. A.R. Gonce } Jury Sworn

#	Juror
1	F. W. Laker
2	B. S. Chirn
3	R. B. Woodward
4	J. D. Bryant
5	W. L. White
6	J. C. Mitchell
7	J. W. Jones
8	R. M. Mohn
9	F. T. Watson
10	Bernard Redmond
11	G. D. Morgan
12	P. Dickerson

---

295 This was the first day of the Trial when the Jury was sworn, not the date the Verdict was returned.

[Greene County Archive Sheet 86]

> We the Jury find the defendant guilty of murder in the second degree and assess his punishment at imprisonment for the term of thirty years in the Penitentiary.
>
> W. L. White, Foreman

In Book 27, Page 140 of the Missouri Archives (not shown here), the verdict shown above is reproduced verbatim, with the additional notation "At the instance and request of the Defendant, the names of the jurors of said Jury were called by the Clerk, and asked, if this was his verdict, each and everyone of said jurors answering for himself in the affirmative."

State of Missouri vs A. R. Gonce: Defendant's Motion for a New Trial: 13 June 1885

[Greene County Archive Sheet 109]

State of Missouri

vs

A. R. Gonce

Motion for New Trial

FILED

June 13 1885

John R. Ferguson, Clerk

By J. M. Smith, DC

Vaughan, Payne,

Patterson, Travers

Attys for deft.

Signed by James R. Vaughan, James M. Patterson, D. M. Payne and P. H. Travers

[Greene County Archive Sheet 110]

State of Missouri
   vs.
A.R. Gonce

S7-153]June 13 – 1885 Overruled

Now comes the defendant and moves the court to set aside the verdict heretofore rendered and grant him a new trial for the following reasons, to wit:

1st The verdict is contrary to law.

2nd The verdict is contrary to the evidence.

3rd The verdict is against the law and testimony.

4th The defendant was not present in the court room during a portion of the trial when the witness Cox was testifying to the jury.

5th One of the jurors that tried the case expressed his opinion as to the guilt or innocence of the defendant before he was qualified as a juror by declaring that the defendant ought to be hung.

6th The prosecuting attorney in his closing argument exhibited the shirt and pants that

[Greene County Archive Sheet 111]

deceased had on when he was killed, and the same were conspicuously exhibited from a table in front of the jury during the trial.

7th The court erred in admitting improper, irrelevant, incompetent and illegal testimony in the part of the State against the objection of the defendant.

8th The court erred in excluding competent and relevant testimony offered on the part of the defendant.

9 The court erred in instructing the jury, and by giving improper instructions of its own motion against the objections of defendant numbered from one to fifteen inclusive.

10th The court erred in refusing proper instructions asked for by the defendant numbered from one to fifteen inclusive.

[Greene County Archive Sheet 108]

11th

The Court erred in permitting certain of the jurors to ask witnesses while testifying in this case impertinent, incompetent and irrelevant questions, having a tendency to excite prejudice against the defendant.

12th-When one of the witnesses was testifying in relation to the reputation of the deceased as a quarrelsome and dangerous man, the juror Mitchell said to him, "if you have always found Kaiser straight in his dealings with you, you can't say he is anything but a good man."

13 - The court in the instructions given of its own motion did not clearly and definitely set forth the doctrine of self defense.

14 - The court erred in instructing the jury as to murder in the second degree.

On 13 June 1885, Doc's attorneys filed a Motion for a New Trial. The illustration below seems to be Doc's actual signature from an affidavit supporting that document.

Signature of Abraham Rudolph Gonce from the 13 June 1885 Affidavit in Support for (his) Motion for a New Trial

Doc's signature on a related affidavit two days later is shown here for comparison.

Signature of Abraham Rudolph Gonce from the above Affidavit of 15 June 1885

[Greene County Archive Sheet 121]

State

vs

A. R. Gonce

Affidavit
of A. R. Gonce in
support of motion
for new trial

Filed June 13 – 1885
John R. Ferguson, Clerk
By J. M. Smith, D.C.

[Greene County Archive Sheet 119]

State of Missouri }
Greene County   }   ss

The said AR Gonce being duly sworn says that he never heard nor learned until after the return of the verdict in this cause in which he is the Defendant that the said J. D. Bryant a Juror had formed or expressed an opinion that he the Defendant was guilty and ought to be hung, and did not know and had not heard prior to the revelation of the said verdict that the said Juror was prejudiced against him or had made any expressions

[Greene County Archive Sheet 120]

of any kind against him the Deft.

A. R Gonce

Subscribed + sworn to before me this 13th day of June 1885

John R. Ferguson, Clerk
By J. M. Smith, D.C.

[Greene County Archive Sheet 114]

State

vs

A. R. Gonce

Affidavit
in Support
of motion for
New Trial

Filed June 13 – 1885
John R. Ferguson, Clerk
By J. M. Smith, D.C.

[Greene County Archive Sheet 112]

State of Missouri } ss
Greene County

George A. Porter being duly sworn says that he is 33 years old, lives in Springfield Mo. And has lived here about seven years, that for several months he was on the police force of this city, that he knows J. D. Bryant[296] and has known him for about four years; that J. D. Bryant and himself were on the police force of this city together for some time and in that way he and Bryant became well and intimately [Reguaintue?], that soon after the killing of Kaiser and when newspaper accounts relating to the affair were being published he heard John D. Bryant one of the jurors who sat and served

---

296 John D. Bryant was Juror Number 4.

[Greene County Archive Sheet 113]

on the Jury in the late trial of Dr. A. R. Gonce say that Gonce was guilty of murder and ought to be hung for it. In saying this he (Bryant) was talking about the killing of Keiser in Christian County about one year ago and the remark above set forth was made by Bryant with reference to the killing of Keiser by Gonce.

I heard Bryant speak about Gonce + the trial for the killing of Charles Keiser at least one other time than that stated above, but cannot now remember just what he said.

G. A. Porter

Subscribed + sworn to before the undersigned a Notary Public within and for Greene County + State of Missouri this June 13th A.D. 1885

Geo. S. Rattibun Jr.

Notary Public

My Commission expires Oct. 30th 1888

[Greene County Archive Sheet 116.1]

State of Missouri

vs

A. R. Gonce

Affidavit of
J. D. Bryant to
effect that he
had not formed
an opinion as to
guilt or innocence
of Deft prior to trial

Filed June 13 – 1885
John R. Ferguson, Clerk
By J. M. Smith, D.C.

[Greene County Archive Sheet 115] [297]

State of Missouri \} ss
County of Greene

J. D. Bryant who being duly sworn according to law states:

That he has no recollection of having heard of the killing of Charles Keyser by Dr. A. R. Gonce prior to the time of his being summoned as a juror to try the case of the State of Missouri against said A. R. Gonce.

Affiant further states that he has never at any time prior to the trial of said case said to J. P. Simpson "that Gonce ought to be hung" and that he has never made a statement to said Simpson or to any other person, of similar import.

Affiant states, that he has a no place or time, formed or expressed an opinion as to the guilt or innocence of said

---

[297] See the image of the original on page 198

Dr. Abraham Rudolph Gonce

[Greene County Archive Sheet 116.2]

Gonce, prior to said time.

J. D. Bryant

Subscribed and sworn to before me this 13th June 1885

John R. Ferguson, Clerk

Greene County Archive Sheet 115

Greene County Archive Sheet 122

[Greene County Archive Sheet 123]

State of Missouri

vs

A. R. Gonce

Affidavit of

J. D. Bryant

to effect that he

at no time said

to G. A. Porter that

A. R. Gonce ought

to be hung

Filed June 13 – 85

John R. Ferguson, Clerk

[Greene County Archive Sheet 122] [298]

State of Missouri } ss
County of Greene }

J. D. Bryant being duly sworn, says that he has never at any time said to George A. Porter that A. R. Gonce was guilty of Murder and ought to be hung for it.

Affiant further states that he and G. A. Porter were on the Police force of the city of Springfield together until about April A.D. 1884, and affiant states to the best of his knowledge and belief he has not had any conversation since said time, with said Porter.

J. D. Bryant

Subscribed and sworn to
before me this 13th June 1885
John R. Ferguson, Clerk

---

[298] See the image of the original on page 198.

[Greene County Archive Sheet 118]

State of Mo

vs

A. R. Gonce

Affidavit for
Support of motion
for New Trial

Filed June 13th 1885
John R. Ferguson, Clerk

[Greene County Archive Sheet 117]

I, J. P. Simpson, make oath and say that just about the beginning or a few days before the beginning of this the present May term 1885 of this Circuit Court of Greene County, Missouri, I had a conversation with J. D. Bryant, one of the jurors now trying in said Circuit Court the case of the State of Missouri against A. R. Gonce for the murder of Charles Kaiser in June 1884 in Christian County Missouri, in which said conversation I remarked to said Bryant "I guess Doctor Gonce's trial will come up this term of the court," meaning by that the present May term 1885 of the Circuit Court of Greene County Missouri; and in his reply the said Bryant said "Well, I guess he ought to be hung anyhow," meaning the said Gonce ought to be hung.

J. P. Simpson

Subscribed and sworn to before me this 13th day of June 1885

J. D. Van Bibber

Clerk, County Court

[Greene County Archive Sheet 125.1]

State of MO

vs

A. R. Gonce

Motion in arrest

of Judgt

Filed June 15 –1885

J. R. Ferguson, Clerk

By J. M. Smith, D.C.

Vaughan, Payne,
Patterson, Travis
Attys for Deft

[Greene County Archive Sheet 124]

State of Missouri

vs

A. R. Gonce

27-156Overruled

Now comes the defendant and moves the Court to arrest the Judgment and that no judgment be rendered him for the following reasons:

1st The record does not show the presence of the prisoner during all the proceedings in the case.

2^{d} Upon inspection of the entire record it appears that one of the jurors that tried the case was disqualified by having expressed an opinion of the defendant's guilt.

3^{d} The facts stated in the indictment constituted no offense.

4th The record does not show that Judge McGregor was properly authorized to try the case.

5th The record does not show the case is properly here on change of venue from Christian County.

[Greene County Archive Sheet 125.2]

Jas R Vaughan
Jas. M. Patterson
D. M. Payne
P. H. Travers
Attys for deft

[Greene County Archive Sheet 127]

State of MO
vs
A. R. Gonce

Affidavit of deft for
an Appeal

Filed June 1885
John R. Ferguson, Clerk

[Greene County Archive Sheet 126]

State of Missouri
vs
A. R. Gonce

A. R. Gonce being sworn on his oath states that his application for appeal is not made for vexation or delay but because he believes he is aggrieved by the judgment of Court on the verdict of the jury assessing his punishment of imprisonment in the penitentiary for thirty years.

A. R. Gonce
Sworn before me this 15 day of June 1885
John R. Ferguson, Clerk

State of Missouri vs A. R. Gonce: Index to Testimony and Affidavits

The following indexes to transcriptions of the trial documents is chronological and references the original documents as well as the pages in this book on which they have been transcribed.

Grand Jury Indictment

Taylor, G. W., foreman	GCAS 56	Pg 117		Pi

Defense Pre-Trial Affidavits

Gonce, A. R.	GCAS 59	Pg 122	Plea and Affidavit for Continuance	Da 1
Cloud, Wiley	GCAS 82	Pg 133		Da 2

Prosecution Testimony

Collins, Dr.	GCAS 197	Pg 135		Pt 1
Norman, Thomas	GCAS 196	Pg 136		Pt 2
Phillips, Mrs. M. C.	GCAS 195	Pg 137	Letter on [GCAS 160] (pg 159)	Pt 3
Cox, Newton	GCAS 194	Pg 139		Pt 4
Gonce, Martha Sims	GCAS 194	Pg 139		Pt 5
Larkins, William	GCAS 187	Pg 142		Pt 6
Larkins, Judge	GCAS 181	Pg 143	recalled [GCAS 167] (pg 155)	Pt 7
Forbes, William	GCAS 181	Pg 143		Pt 8
Brown, Dr. E. B.	GCAS 184	Pg 144		Pt 9
Fulbright, Dr.	GCAS 183	Pg 146		Pt 10
Smith, Spenser	GCAS 177	Pg 148		Pt 11
Clevenger, George	GCAS 179	Pg 150		Pt 12
Kaiser, Sarah	GCAS 180	Pg 150	recalled [GCAS 166] (pg 155)	Pt 13
White, Mr. D. J.	GCAS 169	Pg 152		Pt 14
Keyser, Minnie	GCAS 170	Pg 153		Pt 15

Defense Testimony

Cloud, Wiley	GCAS 168	Pg 156		Dt 1
Nelson, John	GCAS 165	Pg 157		Dt 2
Maples, Pleasant	GCAS 158	Pg 158	recalled [GCAS 144] (pg 171)	Dt 3
Berry, F. P.	GCAS 159	Pg 158		Dt 4
Gonce, A. R.	GCAS 154	Pg 163	recalled [GCAS 139] (pg 172)	Dt 5
Brown, Wm. F.	GCAS 148	Pg 169		Dt 6
Blyen, M.	GCAS 149	Pg 169		Dt 7
Gonce, Martha Keithley	GCAS 145	Pg 170		Dt 8
Masters, G. W.	GCAS 143	Pg 171		Dt 9
Kirk, J. W.	GCAS 143	Pg 171		Dt 10

Post Trial Testimony				
Galloway, Charles	GCAS 139	Pg 172		Pt 16
Vaughan, Wm.	GCAS 139	Pg 172		Pt 17
Hawkins, T. J.	GCAS 139	Pg 172		Pt 18
White, Thomas	GCAS 139	Pg 172		Pt 19
Collins, John	GCAS 139	Pg 172		Pt 20
Owen, C. B.	GCAS 139	Pg 172		Pt 21
Cox, Richard	GCAS 139	Pg 172		Pt 22
Rogers, John C.	GCAS 139	Pg 172	Christian County Circuit Court Clerk	Pt 23
Roberts, M. C.	GCAS 133	Pg 179	Deputy Sheriff, Green County	Dt 11
Travers, P. H.	GCAS 135	Pg 180	Doc Gonce's Lead Lawyer	Dt 12
Wayburn, Jas. R.	GCAS 128	Pg 181		Dt 13
Post Trial Affidavits				
Gonce, A. R.	GCAS 121	Pg 194	Motion for New Trial	Da 3
Porter, George A.	GCAS 112	Pg 195		Dp 1
Bryant, J. D. (Juror)	GCAS 115	Pg 197	Add'l Affidavit [GCAS 122] (pg 199)	Pp 1
Simpson, J. P.	GCAS 117	Pg 200		Dp 2

State of Missouri vs A. R. Gonce: Greene County Summons Issued for Appearance

Issued by Defense	Date	Sheet
Berry, F. P.[299]	18850513	46-47
Blyen, Martin	18850603	36-37
Blyen, Stephen	18850603	36-37
Brazeal, J. J. C.	18850605	38-39
Brown, W. F.	18850513	44-45
Clevenger, Geo.	18850513	44-45
Cloud, Wiley	18850513	46-47
Cloud, Wiley	18850601	40-41
Coin, M. B.	18850513	44-45
Dennis, W. G.	18850605	38-39
Edmondson, W. B.	18850603	36-37

Issued by State	Date	Sheet
Cloud, Wiley	18850603	20-21
Collins, J. D.	18850429	26-27
Collins, John, Sr.	18850504	28-29
Cox, Newton	18850429	26-27
Cox, Richard	18850429	22-23
Fulbright, J. H.	18850429	26-27
Galloway, Chas	18850429	22-23
Geiger, W. F.	18850606	12-13
Gideon, A. C.*	18850429	26-27
Gideon, John A.*	18850515	30-31
Gideon, T. J.*	18850613	10-11

---

[299] Francis P. Berry, whose strange testimony is given on page 158, lived in the area as early as July 1869 when he served as guardian and curator for the heirs and estate of Caleb Harris in Stone County.

Fox, Geo. W.	18850513	44-45		Gonce, Mrs. Mack	18850429	26-27
Garrett, Rob't	18850513	44-45		Hawkins, J. M.	18850429	22-23
Gideon, F. M.*	18850513	46-47		Johnson, J. A.	18850429	26-27
Haden, C. H.	18850513	50-51		Logan, G. W.	18850604	14-15
Hodge, George	18850603	36-37		McCord, John T.	18850429	26-27
Jones, John T.	18850513	44-45		Nelson, Jno T.	18850429	22-23
Keithley, A. S.[300]	18850513	48-49		Norman, Squire	18850429	22-23
Keithley, Wm. G.	18850513	48-49		Owen, C. B.	18850601	24-25
Keithley, Wm. G.	18850513	44-45		Phillips, Mrs. E. T.	18850601	24-25
Kentling, Frank	18850513	44-45		Smith, Spenser	18850523	32-33
Kirk, J. W.	18850506	52-53		Smith, W. E.	18850429	22-23
Lebo, Jos.	18850513	44-45		Stephens, William	18850523	32-33
Lebo, Manon	18850513	44-45		Vaughan, Wm	18850603	16-17
Maples, Pleasant	18850513	44-45		Wade, James	18850515	30-31
Masters, Reverend	18850601	40-41		Wade, Jas.	18850429	22-23
Nelson, John	18850513	46-47		White, Thomas Sen	18850504	28-29
Oliver, James	18850603	36-37		White, W. D.	18850523	34-35
Shelton, George	18850603	36-37		Wilson, Joseph	18850429	22-23
Wade, Louis	18850603	36-37		Winn, Joshua	18850429	26-27
Wade, Pleas	18850603	36-37				
Wade, Wash	18850603	36-37				
Wilhite, Dow	18850513	44-45				
Wilhite, Hamilton	18850603	36-37				
Wilhite, James	18850603	36-37				
Wilhite, John	18850513	44-45				
Wilson, Joseph	18850513	46-47				

* There is also reference to a Jim Gideon on archive sheet 143 (see page 171) The prosecutor's name was also Gideon.

The "Sheets" column indicates the Greene County Archive Sheets on which the front and back of the Summons appeared. The witness Wiley Cloud was summoned to testify by both Prosecution and Defense; images of the front sides of two of the Summonses for Wiley Cloud are shown on the next page.

---

[300] This is Ambrose Keithley; Ambrose and William Keithley are relatives of Doc Gonce's wife Martha Keithley.

Dr. Abraham Rudolph Gonce

[Greene County Archive Sheet 20 and 46]

STATE OF MISSOURI, } ss.
COUNTY OF GREENE.

The State of Missouri, To Wiley Cloud

Setting aside all excuses and delays, you are hereby commanded to be and appear before the Judge of our Circuit Court, at the Court House, in Springfield, within and for said County of Greene, on the 3rd day of June 1885 and then and there to testify to what you know relative to a certain matter of controversy in our said Court pending between State of Missouri plaintiff and A R Gonce defendant on the part of the said State of Mo. and hereof fail not at your peril. And the officer or person serving this summons will return the same at the time and place aforesaid.

Witness, **JOHN R. FERGUSON**, Clerk of said Court, with the seal thereof affixed hereto, at office, in Springfield, this 3rd day of June 1885.

John R Ferguson, Clerk

STATE OF MISSOURI, } ss.
COUNTY OF GREENE.

The State of Missouri, To F. M. Gideon, Berry Wiley Cloud, John Nelson, Joseph Wilson.

Setting aside all excuses and delays, you are hereby commanded to be and appear before the Judge of our Circuit Court, at the Court House, in Springfield, within and for said County of Greene, on the first day of June 1885 and then and there to testify to what you know relative to a certain matter of controversy in our said Court pending between State of Missouri plaintiff and A. R. Gonce defendant on the part of the said Defendant and hereof fail not at your peril. And the officer or person serving this summons will return the same at the time and place aforesaid.

Witness, **JOHN R. FERGUSON**, Clerk of said Court, with the seal thereof affixed hereto, at office, in Springfield, this 12th day of May 1885.

John R Ferguson, Clerk

Section IV:
The Legacy of
Doc Gonce

Gonce Outlaws and other Descendants of
Dr. Abraham Rudolph Gonce

Doc Gonce's Outlaw Descendants: Preface

Like most families of any size, the descendants of Justice and Magdalen Gonce include some interesting characters who crossed over to the wrong side of the law, even if only temporarily.

In her 1986 book referenced earlier, Barbara Gonce-Clepper ID 2805 relates the story of Marion Wilson Gonce's ID 2739 brief connection with what most likely was the infamous Jesse James[301]. Like some of those discussed below, Marion Gonce seemed to be quite intelligent and eventually became a solid citizen.

For whatever reason, however, the descendants of Abraham Rudolph Gonce seem to include a disproportionate number of such figures. Although the questions of "nature vs. nurture," or "genetics vs. environment" are hard to avoid, I'll leave that for others to ponder, and simply tell the stories of several of Doc's children, grandchildren and great-grandchildren – beginning with the tale of my fifth cousins twice removed – the "Baby Bandits."

In order to appreciate both its tragic as well as redemptive aspects, the story of the Colorado "Baby Bandits" and their siblings needs to begin with the backgrounds of their parents.

Lester Olonzo Gonce

The Bandits' father Lester Olonzo Gonce ID 4073, born 2 July 1882, was the second of three children of Abraham Rudolph "Doc" Gonce ID 2883 and Martha Ann[302] "Matt" Keithley ID 4007, whose marriage to Doc, you may recall, resulted in his serving an eighteen month prison sentence for bigamy in 1879. Although Lester was conceived and born after Doc had served this sentence, he could hardly have known his father very well, since Doc entered the penitentiary for the second time after being found guilty of killing Charlie Keyser just after Lester's third birthday.

Martha Ann (Keithley) Gonce
6 MAY 1858 - 10 APR 1899

After Doc was incarcerated, his wife Martha married a man named May[303], became a widow and, by the last

---

301 "Gonce-Wynne Genealogy"; Clepper, page 66.
302 There is another photograph of Martha on page 62
303 Mr. May reportedly had two sons from an earlier marriage; he himself died sometime between 1895 and 1899. I have located no evidence to support either of these statements however.

decade of the century, she and her younger children Lester Olonzo and Anna Belle ended up in Sterling, Kansas[304]. Circumstantial evidence suggests that her oldest son Rolyn [ID 4161], about eleven years old, may have remained in Missouri, at least for a few years. As mentioned earlier, the three children were reported by the Atchison (Kansas) Globe[305] to have been present in the courtroom with their mother during their father's trial and sentencing for murder. Rolyn would have been about 8, Lester 3, and Anna still an infant.

On 10 April 1899, when Lester Olonzo was not yet seventeen years old, his mother Martha died in Kansas of a rapid onset of tuberculosis. Since the family was indigent, Mattie May, as she was then known, was buried in the Potter's Field[306] in the Sterling Community Cemetery[307] on the following day.

Sarah Jane Bright

Lester Olonzo's wife, and the mother of the "Baby Bandits," was Sarah Jane Bright [ID 4094], born on October 7, 1885 in Missouri, the second of four children of John Wesley Bright [ID 4529] and Matilda Gideon [ID 4530]. Sarah's early history was, if possible, more traumatic and certainly less promising than Lester Olonzo's. Because Sarah Jane was born just a few months after Doc Gonce began his sentence for murder, it seems quite unlikely that Lester Olonzo Gonce had met his future wife before his family relocated to Kansas, even though the Gideon, Gonce and Bright families were certainly acquainted in Missouri, although not particularly friendly. The Gideons, in fact, were one of the largest and most prominent families in Taney County, Missouri during the post-Civil War years. Ironically enough, Sarah Jane's mother, Matilda Gideon, was a niece of J.J. Gideon, who was the prosecutor at Doc Gonce's murder trial.[308]

> **Obituary**
> **Death of Mrs. May**
>
> Mrs. Martha A. May, a widow who recently came to Sterling from Colorado, settling on West Main Street, died on Monday, April 10th, at the age of 40 years, 11 months and 4 days. Three children are the only relatives of the deceased, and will probably move to Oklahoma soon. The funeral services were conducted by Elder A.S. Poe, pastor of the Christian Church, and the remains were interred in Cottonwood Cemetery, Tuesday. Quick consumption was the cause of her death.
>
> Sterling Bulletin: April 14, 1899

---

304 Sterling is in Rice County; there are indications that Martha and her children may have spent some time in Colorado before settling in Sterling (see the obituary shown above).
305 June 11, 1885, as recounted by the Globe's local stringer.
306 A potter's field provided a place for burials of strangers, illegitimate children, criminals and suicides, as well as individuals who could not afford a cemetery lot, those who had no surviving family, and sometimes bodies of infants who would later be reburied in a family lot.
307 At the time, it was known as the Cottonwood Park Cemetery, and was an outgrowth of the original unplatted Friends Cemetery; there is a Cottonwood Cemetery near Wichita, but this is not the same cemetery.
308 Several other members of the Gideon family testified or were mentioned at that trial.

In the years following Doc's murder trial, J.J. Gideon became much better known as a defense attorney, however, having defended many of the infamous Bald Knobbers[309] when they faced trial for their extra-judicial hangings of those they deemed worthy of that honor. J.J. himself was reputed to be a member of this group.

Indications are that the Bright and Gideon families (Sarah Jane's forebears) were not the closest of friends either. The Springfield Daily Democrat, for instance, reported that John Wesley Bright was an "anti-knobber" and that "a former Bright was killed by the hands of Knobbers."[310]

John and his wife Matilda, who by many accounts was a beautiful woman, lived on Roark Creek, an "off the beaten path" area about 15 miles northwest of Forsyth in Taney County. Matilda, although already the mother of four young children, was still under 30 years old, and her husband, himself 32, became convinced that she had been showing an inordinate and flirtatious interest in their 33 year old married neighbor Hiram Jones.

So it happened that, on Sunday March 6, 1882, Matilda headed to the nearby spring to fill a bucket with water. Sarah's father John Wesley Bright followed after his wife and, when she arrived at the spring, he shot her in the back – the shot, passing through her heart, killed her instantly.

Rumors of this killing took several days to reach the larger towns, and The Springfield Leader didn't publish their first article until March 11th.[311] At that time, they reported that John Wesley Bright had been arrested for the murder, but had few other details.

By the next day, however, the Leader published the following:

THE TANEY COUNTY MURDER[312]
More Details About the Killing of Mrs. Bright

Later reports about the Taney county murder confirm the first rumor that John Wesley Bright has been caught and lodged in the Forsyth Jail on the charge of killing his wife. The alleged murderer was hunted down by a party of about sixty armed men. Mrs. Bright's maiden name was Gideon, a relative of the family so well known in Christian and Greene counties.

When Mrs. Bright started to the spring just before her death, Bright took his gun and left the house. Soon the children heard a shot in the

---

309 The Bald Knobbers were a rather infamous group of vigilantes operating in this area of Missouri after the Civil War. Their history is very well documented and so not discussed here.
310 The Springfield Daily Democrat; March 15.1892 Vol. 2 # 186 pg. 5
311 The Springfield Leader March 11, 1892 Vol. X #295 pg. 3. This article is reproduced in Appendix I.
312 The Springfield Leader March 12,1892 Vol. X #296 pg. 1. The complete text of this and other articles quoted in this section is given in Appendix I.

direction of the spring. Bright came back to the house in a few minutes and told the children that he had been shot at by someone at the spring. He warned the children not to go near the spring, as they might get hurt. The man then filled his pockets with eggs, took his gun and left the house. After a while, the children went to the spring and found their mother dead. They gave the alarm and the neighbors gathered in and began the search for the suspected murderer.

Regardless of what Matilda Gideon Bright had or had not done to incur her husband's wrath[313], the killing of anyone related to the Gideon family was not likely to be tolerated, and the family's long ties to the Bald Knobbers insured that justice would not likely be left in the hands of the Missouri judicial system. The Daily Democrat observed "some say that the masked men were Bald Knobbers who took this opportunity to kill Bright, who was an anti-knobber."[314] The Leader's article of two days later summarized what took place:

TWO MURDERS[315]
Lynchers Hang John Bright, the Taney County Murderer.
Deputy Sheriff Williams Shot Down While Resisting the Mob.
The Preliminary Trial Was Going on When the Mob Came After the Man.

Mob law, once the terror of the White River region, has again resumed sway in Taney county and John Wesley Bright, the alleged wife murderer, is now beyond the jurisdiction of all human courts. The work was done quickly and thoroughly as such things are always executed at Forsyth. But the mob did more than hang Bright and avenge the death of his wife who was shot in the lonely pine forests of the Roark wilderness. Between the doomed prisoner and the vengeful agents of Judge Lynch[316] stood a brave and conscientious officer, Deputy Sheriff Geo. T. Williams. He would not yield to the demands of the mob and sought to protect Bright from the fury of the vigilance committee. But the mob would not be cheated of their victim. The heroic deputy was shot down and over his bleeding corpse the terror stricken prisoner was dragged to the rude gallows from which his lifeless body soon hung.

Many more details of this incident and its importance in the context of post-Civil War Missouri history are well documented, and so will not be

---

313 I was unable to find any comments concerning her activities; on the other hand, there also seemed to be no indication that her neighbor Hiram Jones encountered any trouble resulting from this incident.
314 The Springfield Daily Democrat; March 15.1892 Vol. 2 # 186 pg. 5
315 The Springfield Leader March 14, 1892 Vol. X #298 pg.1
316 A common term used in this period. The Daily Democrat also used this term freely; one example on March 11th (Vol.2 #183 pg. 1) opining that "Judge Lynch will preside if the murderer is caught."

repeated here. A collection of contemporary newspaper accounts is given in Appendix I, titled "Press Coverage of the Bright Murders," which begins on page 243 of this book.

All four of John and Matilda's children were taken into the home of Isaiah Stewart and his wife Nancy Minerva Gideon[317], who was Matilda's older sister. The Stewarts, who had four children of their own, still had all eight of the children living with them in Jasper Township (Taney County, Missouri) at the time of the 1900 census[318], when Sarah was fourteen years old.

Mysteries And Questions:
- How did Sarah Jane Bright end up in Sterling, Kansas? – It seems like an incredible coincidence that she and Lester Olonzo Gonce ended up in the same town in another state.
- Who is Mr. May, i.e. what is his first name? (There are Mays in the Missouri area of interest, which might indicate that Sarah married prior to leaving Missouri.)
- Where and when did Mr. May and Matt Keithley-Gonce marry?
- Where and how did Mr. May die?

Marriage of Lester Olonzo Gonce and Sarah Jane Bright

I have located no information to suggest how or why Sarah Jane Bright moved from Jasper, Missouri to Sterling, Kansas, or whether either she or Lester had spent any time in Colorado before reaching Sterling. In about 1903, however, Sarah Jane and Lester Olonzo Gonce (pictured on the next page), then a self-employed bricklayer, seem to have been married in Sterling[319]. Lester would have been about 21 years old, and Sarah Jane about 17 at the time.

Lester and Sarah eventually had five children, all of whom were born in Sterling.

---

317 Not to be confused with the older Nancy Minerva Gideon, who was married to Francis P. Berry
318 National Archives Series t623, roll 905, page 60.
319 It is possible that Lester returned to Missouri, married Sarah Jane, and then took her back to Sterling, but there is no evidence I've found to support this either.

- Thelma Irene Gonce [ID 4095] was born in December of 1904. She died on 15 October 1939[320].

- Forrest Elmer Gonce [ID 4096] was born 4 March 1906, and died in June 1982. Forrest was the older of the infamous "Baby Bandits" of Colorado. In the 1915 Kansas census[321], Forrest was listed as "Bud," although that name doesn't appear in any of the contemporary stories about his "baby bandit" escapades.

- Vollie Vernon Gonce [ID 4097] was born on 10 February 1908. Vollie and his wife Kathleen L. Chapman (born 25 Nov 1924 in Boise, Idaho, the daughter of Oscar Chapman) had four daughters. He died on 23 March 1951. As an adult, he was known as "Sam," and in news reports of 1951 was referred to as "V. L. Gonce."

Lester Olonzo Gonce
2 JUL 1882 - 25 DEC 1957

- Lester Gonce, Jr. [ID 4098], born 10 February 1912, was the younger of the "Baby Bandits." He eventually adopted the name "Chet," and married Erma Dean Ruff [ID 4473]. He and Erma raised one son.

- Marion Gonce [ID 4099] was born in October 1915, after the 1915 Kansas State Census was taken; he died in Colorado in 1920.

- An unnamed female infant [ID 4542] was born premature on 5 November 1918 and died 8 days later. The infant was buried in the Potter's Field at the Sterling Community Cemetery where her grandmother Mattie is buried.

More details of the lives of this family are given in the succeeding sections, but their story begins with the recession that followed the end of World War I.

Sometime in mid-1919, with construction work declining precipitously, Lester Olonzo and his family decided to relocate to Olney Springs, Colorado, a town about thirty miles east of Pueblo. Stories passed down through that branch of the Gonce family say that they packed their belongings into a covered wagon, with Lester, Jr. riding along on their donkey.

---

320 More information about her untimely death is given later.
321 Kansas State Census; microfilm roll ks1915-202.

Once in Olney Springs, things began looking up, but only momentarily. Lester and Sarah acquired a piece of land there, and began to farm grain and hay. Although their first crop looked quite promising as it was coming near to harvest time, a herd of range cattle broke down their fences and devoured most of the crop.

Shortly thereafter, while working on a nearby ranch, Vollie Vernon "Sam" Gonce, then about seventeen, lost control of a team of horses, got thrown under a wagon, and crushed one of his legs. This injury was serious enough that it left him a cripple for the remainder of his life.

In the same year, several members of the family contracted diphtheria – attributed at the time to unsanitary water in the cistern they had been using. Although most of them recovered, Marion, not yet five years old, died from the disease. Lester and Sarah acquired a cemetery plot in the Olney Springs Cemetery where they buried Marion. Although they left the area very shortly thereafter, many of the family would be buried there in later years.

The Baby Bandits of Colorado

In 1921, Lester Olonzo and his wife Sarah Jane moved their family to the nearby town of Pueblo. Their descendants report that they first lived in various transient rooming houses on Santa Fe Avenue. By 1923, however, we find them living at 106 East 4th Street there[322]. By early 1926, Lester Sr. and his three living sons (then aged about 19, 17 and 14) were unable to find enough work to support the family, and poverty forced their move to what was described as a "shack on the outskirts of East Pueblo."[323] Thelma, was by this time married to

1923 Pueblo Telephone Book, Top of Page 139

---

322 See the Pueblo City Directory for that year. Forest was just 16 years old at this time, so the fact that he had a separate listing probably indicates that he had already joined the work force, although his occupation isn't listed (see illustration above).
323 The quote is from Ralph C. Taylor, a Pueblo Star-Journal reporter who covered these events as they happened, and continued to follow the participants for sixty-five years; he published his last column about Chet/Lester Gonce on 13 October 1991.

Clarence Leonard, and they were also living in East Pueblo. The population of Pueblo at that time was a little over 60,000.

During the summer of 1926, Forrest and Lester Jr. decided to explore some alternative sources of income. Vollie's name is never mentioned in conjunction with all the publicity surrounding the "Baby Bandits," most likely attributable to his disability. He eventually stepped outside the law as well, but doesn't appear to have been actively involved with his brothers during their crime sprees of 1926.

Forrest and Lester began their activities innocuously enough – going out into the desert to shoot rabbits for the family's dinner, for example. Before long, they began stealing bread and other groceries.[324]

The boys' first genuinely outlaw experiment, however, was an ill-conceived theft of two horses from Roy Ortner. On the shore of Minnequa Lake in Pueblo, there was a country club known imaginatively enough as the Minnequa Club that was popular for various activities such as weddings, showers, and the like. It also was the location for many outdoor activities including swimming, water skiing, and horseback riding. "Country Club" is perhaps a pretentious description, since the local press sometimes referred to it as the "working man's" or "poor man's" country club[325]. To Forrest and Lester Jr., however, the Minnequa Club likely seemed to represent an attractive opportunity for some surreptitious pilfering. Although they managed to steal two of Mr. Ortner's horses and remove them from the club, the boys were captured after being tracked into the hills for two days by a local posse.

Colorado State Penitentiary at Buena Vista

Because he was over eighteen, Forrest was sentenced to the nearby prison in Buena Vista. Lester, because of his younger age and the presumption that he was simply led astray by his older brother, was placed on probation.

With the exuberance of any fourteen year old who believes he has acquired some adult skills, Lester and a fifteen year old acquaintance named

---

324 Years later, Chet/Lester told Ralph Taylor "We never killed anybody – we just wanted to get food for our family."
325 For a little perspective on what constituted "poor man's country club" in Pueblo, the August 16th issue of the Chieftain described a car accident involving people returning from "a Dance being held at a nearby mining camp."

Dick Adams, another Pueblo boy, then joined up with two other slightly older boys – Bill Edwards and George Wilfong – both of whom had recently been paroled from the Buena Vista facility where Forrest was now incarcerated.

On Saturday June 5, 1926, the group stole two cars in Pueblo and headed for Colorado Springs; spotted almost immediately, a "special county officer" named Roy Arnold began chasing them along the highway. The boys managed to run Arnold's car off the road during the chase and continued on their way. Officer Arnold's car rolled over into a deep arroyo[326], although he was not seriously injured. Edwards and Wilfong were apprehended shortly after they arrived in Colorado Springs, but Lester and Dick Adams eluded capture, stole another vehicle, and headed across the Rocky Mountains towards the Grand Junction area in western Colorado.

Lester and Adams apparently separated after arriving there on Monday June 7th, and Lester stole another car shortly thereafter. He began to drive off, but someone, realizing that the boy was stealing the vehicle, notified the police. A posse was formed to capture him but, although Lester managed to elude them for four days, he eventually fell asleep at the wheel and drove the car over a fifteen-foot embankment. Apparently uninjured, he pulled out his .44 Colt and pointed it at his pursuers. W. E. Cotton, a member of the posse, then fired two shots at Lester's feet, whereupon Lester dropped the gun and was arrested by Marshal W. J. Bancroft of Palisade. The arrest took place on Friday night, June the 11th. During the four days he remained awake while eluding capture, reports suggest that he engaged in several holdups in Grand Junction, Fruitvale, and Clifton – his largest haul being about $200[327].

Although charges of robbery, grand larceny and hijacking were filed against Lester in Grand Junction's Juvenile Court, his probation for the earlier crimes he committed with Forrest was revoked and he was sent to the juvenile reformatory in Golden in the far western suburbs of Denver in order to spare the State the expense of a trial.

The Boys Escape

In late July, Forrest managed to escape from the prison at Buena Vista, although I have as yet been unable to locate any published details of this.

In early August, Lester Gonce, Sr. visited his youngest son at the Golden Reformatory. Some hours after he left, it was discovered that Lester Junior was no longer at the facility. The brothers' escapes were certainly related and, although it seems very likely that the boys' father must have had some involvement in both, he never seems to have been charged.

---

326 For those who haven't lived in the southwest, an arroyo is a usually dry gully formed by a river or stream that only flows as a result of periodic flash flooding.
327 As reported in the 13 June issue of the Pueblo Chieftain.

Having apparently decided that the move to Colorado wasn't working out well for them, the family was attempting to make their way back to their earlier home in Kansas. On August 9th, they were discovered attempting to steal a car in Garden City, about half way between the Colorado-Kansas border and Sterling. The Gonces, or at least Lester, Forrest and Lester Sr., ended up getting into a gunfight with police. The three of them managed to escape. No one seems to have actually been shot during the fray, "but women said to have been with them and a younger Gonce boy were taken into custody."[328] Since the article from which this quote is taken clearly refers to multiple females, my assumption is that those taken into custody included Sarah Jane, her daughter Thelma, and her second son Vollie, then seventeen years old. They were eventually released and returned to Colorado.

The activities of the Gonce brothers had by now become well publicized and had earned them the sobriquet of "Baby Bandits," and they appeared as such in almost every issue of the Pueblo Chieftain newspaper during the middle of August 1926. With a warrant issued for the car theft across the border in Kansas, the Federal authorities now became involved. Two agents named Funston and Morris[329] were assigned to pursue the "Baby Bandits."

Some time in the very early morning of Friday, August 13th, W. P. Beauchamp's store in the town of Rye[330], Colorado was burglarized, and a Chandler automobile parked nearby was missing and presumed stolen. The general consensus was that the "Baby Bandits," now back in Colorado, had struck again.

The Pueblo County Sheriff, Samuel A. Thomas, organized a posse and began searching for the boys in the areas north of Pueblo, but failed to locate them. Although they were in fact heading north, I was unable to determine how the sheriff had become aware of this.

One of the more interesting incidents – one that would eventually have significant and long-lasting ramifications for many of the participants – occurred later that day (Friday). A report was called in at about 9:00 am from Stone City, near present day Fort Carson north of Pueblo, by W. H. Potter, who was driving his work crew out to the site of some railroad construction. He had been flagged down by Forrest and Lester from a Chandler parked on the side of the road. Potter promised to send someone back with gas, but Forrest told him not to bother since someone else would likely be along soon. Under-Sheriff F. P. Daniel and a Deputy Sheriff named Charles Fiscus immediately went to investigate, driving a new Star Coupester that belonged

---

328 "The Gonce Brothers, Dubbed the 'Baby Bandits,' wreak Havoc," by Jeff Arnold; Pueblo Lore, September 2002.
329 I was unable to find any source that mentioned either of their first names.
330 Rye is about five miles west of Colorado City, which itself is about twenty-five miles south of Pueblo. The items reported stolen were mostly "foodstuffs ... clothing, cutlery and an army rifle."

to Deputy Fiscus. When the two lawmen arrived at the location, Forrest and his brother Lester were hidden behind the Chandler waiting for them. Using the element of surprise, the boys were able to steal all of the officers' money, their weapons (including two hand guns and a 30-30 Winchester rifle), and Fiscus' new vehicle[331]. Compounding Deputy Fiscus' embarrassment, the boys took his shield and watch as well. Although there is no explicit statement of such in any of the extant reports I was able to locate, there is a clear sense that Deputy Fiscus seemed to be viewed (at least by the press) with the same respect given to Deputy Barney Fife in Mayberry. After the boys escaped[332], Daniel and Fiscus attempted to start the abandoned Chandler but discovering the empty gas tank, were forced to walk for five or six miles before encountering someone who would give them a ride.

The next day, Deputy Fiscus' Star Coupe was found abandoned on the road between Beulah and Rye – out of gas, and with its tires blown out. Inside the car were items purportedly taken from the burglary of W. P. Beauchamp's store in Rye. Reports of the car's recovery mention that "no trace of the boys' father, who was thought to be in the vicinity of Rye, and to whom the boys were thought to be making their way, was found Saturday."

With the local sheriff's office now thoroughly embarrassed by the crime spree, more posses were formed to search the foothills of Greenhorn Mountain[333] about five miles southwest of Rye, where it was assumed the boys had fled. Not only were some experienced trackers[334] drafted, but a team of bloodhounds and a search plane[335] were employed. Sheriff Thomas declared: "we have every reason to believe that we have the boys cornered, and while we had not finally located them by this evening, it is but a matter of a few hours more before we will have them in custody."[336]

Nothing further seems to have been heard from the boys until about 7:00 pm the following Tuesday, August 17th, when Forrest and Lester, apparently bored by their weekend living in the great outdoors, decided to hold up the campers and staff at Camp Crockett[337], a popular campground run by the Y.M.C.A.. According to the Pueblo Chieftain report of August 18th, "The boys crept down from their hiding place ... All the members were searched and their money and jewelry ... were taken ... the two bandits ransacked the cook shack and made off into the mountains with their loot."

---

331 This was described in the August 14th issue of the Pueblo Chieftain.
332 According to the account in the 8/14 Chieftain, Forest forced the two lawmen across a barbed wire fence using his weapon and made them face away from the road, while Lester went and got the Star started.
333 This is located in the San Isabel National Forest.
334 Or, as the August 18th Pueblo Chieftain put it, "old-timers, well versed in manhunts and the pursuing of fugitives in the mountain country".
335 This was 1926, and so is quite worthy of note!
336 His quote of Sunday evening was given in the Chieftain on Monday August 16th.
337 This still exists, and is still run by the Y.M.C.A., but is now called Camp Jackson.

The witness impressions of the campground robbery were incorrect, however. In spite of what it appeared to the victims, the boys did not "make off into the mountains," but managed to elude the search parties and begin making their way out of the forest and back toward the town of Rye.

Pueblo Chieftain Headline of Wednesday 18 August 1926

Upon arriving in Rye, the boys made no attempt to avoid being seen. As the Chieftain reported in its Thursday issue: "… jauntily shouting a farewell at a girl schoolmate, a young man said to be Lester Gonce, notorious 'baby desperado,' cut out the muffler of a blue sedan car and thundered past Rye at 7 o'clock Wednesday evening." The girl, Virginia Thomas, was actually an ex-classmate of Lester's, since he had dropped out of school several months before the end of the prior school year.

So while the posse was still scouring the mountains southwest of Rye, the boys were making their way back north to Pueblo. In a later interview, Forrest Gonce said "the bloodhounds they had in the mountains after us were a joke, for they were always on the wrong trail, and readily assisted us in leading the posse away from us."

Forrest and Lester reached Pueblo without incident, and spent the night concealed in the stockyards there, then went to their sister Thelma's house the next morning.

Ralph C. Taylor, the Pueblo Star-Journal reporter, writing many years later, said that the boys' uncle[338] came to Pueblo from Denver to arrange Forrest's surrender to Sheriff Sam Thomas. Nonetheless, at about 4:00pm Thursday, Forrest, offering no resistance, was arrested by Patrolman Smith near the Eighth Street Bridge in Pueblo.

---

338 The uncle is never identified, but Conrad Bright, Sarah's younger brother, who was born in November of 1889, seems the most likely suspect.

Thelma Gonce, meanwhile, drove the stolen car into town with her brother Lester while she was attempting to convince him to surrender, and later said that she had almost convinced him to give her the revolver he had and turn himself in. She wasn't convincing enough, however, and he left the car, keeping the weapon, which he said he might need in order to make his escape, and headed up the street on foot. After turning over the stolen vehicle to the authorities, Thelma met with the previously mentioned federal agents Funston[339] and Morris, who were now in Pueblo, in an attempt to assist them in persuading Lester to surrender.

Funston later said[340]:

> *"We let the sister out of the Federal building, and then started on a search for the bandit. We saw him standing on the corner of Fifth and Court streets and drove our machine up to the curbing where we could talk to him. He saw us and placed his hand on the handle of the revolver he was carrying in the large leather belt, or protector, that he had girded about his body. He told us that he would shoot if we tried to capture him. We informed him that we were not his enemies, but were only trying to help him. Morris told him that we had no guns and we showed him our hands and opened our coats. He walked over the car and looked to make sure, telling us to keep our hands in sight. When he was convinced that we would not try to shoot him, he allowed Morris to get out of the car and talk to him. Morris stepped to the curbing and commenced to persuade him that he should give himself up, and it might save his being shot or his shooting some one else."*

At about the time the Federal authorities were setting out to locate Lester, someone had reported to the Sheriff's office that he had been seen walking north on Court Street. It was now a little after 10:00am on Thursday.

Sheriff Thomas and the hapless Deputy Fiscus quickly drove to the scene. Sheriff Thomas spotted Lester, claimed that Lester had his hand on his pistol grip, and fired his shotgun at the young man[341]. Deputy Fiscus jumped out of the car from the other side and reached Lester just as he had fallen to the ground. With the federal agent Morris still standing there, Fiscus fired his pistol five times at point blank range into Lester's midsection. By all accounts[342], Lester had never removed the pistol from his belt.

---

339 In Funston's account of the incident when interviewed by the Colorado Springs Gazette for their August 21st issue, he referred to Thelma only as "the married sister of the outlaw youth."
340 This quotation was given in the Colorado Springs Gazette of 21 August 1926.
341 This is, of course, giving Sheriff Thomas the benefit of the doubt. Why he took such a shot, particularly with a gun that had a wide shot pattern, while someone was standing next to Lester (even assuming the Sheriff was unaware that the man was a Federal agent) was never explained.
342 ... except for Deputy Fiscus' account, of course.

Pueblo Chieftain Headline of Saturday 21 August 1926

There were numerous eyewitness accounts. Here are two of them[343]:

> "Marie Kelly, employed in the drug department of the city market, across the street from the scene, who claimed to see virtually all the affray, said: "I was standing here arranging a counter when I was startled by a shot. It was different from the explosion of an exhaust from an automobile and I knew immediately that it was gunfire. I looked out of the big window on the west just in time to see the boy falling. His legs and arms were all spraddled out as he was falling. After he slumped to the sidewalk, an officer, I don't know who, rushed to the lad, stood over him and fired a revolver several times, the bullets evidently going into his body. I screamed, 'It's the boy!' and frightened everyone in the building. I said 'It's the boy' because I was frightened and meant by the term that it was the 'baby bandit.' I saw no one standing near the boy when he fell."[344]

> "Blanche Edvis related that she was standing in a doorway only a few feet from where the shooting took place and saw the whole affair. "When I first recognized that something was about to take place, I noticed a car pass the door and the two men in it got out. It seemed to me that the one who was not driving pointed a revolver toward the sidewalk and commenced shooting. I never heard them say a word."

---

343 These are both quoted in the Colorado Springs Gazette on 21 August 1926.
344 This seems to conflict with Agent Morris' presence, but perhaps he was quick enough to remove himself from the scene when he saw Thomas and Fiscus arrive.

Fiscus, who was never charged with any crime, immediately left the scene and presumably went home. The Sheriff and a bystander carried Lester, by then unconscious and bleeding profusely, about a block away to the Thatcher Building, where a Doctor named Low had his office. After being stabilized, Lester was transported to Parkview Hospital twelve blocks away, although no one expected him to survive through the night.

The two federal agents Funston and Morris, who seem to have been caught off-guard by the local lawman's actions, left the scene fairly quickly; although their interviews with the Gazette seem to confirm everything that the eyewitnesses reported, they made no attempts to remain involved with the "Baby Bandits" case, and don't appear in any later news accounts.

Reports of the shooting quickly drew some large crowds (described by the Gazette as "mobs") to the scene; the crowds became more incensed as the details of the shooting began to spread, and more police were called in to disperse them. Ralph Taylor describes the subsequent response of a group of steel workers who had gathered at the site of the shooting:

> "The target now became Fiscus. Soon after darkness, the armed posse started eastward on Highway 96 toward the Baxter farm where the deputy lived. Some friend got word to Fiscus and he scrambled into the heavy underbrush along the Arkansas River. By midnight the posse suspended the search and returned to town."

The next day, Friday, August 20th, Forrest was arraigned, without counsel[345], and pled Guilty to robbery with a gun. He was tried by District Attorney J. Arthur Phelps and sentenced by Judge James A. Park of the Federal District Court to 25-to-30 years[346] in prison. Family stories relate that one of the reasons for Forrest's easy acquiescence to this treatment was that he had been told that the mob (which he would have been aware of) had gathered to lynch him. According to this account, "officers suggested he'd better plead guilty to highway robbery as quickly as possible so he could be afforded protection by the State Penitentiary." By the end of the day, Forrest had become Colorado Prisoner number 13596.

On Thursday, August 26th, it happened that the Colorado Sheriff's Association opened their annual meeting in Colorado Springs. Their first order of business was to issue a statement denouncing the media reporting of Lester Gonce's shooting, accusing the papers of generating "maudlin sentiment."[347] They then voted unanimously to vindicate Deputy Fiscus' shooting, arguing that it was entirely appropriate. The newspapers reported the Association's proclamations in a matter-of-fact fashion, highlighting some

---

345 Ralph Taylor reported this. Although he seemed concerned by this, it wasn't unusual at the time that defendants faced hearings without any legal advice.
346 He ended up serving a total of 14 years and 3 months in prison.
347 Apparently, reporting eyewitness observations was considered inappropriate.

of their sillier remarks, although none of the media overtly pointed out that the association's attendees had no first-hand knowledge of the incident.

There don't seem to be any accounts of Lester Gonce Sr., his wife Sarah Jane, and their middle son Vollie during this period, but with Forrest now in prison – apparently for a long term – and the younger Lester apparently close to death, it isn't surprising they were keeping a low profile. One exception to this was reported by Taylor:

> *"There was deep bitterness in the hearts of the parents of the boys. While all the Baby Bandit publicity was at a peak, Mrs. Gonce hunted me down and vowed to kill me if I wrote another word about her sons. She meant it, but fortunately, we never met again. The father, however, brooded over two sons in prison."*

Dr. Eugene Brown had been responsible for Lester's treatment, but once he was stabilized, the doctor left with his family for a short vacation. During this period, the Sheriff's department took Lester from Parkview Hospital back to the jail. When Dr. Brown returned on Monday August 30th, he found that Lester had developed an infection in his hip (where one of Deputy Fiscus' bullets was still lodged) and was running a 101° fever. The doctor ordered that Lester be taken to St. Mary's Hospital and, a few days later, attempted surgery to remove the bullet, but wasn't successful in extracting it.

LESTER GONCE SHOWS IMPROVEMENT; MEDICAL HEADS BAFFLED AT CASE

Hospital attendants at Parkview hospital reported Tuesday evening that the condition of Lester Gonce, 14-year-old "baby bandit," who was shot by Deputy Sheriff C. L. Fiscus Friday morning, was better than it had been Monday.

Gonce has as yet undergone no operation for removal of the bullets which penetrated his body, arm and lungs, and considerable wonderment has been expressed in medical circles, as well as generally, that he has survived under the circumstances.

While the announcement was made that his condition was better than it had been Monday, no definite statement was made by those caring for him that he had a certain chance for recovery. It seems to be the opinion of attending physicians that he may live, but chances are declared equal that he may not live.

To most peoples' surprise, Lester not only survived[348], but eventually recovered, although the shooting left him severely crippled due to his hip injury. The Pueblo Chieftain's initial report on Wednesday (25 August) of Lester's recovery (shown above) stated: "considerable wonderment has been expressed in medical circles ... that he has survived."

Lester had a mechanical hip replacement implanted around this time, but I was unable to determine exactly when this occurred or how it was paid for[349]. The steward of the local Elk's Club[350] and a local plumber named William A. Cody and his wife Grace posted a five thousand dollar bond for Lester's release. For reasons not explained in any of the accounts I was able to find, Lester was then released from the hospital into the care of Mr. Cody and his wife rather than being sent back to live with his own family. The Codys, who had moved their family from Iowa in the first decade of the century, took him into their household for two years and managed to get him enrolled in Centennial High School. The Codys had another son, William Jr., living with them at the time, who was 16 years old, less than two years older than Lester. Bill Junior was a communications operator at a radio station, and began instructing Lester in what was then still a cutting edge technology, and for which Lester showed an aptitude. Perhaps not surprisingly given all the negative publicity surrounding his shooting, the authorities declined to press any further charges against the younger Lester, and he doesn't appear to have been returned to the reformatory[351]. Lester evidently developed a strong connection to the Cody family that would manifest itself some years later.

At age seventeen, Lester found employment at station KGIW in Trinidad, Colorado for about a year.

By the time of the 1930 U.S. Census[352], though, Lester, Jr. was back at home with his parents Lester, Sr. and Sarah; he was now eighteen, and working as a radio operator for station KGFL[353]. Forrest was, of course, still in prison[354]. Thelma was no longer married, but was listed as a head-of-household in Pueblo[355]; she was living alone under the name Gonce and

---

348 Accounts by members of his family say that, at one point, Lester was actually pronounced dead, but I haven't been able to locate any evidence to confirm that.
349 Such operations were not very common at that time; although it would seem reasonable to suspect that the State or County may have paid for this given the circumstances, I haven't located any evidence to support that.
350 ...whose name I have been unable to determine.
351 A relative of Lester's told me that the family had been told that Lester was tried and acquitted of the charges against him, but I found no record of any trial.
352 National Archives Microfilm Series t626, roll 241, page 2b.
353 KGFL is currently located in Clinton, Arkansas – too far away for him to commute – but a family member reports that, at the time, it was located in Raton, New Mexico, about 70 miles south of Pueblo just across the border.
354 National Archives Microfilm Series t626, roll 241, page 21b.
355 National Archives Microfilm Series t626, roll 249, page 1a.

working as a waitress. Vollie had by this time moved to Denver[356] and was working as a postal clerk there.

Although Lester was now gainfully employed, he was planning how to help his older brother Forrest to escape[357]. On Saturday, 8 August 1931, he succeeded, and he and Forrest left the area.

Both were eventually captured, and on October 31st, Lester was convicted of robbery in Saguache County. On November 2nd, he was given a sentence of six to ten years for aiding an escape. Lester now became known as Colorado Inmate 16472.

By Thursday, 11 February 1932, Forrest had been returned to prison with several more years added to his original sentence.

Lester Olonzo Gonce kills the Deputy Sheriff

The boys' father, Lester Sr., had by now become quite despondent, and this latest incident only served to exacerbate his anger. He brooded for several months and then one day walked out to the home where Deputy Sheriff Fiscus lived with his wife Bertha and their sixteen year old daughter Augusta. When Fiscus opened the door, Lester immediately shot and killed the Deputy without apparently saying anything.

Lester Sr.'s arraignment on murder charges took place on November 9th, but rather than schedule a trial, the judge ordered that he be placed under observation at the Colorado State Hospital for thirty days. Two of the doctors there, Superintendent F. H. Zimmerman and J. L. Rosenbloom declared that Lester was sane (as the prosecutors had hoped), and testified to this when the case was returned to court. The judge therefore permitted the County to proceed with a murder trial.

The jury apparently disagreed with the doctors[358] and on May 5th 1933 returned a verdict of not guilty by reason of insanity. At the prosecutor's request, the judge ordered that Lester be sent back to the State Hospital, although his authority for doing so seems somewhat murky[359]. It was inevitable then, that on June 20th, Lester Olonzo Gonce was discharged. The local authorities attempted to use the jury's declaration that he was insane to have him committed once again. Since the two most senior psychiatrists in

---

356 National Archives Microfilm Series t626, roll 239, page 1a. He was one of several boarders living at 1015 15th Street there.
357 I was unable to locate any details of how he accomplished this however.
358 Or perhaps simply didn't find the killing of Charlie Fiscus all that reprehensible. In spite of the Colorado Sheriffs' earlier support for Fiscus, public support was almost non-existent.
359 Juries have the authority to declare some one "not guilty" for whatever reason, but their stated reason for this decision could hardly be described as a medical finding.

Colorado had already declared him sane, however, the judge ended the whole episode and released him unconditionally.

Lester "Chet" Gonce, Jr. Paroled and Married

At District Attorney Phelps' recommendation[360], the younger Lester was paroled on 12 April 1934, having served two and a half years of his sentence for aiding Forrest's escape. He was given a job with the Pueblo radio station KGHF (1350 AM) by its owner, Curtis P. Ritchie.

Not long after, while climbing the station's tower at the Congress Hotel, Lester fell; already physically disabled, he now became more so.

On the 19th of February 1935, Lester married Erma Dean Ruff [ID 4473], known as Dean, in Clayton (Union County), New Mexico. Erma, born on 13 November 1915, was the daughter of Arthur Ruff, a locomotive engineer, and his wife Ellen of that town.

Contemporary sources report that Lester violated his Colorado parole and was returned to prison on 24 June 1935; his parole was formally revoked[361] on the following July 2nd.

Lester was again released from prison on the 27th of October in 1936. Shortly thereafter, he and Dean moved to Montana, where Lester took a position as a radio announcer. He and Dean had a son, Lester, who died on 25 October 1938, almost immediately after birth. This was Dean's second child[362] and, as a member of this family explained to me:

> "She was Rh Negative. Her first child lived and the second one did not. I understand that is the way the negative Rh factor works and therefore why a second child is now immediately given a total blood transfusion."

Lester's namesake infant is buried outside Butte, Montana.

---

360 This was the same J. Arthur Phelps who had gotten Lester's older brother Forrest a 25-30 year sentence back in 1926.
361 I have been unable to locate any information concerning what he might have done to violate his parole other than possibly working out of state or setting up residence out of state after his marriage.
362 Dean's first son, born in New Mexico, is still living and therefore not discussed here.

Vollie Vernon "Sam" Gonce Serves Time

Between 1932 and 1937, Vollie Gonce served two terms in the Colorado State Penitentiary as prisoner number 18596, then as 20257[363]. I haven't yet been able to determine what his convictions were for, but they seem to be late enough that they are likely unrelated to his brothers' earlier activities.

After his release from prison, Vollie moved to the northwestern United States, and at some point between 1937 and 1940, married Lucille M. Adams[364] in Jackson County, Oregon. I'm unaware of any children from this marriage.

Vollie eventually divorced and

Vollie Vernon "Sam" Gonce ID 4097

moved to Nevada where, now known by his childhood nickname of Sam, he was employed as a dealer for a series of casinos in the town of Hawthorne[365]. Although I've been unable to locate any details, subsequent events suggest that, unlike his brother Lester, Vollie likely continued to have run-ins with the law even after settling in a new state.

---

363 Colorado State Penitentiary Index 1871-1973. Based on the numbers given to his brothers and the dates of their entrance, simple mathematics might imply incarceration dates of July 1935 and June 1938, but this would only be a very rough guess.
364 Oregon Marriage Book #19 (1937-1940); certificate 435.
365 Hawthorne, Nevada is about 250 miles northwest of Las Vegas and about 150 miles due east of Sacramento, California.

Thelma Irene Gonce Dies

Thelma Leonard, sister of the "Baby Bandits," had moved to the outskirts of Gunnison Colorado, having been divorced for some time from Clarence Leonard. In any case, being a good contemporary Colorado woman, she apparently kept a loaded .22-caliber rifle hanging on her wall. As it turned out, the rifle was not mounted as securely as it might have been.

On 15 October, 1939, when she was not yet thirty-four years old, she was driving more nails into her wall to hang another weapon when the .22 dropped to the floor and discharged, hitting her in the stomach and, according to the Denver Post article reproduced above, causing further damage as the bullet traveled upwards.

from page 12 of the Denver Post – 16 October 1939

Thelma survived long enough to walk more than a mile to a neighbor's ranch to seek help, but died later that evening in the hospital. Thelma was buried in the family's plot in Olney Springs.

Forrest "Bud" Gonce Released from Prison

Forrest Gonce was finally released from the Colorado Penitentiary on Saturday, May 11th, 1940. According to later interviews with Ralph Taylor, Forrest claimed to have spent a great deal of his free time in prison reading the Wall Street Journal. Like his younger brother Vollie, Forrest also moved to the northwest.

Lester "Chet" Gonce, Jr. Pardoned

Lester was given an unconditional pardon by the Governor Ralph L. Carr of Colorado on the 23rd of April 1942. This seems to have been related to his wish to enlist during World War II but, due to his physical disabilities, that never came about.

Although Chet became a life-long member of the AFIO[366], he was never actually in the military, much less the intelligence sector, as this might suggest. His daughter-in-law, after reading of this association in his obituary years

---

366 Association of Former Intelligence Officers

later, received the following response to her query of the AFIO: "Mr. Gonce was an 'Associate' member of the Association. Associate members are those with no proper service in a federal or military intelligence capacity, but private citizens who support the principles of the Association for a strong intelligence capacity in US policy."

Forrest "Bud" Gonce Joins the Military

On September 3rd 1942, Forrest went from his home in Silver Bow County, Montana to enlist in the Army from Portland, Oregon[367]. According to his family, Bud was honest from the start about his background and incarceration but these concerns were conveniently overlooked – as many draft boards were doing in the year following the attack on Pearl Harbor.

Once his basic training near Little Rock, Arkansas was complete, he was sent to Fort Carson, Colorado, where he served as a rifle instructor. Since he was back in familiar territory, however, it was inevitable that he was finally recognized as one of the "Baby Bandits" and he was given a dishonorable discharge. Because his Draft Board intervened and filed an appeal to the Department of the Army on his behalf, this was subsequently changed to an honorable discharge.

Ralph Taylor reported that Forrest eventually became quite wealthy investing, although he remained something of a recluse. Bud worked in Klamath Falls, Oregon[368] as a night guard in a lumber mill for many years[369].

Sarah Jane (Bright) Gonce Dies

In March of 1946, the mother of the "Baby Bandits," Sarah Jane Bright Gonce, passed away in Sparks, a suburb just east of Reno, Nevada; she was buried in the family plot in the Olney Springs Cemetery, about 40 miles east of Pueblo. Sarah Jane was 60 years and 5 months old at the time she died.

Lester "Chet" Gonce, Jr. Begins a New Career

After World War II, Lester relocated to Las Vegas, at which time he began using the name Chet almost exclusively. After being associated with the radio broadcasting industry for many years in almost every capacity from technician to station owner, he now entered what would become a long career in the city's gaming industry, beginning with Del Webb's Sahara-

---

[367] National Archives and Records Administration; U.S. World War II Army Enlistment Records, 1938-1946 (Record Group 64). This source gives his marital status as single, his education as high school, his height as 69" and his weight as 126 lbs. Since he is classified as a "selectee," it seems safe to assume that he was drafted.

[368] He received his Social Security number 544-16-5322 in Oregon.

[369] In his 1991 retrospective article about the "Baby Bandits," Ralph Taylor said "Forest went into the Washington forests to work in logging," but this seems to be a misunderstanding.

Nevada Corporation, where he was an assistant manager for ten years. He left with the General Manager of that facility when he took a new position operating the Eldorado Club in Henderson.

He subsequently began a long association with Sam Boyd's organization, starting as a Keno Game Manager, and eventually becoming a trusted financial advisor and sometime investment partner to Boyd.

Lester "Chet" Gonce

> **Sam Boyd**
>
> *Samuel A. "Sam" Boyd (23 Apr 1910 – 15 Jan 1993), an Oklahoman like Chet (Lester) Gonce, came to Las Vegas in 1941 with, as legend has it, just $80 to his name. He found employment as a dealer, and worked his way up through various positions until he was able to purchase an interest in the Sahara Hotel. An astute businessman, he subsequently introduced many innovations into the Vegas gambling scene.*
>
> *His eponymous Boyd Gaming Corporation, which maintained a reputation for honesty even during the worst of the skimming scandals of the 1950s, was eventually tapped by federal regulators to take over the operations of some of the shadier businesses there, and his conglomerate became one of the largest gaming operations in the country.*
>
> *The company still exists, and Sam is remembered by many facilities that bear his name, e.g. the Sam Boyd Stadium, home field of the UNLV football team.*

A relative of the Cody family, with whom Lester had stayed for a time after his time in the hospital following the Fiscus incident, related to Ralph Taylor that, after the death of William Cody, his wife Grace was facing foreclosure on their Pueblo house. Chet/Lester heard about this, and returned to Pueblo to visit her. He then purchased the house outright and gave it to her.

Vollie Vernon "Sam" Gonce

Once in Hawthorne, Nevada, Vollie married again, this time to Kathleen Louise Chapman [ID 4524], a mother of two young daughters Katherine and Theresa, who were adopted by Vollie. Vollie and Kathleen, who was seventeen years younger than Sam, then had two more daughters of their own named Sandra Jane (Sandra) [ID 4527] and Georgia Irene (Irene).

Based on the following incident, it is evident that there are significant gaps in what we know about Vollie's life. On the 23rd of March in 1951, Vollie went into Hawthorne's 222 Club at about 1:30 am, took a seat at the bar, and ordered a drink. When the bartender, Leonard E. Erickson, placed the drink on the bar, Vollie pulled out a pistol and, according to one witness, said: "I've promised this for a long time and here it is." The shot hit Erickson in the chest, although the wound wasn't fatal[370]. It doesn't seem a coincidence that, before working at the 222 Club, Leonard Erickson had been a Deputy in the Mineral County Sheriff's office, and had run for Sheriff himself.

A 35 year-old civil service worker named Marie Diggins, another patron at the bar, began to intervene, but Vollie shot her as well. She also survived. Vollie immediately took off, and the local authorities mounted a search for him with armed pursuers in jeeps and an airplane to sweep the area, which is fairly rugged.

The next day, Saturday, members of the posse located Vollie's body on the side of Pamlico Road about ten miles southeast of Hawthorne with a single bullet wound in his chest. He had apparently shot himself with the same .32-20 revolver that he had used to shoot Leonard Erickson and Marie Diggins in the 222 Club. This gun and a 30-30 Winchester carbine were also found at the scene. The posse members also found a Keno ticket with the body. Vollie, then 43 years old, had the forethought to write a will on the back of this ticket in which he simply left all of his property to his wife. He also wrote a note – apparently referring to Marie Diggins – saying, "It is too bad that the girl, whoever she is, couldn't mind her own business."

The Mineral County Independent News reported on Vollie's funeral – held the following Tuesday the 27th; Vollie is buried in the Hawthorne Cemetery. Just about two months after Vollie's burial, his wife was buried next to him. Details of Kathleen's death were not given, but she was just twenty-six years old, and the Mineral County Independent News reported that, "she died 26 or 27 May 1951," suggesting that her suicide[371] might have gone undiscovered for several days. The four girls   were picked up by Kathleen's parents Oscar Chapman[372] and his wife; Lester and his wife Dean quickly adopted his brother Vollie's daughters Sandra and Irene, who went to Las Vegas to live with them.

On Christmas day of 1957, Lester Olonzo Gonce, father of the "Baby Bandits", passed away, and was buried alongside his wife Sarah Jane in the Olney Springs Cemetery.

---

370 This incident and the subsequent events were related in the Nevada State Journal, a newspaper published in Reno. The only explanation I've located is a vague comment in the Journal that the shooting resulted from "an old grudge between the two men."
371 Although the circumstances themselves suggest suicide, this was confirmed by a relative.
372 She also had two married sisters and a brother, all of whom lived in Hawthorne.

Denoument

The next twenty years passed relatively uneventfully, with Chet's career and reputation growing. In the early 1980s, however, his older brother Forrest developed stomach cancer, and moved to Las Vegas to live with Chet and his wife Dean. In June of 1982, Forrest died there. His death certificate, rather than mentioning the stomach cancer, lists the cause as "Cerebrovascular Accident" – a result of his decision to shoot himself rather than face the increasingly painful effects of the cancer.[373] He was buried with his parents in the Olney Springs Cemetery – the last of the Gonces to be interred there.

Two years later, Chet's wife Erma Dean died on 27 June 1984; she is buried at the St. George City Cemetery in St. George, Utah.

Through the "Chet L. Gonce/Dean Gonce Trust[374]," Chet continued his investments and, as late as 1988, the Trust became a part owner of Boyd's California Hotel and Casino in Las Vegas.

Chet finally retired to St. George in 1989. Because of the prominence he had gained in the Las Vegas business community, his retirement was featured in the local papers. He had one of these with him when he encountered his long-time acquaintance Ralph Taylor and, as Taylor reports:

> "Chet greeted me by waving a newspaper – a Nevada newspaper with the banner headline 'Chet Gonce Retires.' He laughingly said 'Well, I made the headlines again'."

Not long after, on 8 April 1991, he married for a second time to the widow Velma G. Kimbrough ^{ID 4523}. He had apparently known Velma for many years; she had worked as an accountant in Raton, New Mexico during Chet's early days in radio. At the time of their marriage, Chet and Velma were almost eighty years old.

Chet died on 2 March 1992, and was buried in the St. George City Cemetery[375] with his first wife Erma Dean. Velma died on July 10, 2004.

Chet Lester Gonce's headstone in the St. George, Utah cemetery.

Erma Dean Gonce's headstone in the St. George, Utah cemetery.

---

373 The actual meaning of this euphemism was provided by Chet's daughter-in-law.
374 The Trust was dissolved on 19 November 1992, after his death.
375 Chet is in plot M-1-9-NH; Erma is buried next to him in plot M-1-9-SH.

The "Baby Bandits" Tale Comes to an End.

Ralph C. Taylor, whose articles have been quoted extensively above, wrote his final piece on the "Baby Bandits" for the Pueblo Star-Journal on October 13, 1991 – more than sixty-five years after his first article appeared. By this time, as described above, Chet had become a well-respected businessman. This article is reproduced below:

'Baby Bandits' tale finally completed after 65 years

By RALPH C. TAYLOR

Sixty-five years ago I was a young reporter for *The Pueblo Star-Journal* when Pueblo's "Baby Bandits" story made headlines. I have never been able to complete that story until now.

It began in 1926 when the Gonce family moved their few possessions into a shack on the outskirts of east Pueblo.

They had only a willingness to work, but were unable to find employment. Forrest, 17, and Lester, 14, engaged in a series of holdups and thefts that summer.

"We never killed anybody — we just wanted to get food for our family," Lester explained.

An uncle of the boys came to Pueblo from Denver and arranged Forrest's surrender to Sheriff Sam Thomas on the night of Aug. 19.

The next day, word reached the sheriff that Lester was walking north on Court Street. It was noon.

The sheriff started driving his car north on Court and Deputy Charles Fiscus was coming south on the same street. As Lester reached the southwest corner of the intersection, Thomas fired his rifle from his car. The bullet struck Lester. Fiscus ran up to the wounded boy. Versions differ about whether Lester was on his feet or on the ground, but Fiscus fired five bullets into his body.

The bleeding and unconscious boy was rushed to Parkview Episcopal Hospital 12 blocks away.

It was known that Fiscus was angry with the brothers, who had disarmed him and stolen his car a week earlier.

Word of the shooting spread. Immediately the wrath of a posse of steel workers changed. The target now became Fiscus. Soon after darkness, the armed posse started eastward on Highway 96 toward the Baxter farm where the deputy lived. Some friend got word to Fiscus and he scrambled into the heavy underbrush along the Arkansas River. By midnight the posse suspended the search and returned to town.

After Forrest's capture on Thursday, law enforcement agencies moved swiftly. Criminal charges were drawn Friday, and court was called into session. Forrest, without counsel, was sentenced that day to serve 14 years in prison.

Lester recovered, but became a cripple for life. When he was able to leave the hospital, he was taken into the home of Mr. and Mrs. William Cody, who operated a Pueblo plumbing business. Gonce lived with the Codys for two years and attended Centennial High School.

Never able to forget his brother in prison, Lester engineered Forrest's escape. The two were captured quickly. Forrest was returned to complete his 17 years behind bars. Lester faced unsympathetic jurors who found him guilty of aiding in the escape. He was given a four-year prison sentence.

Chet Gonce
... formerly known as Lester

There was deep bitterness in the hearts of the parents of the boys. While all the Baby Bandit publicity was at a peak, Mrs. Gonce hunted me down and vowed to kill me if I wrote another word about her sons. She meant it, but fortunately we never met again. The father, however, brooded over two sons in prison.

Six years later, the father walked out to the Fiscus place. As Fiscus responded to Gonce's knock, he was shot dead. Gonce made no effort to flee.

He was arraigned Nov. 9, 1932 on murder charges.

For 30 days Gonce was under observation at the Colorado State Hospital. Superintendent F.H. Zimmerman and his assistant, Dr. J.L. Rosenbloom, testified that Gonce was sane at the time he shot Fiscus.

The following spring, on May 5, 1933, a jury of 12 men found Gonce innocent by reason of insanity and he was sent back to the state hospital. Six weeks later, **Please see Gonce, Page 4B**

Pueblo (CO) Star-Journal; 13 Oct 1991; pg 1B

Gonce

Continued from Page 1B

on June 20, he was released.

Within weeks, the case was in court again. It was noted that Colorado statutes provided that criminally insane people can be released only on order of the superintendent.

In this case the two top psychiatrists at the hospital already had testified as to the man's sanity. The court gave the senior Gonce his freedom.

When Lester completed his sentence he was employed by Curtis P. Ritchie, owner of radio station KGHF. Lester was working on the radio tower atop the Congress Hotel when he fell, further disabling his body. Upon his recovery he began making the rounds of area radio stations, working on some and owning others.

Lester changed his name to Chet Gonce upon leaving Pueblo.

Forest served his 17 years, spending much of his time reading the Wall Street Journal. From prison he went into the Washington forests to work in logging. A recluse, he invested his money, becoming a millionaire. He never married and lived alone until he became ill. He lived his last years in the Las Vegas home of Mr. and Mrs. Chet Gonce.

Chet Gonce entered the Las Vegas world by managing keno games in casinos operated by Sam Boyd. In time he became a financial associate of Boyd's. He built a nice suburban home. He and his wife reared two nieces, daughters of another Gonce brother, Volley, after he died.

Chet became a prominent and successful citizen.

More than 20 years ago, I heard about the "other lives" of the Gonce brothers. I spent an afternoon in the Gonce home. I asked for details of the complete story. Chet was agreeable, but wanted to talk to Forrest to seek his approval. The elder brother agreed, with one provision — that Colorado's governor grant him a pardon.

I wrote Gov. John A. Love. He said he would grant the pardon if I would obtain letters of recommendation from three reputable citizens of Pueblo. That was impossible since Forrest never lived in Pueblo as an adult. Forrest died without the pardon.

Several years ago, after his retirement, Chet greeted me by waving a newspaper — a Nevada newspaper with the banner headline "Chet Gonce Retires." He laughingly said, "Well, I made the headlines again."

This past Aug. 22 he tried to call me from his retirement home in St. George, Utah. Failing to reach me he phoned Tony Bacino, another Pueblo friend. He asked Tony to remind me it was 65 years ago that he was gunned down.

Presently, he is looking forward to seeing his Pueblo friends in the spring.

The only member of the Cody family still alive is Mrs. John Cowen, a widow living on Pueblo's East Side. She is 92 years old.

She remembers when Mrs. Cody's home was lost through a foreclosure. Chet Gonce learned about it, came to Pueblo, purchased it and gave it to Mrs. Cody.

Chet uses a cane, but says he walks on the same mechanical hip that was implanted 65 years ago.

It never has been replaced.

Chet is the last of the Gonces. His parents and brother are buried in an Olney Springs cemetery. Many times he has gone there to place flowers.

Everyone closely related to the Pueblo Baby Bandits is gone, except Mrs. Cowen, Chet and this writer.

Pueblo (CO) Star-Journal; 13 Oct 1991; pg 4B

A little over six years after this article appeared, and five years after Chet's death, two of his first-cousins-twice-removed became involved in another crime that attracted wide attention – this time in Las Vegas, Chet's adopted hometown. Their story follows.

The Senior Citizen Burglars of Nevada

Fain Terrant Gonce [ID 4536] was born in Ottawa[376], Kansas on the 23rd of July in 1935; his younger brother Richard Alan Gonce [ID 4538] was born about five years later. The brothers were first cousins twice removed of the Colorado "Baby Bandits," although there is no indication that any of these cousins ever knew each other. A member of Chet/Lester's family with whom I have corresponded had never heard of Fain and Richard.

My seventh cousins Fain and Richard were the sons of Loral E. Gonce [ID 3826] and his second wife Dorothy R. Taylor [ID 4537], and were also therefore descendants (2nd great-grandsons) of Abraham Rudolph "Doc" Gonce. William McClellan Gonce [ID 3480], Doc's first son, was born in August 1851, and was already married to his wife Martha Sims [ID 3481] by the time Doc's troubles with the law began. Martha and Mac, as he was known, had their sixth[377] child, Fred Harrison Gonce [ID 3686], on March 19th, 1885. Fain's father Loral was the second child of Fred and his wife Rosa Sanders [ID 3687].

For most of their lives, the two brothers led fairly straightforward lives. Fain was married twice, first to Misa Mugge [ID 4539] on 15 January 1987, from whom he was divorced a little over eight years later on 21 November 1995. Richard was married to Pamela J. Salter [ID 4541] on 17 November 1979. Both of their marriages and subsequent divorces took place in Clark County Nevada. Then, in late 1997, when Fain was already in his sixties, the brothers were apparently convinced that they needed to spice up their lives.

The Target

The United Coin Machine Co. (UCMC) in Las Vegas was founded in 1957 to install, service, and collect the money from "gaming" machines across Nevada[378].  The company continues today to be a significant beneficiary of the Nevada gambling industry and has introduced much new technology to that market.

---

376 Ottawa is in Franklin County in east-central Kansas, a little southwest of Independence, Missouri and about 180 miles east of Sterling, where Lester and his family had lived.
377 Possibly their seventh child.
378 I was unable to determine if Boyd Gaming was a client of UCMC at this time.

The Heist

Shortly after midnight on the morning of December 28, 1997, a pickup truck drove up to the UCMC's Las Vegas facility at 600 Pilot Road, and two men wearing ski masks and jumpsuits got out. They approached the security guard and two female workers who were taking a smoke break outside the facility and forced them at gunpoint into the building.

One of the burglars stood guard while the other managed to place what was reportedly $1.6 million in cash into several duffel bags. The burglars took the bags, loaded them into the back of the pickup truck, and were driven away.

Although the robbery prompted significant media attention, the police had virtually no information with which to pursue the case. Before very long, a reenactment of the heist was shown nationally on the "America's Most Wanted" television program[379]. Once again, however, no useful information was forthcoming, and the authorities had no idea of the burglars' identities.

Shortly after the United Coin robbery, the Gonce brothers Fain and Richard left Las Vegas and relocated to New Mexico. On May 22, 1998, Fain's fiancée Andrea Jane Thomas [ID 4540], whom he would marry on 26 June 1998, filed a deed for the purchase of 127 acres of land[380] in Quemado[381], suggesting that they had recently come into a substantial sum of money. While temporarily living in a trailer on this property, the brothers began construction of a "log cabin" on the site; a later audit indicated that the structure was worth about $44,000. Clearly, this was a high-end cabin when compared to the cost of the average home in New Mexico at the time.

New Investigation

In early 1999, a detective named Anthony Plew was assigned to the Las Vegas Metro Robbery Division, and began looking into the United Coin Burglary with fresh eyes. Detective Plew began reviewing the security tapes and conducting further questioning of UCMC's employees. The television show "America's Most Wanted" featured the robbery in a new episode[382] and, within a short time, he had received a tip suggesting that someone within the company had had been involved in planning the burglary.

He soon settled on fifty-five-year-old Kathryn Toledo, who by now was a "former employee," as the most likely suspect and, within a short time, she confessed to having assisted in the planning of the robbery. A search warrant of Toledo's home and bank accounts, along with further questioning,

---

[379] This episode was first aired on 25 September 1998.
[380] This according to Catron County records.
[381] Quemado is a town off Route 60 about 150 miles southwest of Albuquerque near the Gila National Forest.
[382] This episode aired on 11 March 1999.

revealed that she had very little of her proceeds from the heist remaining, having gambled most of it away. As far as I'm aware, the irony that she had thus "returned" this money to the folks from whom it was stolen wasn't commented on by the police or the press.

After being granted immunity from prosecution by Deputy District Attorney David Wall, Kathryn gave the Metro Robbery detectives the names and current whereabouts of all three of the burglars, and agreed to testify in any resulting trials. In addition to Fain and Richard Gonce, who had no previous records, she named Eric William Zessman as a participant. Zessman, who was born on July 9th of 1954, had earlier been convicted of second-degree murder (on June 21, 1976), forgery (in 1983), firearms violations (in 1990), and armed robbery (on May 21, 2003). Fain Gonce, it turned out, had been the getaway driver, while his younger brother Richard and Eric Zessman entered the UCMC building to collect the money.

The Arrests and Recovery of the Loot

On Thursday, April 8, 1999, acting on information supplied by the Las Vegas police and prosecutors, authorities in New Mexico raided the Quemado site and arrested Fain and Richard Gonce, who were now living under assumed names. Records indicate that more than $400,000 in cash, silver, property and weapons was found in the Gonces' trailer. $32,000 of this amount was in cash, much of which was still in the form of gold and silver coins; there were receipts showing the purchase of $50,000 in mutual funds, as well as the deed for the property. Police also recovered more than twenty-five weapons of various types, including a shotgun and a 9mm semiautomatic pistol that matched the descriptions of weapons used in the robbery.

The raid on Eric Zessman's residence yielded an additional $200,000 in property, cash and gold. Newspaper reports stated that evidence confirming Zessman's connections to the Gonce brothers was also located there, but never specified what that information was.

Altogether, the police claimed to have recovered more than a million dollars of the $1.6 million that was purportedly[383] stolen.

The Indictments

In early May, indictments were handed down in Clark County Nevada charging the three with conspiracy to commit robbery, burglary, robbery and first-degree kidnapping with the use of a deadly weapon. The kidnapping charge seems to have been a technicality based on the fact that some of the

---

383 I only use the word "purportedly" because of the contrast to the amounts recovered; if $1.6 million was an accurate figure, it seems that a fair amount of money must have been completely unaccounted for.

employees were held hostage while the money was being loaded; no one was actually taken from the site that I could determine.

The Chief District Judge, Lee Gates, set bail at $250,000 for Fain and Richard Gonce but, because of his earlier murder convictions and the fact that engaging in armed robbery is apparently considered a parole violation in Nevada, Eric Zessman's bail was set at $500,000. "America's Most Wanted" aired an update to their earlier stories on 15 May 1999.

The Sentencing

An article by Bill Gang that appeared in the Las Vegas Sun on Tuesday, November 9, 1999 describes the sentencing:

> *Sometimes crimes of great magnitude deserve punishment no matter the circumstances, a district judge concluded before sentencing two aging New Mexico brothers to prison for their roles in the $1.6 million United Coin Co. heist in 1997.*
>
> *Despite their gray hair, wrinkles and lack of criminal records, Fain Gonce, 64, and Richard Gonce, 60, were told Monday they are going to be wearing prison garb for at least the next couple of years.*
>
> *District Judge Jeff Sobel said probation for the pair might have been possible for a crime of lesser proportion, but the amount taken and the "real terror" experienced by the victim[384] warranted prison time.*
>
> *"You know you can't take a shot at the big prize" without knowing that a prison sentence is the consequence of being caught, Sobel said.*
>
> *Fain Gonce, who admitted being the getaway driver, was sentenced to two to five years in prison. Richard Gonce, who admitted carrying a shotgun as he helped a third man steal bags of $20 and $100 bills, was sentenced to 2 1/2 to six years.*
>
> *The third man, convicted murderer Eric Zessman, 45, was alleged by the attorneys for the Gonces to be the mastermind behind the holdup. He is scheduled to stand trial Dec. 20 on charges that could put him in prison for the rest of his life if he is convicted.*

As far as I could determine, Andrea Jane Thomas, who had married Fain Gonce 26 June 1998, was never charged with any crime, although it seems very unlikely that she had no suspicions concerning the sudden influx of wealth, the quick move to New Mexico, and the change of names.

---

384 The use of the singular "victim" isn't explained, and none of the material I was able to review seems to justify the word "terror," so there may be more to this story than I have discovered.

Aftermath

Zessman, acting as his own attorney, later sued[385] Detective Plew and other officers, as well as the Las Vegas Police Department and his own attorneys from the trial, claiming the search of his premises exceeded the bounds of the search warrant that had been issued. Zessman had a history of filing such lawsuits prior to this incident, having earlier sued William S. Sessions, then Director of the Federal Bureau of Investigation, for maintaining records that were later used to revoke Zessman's parole, claiming that this constituted double jeopardy. Like many "jailhouse lawyers," though, he wasn't very effective.

After her new husband was sent off to prison, Andrea Jane divorced Fain. He died on 3 January 2003.

Summary: The Legacy of "Doc" Gonce

Whether a result of nature, nurture, or simply coincidence, then, we see the following:

- Doc's son Lester Olonzo shot and killed Charlie Fiscus. Lester had also been involved in at least one gunfight.
- Doc's grandson, Lester Olonzo's oldest son, Forrest engaged in multiple gunfights in the course of his early escapades. Forrest committed suicide.
- Doc's grandson, Lester Olonzo's middle son, Vollie Vernon "Sam" shot Leonard Erickson and Marie Diggins. Sam also committed suicide.
- Doc's grandson, Lester Olonzo's youngest son, Lester/Chet engaged in multiple gunfights in the course of his early escapades.
- Another of Doc's sons, James Tilford [ID 4001] also committed suicide.

  Although not discussed in this appendix, James Tilford Gonce (born 10 Nov 1900) was the middle of five children from Doc's final marriage to Susan Hargrove. After serving in World War I, Tilford (as he was known) married and had at least one son, but after his wife Ruth divorced him, he checked into a hotel in St. Louis, Missouri on April 21, 1942 and swallowed a jar of strychnine.

- Doc's second great grandsons Fain and Richard participated in armed robbery.

  The story of these brothers seems more difficult to attribute to nurture or some environmental stress passed down from their ancestor. William McClellan Gonce [ID 3480], Doc's first son and the great grandfather of Fain and Richard, was born in August 1851, and was already married to his wife Martha Sims by the time Doc's troubles with the law began.

---

385 March 18, 2003. CV-99-01693-LRH. Resolved by 2003 U.S. App. LEXIS 4958,*;58 Fed. Appx. 754; 9th Circuit Court of Appeals.

Appendix I: Bright Murders Press Coverage

Published Accounts of the Murder of Matilda Gideon Bright and the lynching of John Wesley Bright

Press Coverage of the Bright Murders

This appendix provides transcriptions of many published news accounts of the incidents described in Section III. Missouri journalism had advanced quite a bit since the reporting of the murder of Charlie Keyser described earlier in this book. Although these events took place in what was a rather remote corner, modern inventions such as the telegraph, coupled with the more frequent travel associated with increased commerce, brought these stories to the major center of Springfield within hours.

The two competing newspapers of central Missouri in the last decade of the century were the Springfield Leader and the Springfield Daily Democrat; selections from both these publications[386] are given here. A synopsis of relevant sections of a later book discussing the Gideon-Bright tragedy is also provided.

The Springfield Leader; Friday, March 11, 1892; Vol. X #295 pg 3

BULLET THROUGH HER HEART

Wife of John Westly (sic)[387] Bright of Taney County Shot

The Lifeless Body of the Woman Found at the Spring- The Husband the Supposed Murderer

A number of persons from Taney County were in the city last night and rumors of the murder of Mrs. John Wesley Bright, who lived on Roark Creek, about 15 miles northwest of Forsyth, was the subject of much comment, though no exact details of the alleged crime could be learned as these teamsters had left home early in the week.

It was not definitely known that the woman had been killed, the lifeless body being found at the spring last Sunday morning pierced through the heart with a bullet.

Roark, one of the small mountain tributaries of White River, flows through the rugged section of the western border of Taney county. The Bear Creek road, running from Highlandville through to Harrison crosses

---

386 The Springfield Express, not one of the major papers, often reprinted stories from the other papers verbatim.
387 As with earlier publications, the reporters were generally not too concerned with consistent spellings of proper names. John Wesley Bright's name is spelled correctly in the first paragraph of the story.

the table land west of the Roark rivulet on which the Bright family resided. This section of Taney county is remote from railroads and daily mails and news from its pine woods reaches the outside world slowly.

When the woman was found dead suspicion at once rested on the husband of the deceased as the probable murderer. Just what circumstances led to this belief could not be learned from fragmentary rumor of the tragedy. It was reported, however, that Bright had been arrested on the charge of murder and lodged in the new Forsyth jail, a substantial stone building from which no criminal has yet escaped.

The Brights are a numerous family living in the southern part of Christian and the northern and western sections of Taney counties. The father of John Westly (sic) Bright was a well to do farmer of Bull Creek a few years ago till trouble among his boys involved the old man in heavy losses incurred in their defense in courts. Andy Bright, a brother of the alleged uxorcide, was a conspicuous witness in the trial of the Peyton boys for the murder of the infant child of Bub Mathis several years ago, a crime so well remembered by all the people of Christian and Taney counties.

The Springfield Daily Democrat; Friday, March 11, 1892; Vol.2 #183 pg 1

MURDERED HIS WIFE

John Bright of Taney County Takes His Wife's Life in a Cowardly Manner

(By telegraph to the Democrat)

Ozark, Mo. March 10- News reached here today that John Bright living in Taney county shot and killed his wife early this week. Bright sent his wife to the spring after water, then got his revolver and followed her. Coming upon her, he shot her through the head[388], killing her. Bright fled. A posse is after him. Judge Lynch will preside if the murderer is caught.

The Springfield Express; Friday, March 11, 1892; Vol. XI pg 52

(reprint of Daily Democrat article above)

Ozark, Mo., March 10. - News reached here today that John Bright living in Taney county shot and killed his wife early this week. Bright sent his wife to the spring after water, then got his revolver and followed her. Coming upon her, he shot her through the head, killing her. Bright fled. A posse is after him. Judge Lynch will preside if the murderer is caught.

---

388 This conflicts with other accounts, all of which say that Matilda was shot in the back and through the heart.

The Springfield Leader; Saturday, March 12, 1892; Vol. X #296 pg 1

THE TANEY COUNTY MURDER

More Details About the Killing of Mrs. Bright

Later reports from the Taney county murder confirm the first rumor that John Wesley Bright has been caught and lodged in the Forsyth Jail on the charge of killing his wife. The alleged murderer was hunted down by a party of about sixty armed men. Mrs. Bright's maiden name was Gideon, a relative of the family so well known in Christian and Greene counties.

When Mrs. Bright started to the spring just before her death, Bright took his gun and left the house. Soon the children heard a shot in the direction of the spring. Bright came back to the house in a few minutes and told the children that he had been shot at by someone at the spring. He warned the children not to go near the spring as they might get hurt. The man then filled his pockets with eggs, took his gun and left the house.

After a while, the children went to the spring and found their mother dead. They gave the alarm and the neighbors gathered in and began the search for the suspected murderer.

The Springfield Leader; Monday, March 14, 1892; Vol. X #297 pg 1

TWO MURDERS

Lynchers Hang John Bright, the Taney County Murderer.
Deputy Sheriff Williams Shot Down While Resisting the Mob.
The Preliminary Trial Was Going on When the Mob Came After the Man.

Mob law, once the terror of the White River region, has again resumed sway in Taney county and John Wesley Bright, the alleged wife murderer, is now beyond the jurisdiction of all human courts. The work was done quickly and thoroughly as such things are always executed at Forsyth. But the mob did more than hang Bright and avenge the death of his wife who was shot in the lonely pine forests of the Roark wilderness. Between the doomed prisoner and the vengeful agents of Judge Lynch stood a brave and conscientious officer, Deputy Sheriff Geo. T. Williams He would not yield to the demands of the mob and sought to protect Bright from the fury of the vigilance committee. But the mob would not be cheated of their victim. The heroic deputy was shot down and over his bleeding corpse the terror stricken prisoner was dragged to the rude gallows from which his lifeless body soon hung.

PRELIMINARY TRIAL

It was last Saturday that the people of Taney assembled at Forsyth to attend the preliminary trial of John Wesley Bright charged with murdering his wife about a week ago. The crime was revolting, the circumstances pointing to the guilt of the prisoner convincing. On Sunday morning, March 6 the report of a gun vibrated through the pine hills of Roark, a small tributary of White river that flows along the northwestern border of Taney county. This shot was fired near John Wesley Bright's spring. But a few minutes before Mrs. Bright had gone to the spring after a bucket of water. The woman's husband left the house with his gun a short time after the woman's departure. A number of small children constituting the rest of the family at the house. They heard the report of the gun in the direction of the spring. Soon the father came back to the house and told the children that some one had shot at him down at the spring. "Don't go near the spring children, you might get hurt," were the strange words of the man as he hastily prepared to leave the house. The children

WATCHED THEIR FATHER

as he went about the house filling his pockets with eggs and other articles of food. He had his gun and ammunition still and the little ones wondered what strange mission could call their father from home so suddenly on a Sunday morning. The report of the gun, the prolonged absence of their mother and the mysterious words, "Don't go near the spring" filled the minds of the children with shuddering terror. What could all strange events mean? Why did not mother return from the spring? Without explaining his strange conduct the man left the house and the children looked at one another first in mute alarm. Then they began to seek an explanation of the horrid mystery. They thought of the warning given them by their father, "Don't go near the spring", but thither the little ones soon ran and the awful tragedy was revealed. There lay the lifeless body of their mother, her heart pierced with a bullet. Then the report of the gun, the father's "Don't go near the spring," his hasty departure from the house, all the strange events of the morning began to assume in the minds of three motherless children the coherence of an awful story. Father had murdered mother and left the little ones to discover the terrible crime. The children gave the

CRY OF ALARM

To their neighbors. The farmers and their wives hurried to the scene of the tragedy. The grathering (sic) crowd saw the body of the murdered woman and heard the story of (the) children. Quickly a party of pursuers took the trail of the fugitive uxorcide. At each mountain pass the party of hunters received new recruits. Soon the woods were full of armed men, on horseback and on foot armed with winchester rifles, shot guns and revolvers, bent on capturing the murderer at whatever cost. The pursuit was swift and sure. The country was alive with enraged men. Every ravine and cliff where the fleeing criminal might hide was searched. No terror stricken fugitive from justice could escape that army of men who pressed so resolutely on the heels of John Wesley Bright. Nemesis guided the eye and sped the foot of each member of the pursuing party. The murderer was run down and captured, taken to Forsyth and lodged in jail.

The news of the crime spread all over the county. On Saturday a crowd of unusual size gathered at Forsyth to hear the preliminary trial of Bright. The expression of vengeance was clearly written on the faces of many of the citizens of the county who remained in town all day. Deputy Sheriff George T. Williams had the prisoner in charge. Mr. Williams was a brave young man from Louisville, Kentucky, who had been in Taney county only a few years. He had been deputy sheriff since the election of J. L. Cook, the second term. At dusk the town became quiet, and some persons hoped the storm cloud of vengeance had vanished and the law would be allowed to deal out justice to the alleged murder. But this feeling of security was soon to be rudely displaced by the presence of a relentless mob.

THE MOB

At nine o'clock armed men disguised beyond recognition, appeared in all parts of town. They moved quickly toward the jail under the direction of conspicuous leaders and demanded possession of the prisoners (sic), John Bright, the alleged wife murderer. Deputy Sheriff Williams refused to surrender the prisoner to the mob. The crowd surged around the officer and sought to compel him to yield to their demands. Williams was firm in his adherence to the line of duty and withstood bravely the mob. While the deputy was thus defending so nobly the life of his prisoner, the mob shot him down and dragged Bright away to the old grave yard near the town. Here the doomed man was quickly hanged to a tree. When life was extinct in the body of the suspended victim, a pistol shot from the leader of the mob gave the signal to disperse and the crowd disappeared. No one in the mob was recognized.

OTHER LYNCHINGS

John Bright is the third man executed by Judge Lynch in Taney county, while Forsyth has never witnessed a legal hanging. In the Spring of 1886 George and Tubal Taylor, two brothers were lynched by the Bald Knobbers for shooting Mr. T. J. Dickison and wife, merchants of Taney City. The shooting resulted from the refusal of Dickison to sell the boys a pair of boots on credit. The merchant and his wife were not dangerously hurt by the shots received, but the young outlaws failed to get the benefit of their erring aim, and met the terrible vengeance of the Bald Knobber legions, then just organized. This was the first work of tae (sic) secret brotherhood that afterwards gave the White River country such a name of terror. Beginning with the Taylor boys three lynchings and eight or nine other homicides have occurred in Taney county up to the present hour.

WHO WILLIAMS IS

Dr. S. A. Johnson, of this city, is well acquainted with the family of Deputy Sheriff Geo. T. Williams, who so gallantly met his death in defense of the laws of Missouri. Dr. Johnson said to a LEADER reporter this morning "I was raised with Deputy Sheriff Williams in Louisville and know his family well. He was a sober, industrious young man and very courageous. He could always be relied upon to do his duty. He was well educated and of a literary turn. He has hosts of friends wherever known who will be greatly grieved at his sorrowful end."

The Springfield Leader; Monday, March 14, 1892; Vol. X #297 pg 2

Taney's Brave Deputy Sheriff

A few days ago a terrible murder took place in Taney county. John Wesley Bright killing his wife without any known reason. The people of Taney county retaliate by committing two murders, one man killed who was guilty of no crime and died in the discharge of his duty. All honor to Deputy Sheriff Williams who had the courage to defy a band of murderers when he knew that it would likely cost him his life. For years Taney county has been known as one of the most lawless in the West and while this is a slander on the good people of that county it must be admitted that the name is not wholly undeserved. The overzealous citizens of Taney have not made a right by committing two wrongs and every member of that mob is as guilty of murder as was John Wesley Bright. The good citizens of Taney should see that the law is enforced and the murder of Deputy Sheriff Williams, who died defending Taney county and Missouri is avenged, but legally. Southwest Missouri wants no mob law and is not in sympathy with those who are. An example should be made of the lynchers, who have banded together for unlawful purposes, and Southwest Missouri is a good place to begin the work.

A few years ago there existed in this same section of country a band of the same kind who called under a different name though – "Bald Knobbers," (*remainder of article is illegible*)

The Springfield Leader; Tuesday, March 15, 1892; Vol. 298 pg 1

TANEY COUNTY MURDER

Gov. Francis Will send the Militia There if Necessary.

St. Louis March 15 - Gov. Francis has taken official notice of the Taney county Missouri outlawry and has ordered the sheriff to summon a posse sufficient to arrest and hold all concerned in the murder of Deputy Sheriff Williams and the lynching of Bright Saturday last. The governor says if the sheriff is unable to get a posse, he will send State aid. There is much excitement in Southwest Missouri and more blood shed will undoubtedly follow.

Springfield Daily Democrat; Tuesday, March 15, 1892; Vol. 2 #186 pg 5

JOHN BRIGHT, THE TANEY COUNTY UXORCIDE, HUNG BY A MOB

Deputy Sheriff Williams Shot Down for Offering Resistance.
Various Theories of the Composition of the Mob- Great Indignation.

A lynching and a murder are added to the list of Taney county's crimes. Reports of the lynching of John Wesley Bright at Forsyth last Saturday and the murder of Deputy Sheriff Geo. T. Williams, by the same mob, were confirmed yesterday. Bright, it will be remembered, murdered his wife Sunday March 6th under peculiar circumstances. Monday the searchers who had turned out to hunt him by the hundreds after the revolting crime, found him in the woods near his home and he was taken to the Forsyth jail. Threats of lynching had been heard through the week but few regarded them as serious. Saturday, it was noticed that an unusual number of drunken men were in the streets of Taney's county seat and hints of lynching were more frequent. Deputy Sheriff Williams had said in conversation that he would resist any such attempt with his life and this remark is the only explanation of his uncalled for murder.

Last evening a reporter from the Democrat received the following story of the crime from a traveling man who had just arrived from Forsyth: At 9 o'clock Saturday night a small body of men suddenly appeared at the jail door and demanded admittance. Some claim the crowd numbered twelve and some that there were fourteen of them. Williams was outside the jail at the time, and planting himself on the doorstep, fearlessly replied, 'You can only get Bright by crossing over my dead body." The accounts at hand, say no one spoke a word in answer, but a single shot was fired and the next moment the brave officer was lying a dead man, shot through the heart.

The mob was supplied with hammers and crowbars and speedily broke through bolts and bars until the victim they sought was reached.

Bright was brutally seized, hustled to a tree near by and hung without ceremony. Sheriff Cook and others are said to have been near by when Williams was shot, but taking warning from his fate offered no resistance. The mob disappeared from whence they came with no effort made to intercept them.

Who composed the lynching gang is a mystery. One report is that they came from Christian County, another is that they were close neighbors of the Brights who came to avenge the horrible crime of the uxoricide. Some say that the masked men were Bald Knobbers who took this opportunity to kill Bright, who was an anti-knobber. In support of this theory it is said that a former Bright was killed by the hands of Knobbers.

The shooting of Williams seems to have been entirely unnecessary. An examination of his person after his death, it is said, proved that he carried no weapons. Why the mob did not first attempt to seize him and put him aside with their superior force is hard to explain, unless the heads of the mob were turned by liquor or they were evening up with him for some unknown reason. Williams was a comparatively young man who came originally from Louisville, Kentucky. He was president of the Farmer's and Laborer's Union of Taney county and all accounts of him say he was a man of superior intelligence and courage.

The Coroner's inquest held yesterday developed no explanation of the affair besides the customary "by parties unknown." There is said to be just indignation at the rash shot which killed Williams, and if the participants are ferreted out they may meet a like fate.

After the above was written the following account which corrects the former in several particulars came from a correspondent of the Democrat:

ANOTHER ACCOUNT

Forsyth, Taney County, Mo. March 12 - Tonight about 10 o'clock, John W. Bright, a man who murdered his wife in this county on Sunday, the 6th inst., on Roark Creek in the west part of this county, was taken from the county jail here by a mob from that region and hanged to a tree about one half mile north of town.

Last Sunday morning Bright's wife started from her house to the spring to get a pail of water and on her return from the spring was shot and killed by her husband. The preliminary trial commenced here today before Esquire W. R. Cox, but the defense took a change of venue, causing a delay of several hours, when the case was changed to Esquire W. H. Jones. Two witnesses were examined this afternoon on behalf of the State and gave very damaging testimony against the defendant, which pointed closely to his guilt. George Gideon, brother of the murdered woman, was in town all day and was frequently seen conversing with small squads of men on the public square until a suspicion was aroused among the inhabitants of the town long before night that Judge Lynch would likely terminate the case before Monday morning, the time to which the case was adjourned by Judge Jones.

About 10 o'clock some thirty or forty persons on horseback rode into town from the north and surrounded the jail. Deputy Sheriff George T. Williams rushed out to the jail and stationed himself in front and asserted that he recognized the leader of the mob and demanded that they disperse. At the same time he fired one shot into the crowd, but fortunately no one was hurt. Immediately after the shot was fired by Williams some in the crowd retaliated by firing two shots back in rapid succession, the first of which shots took effect just under the left arm of Williams and ranged upward, passing through the heart and causing death almost instantly. Williams was heard to make the remark just a few minutes previous to the arrival of the mob that it was a scheme of McConley and Taylor, attorneys, to take Bright out of jail and hang him and that he intended to bluff them in their undertaking if they attempted to carry out their plans. But some one of the crowd was too quick for him and tonight there is a double corpse lying in the town awaiting a coroner's inquest.

The identical summary of a section of "The Bald Knobbers – Vigilantes on the Ozarks Frontier"[389] that is relevant to this story appears on several web sites[390], but no name is provided for the person who did the summary. I

---

[389] I have been unable to locate a copy of this book, written by Mary Hartman and Elmo Ingenthron (mentioned earlier) and published in 1986, so I assume it is out of print. I have also been unable to borrow a copy through inter-library loan.
[390] Some of these are: http://www.genealogysource.com/gideonmatilda.htm;
http://mrcio.tripod.com/index-718.html; and
http://familytreemaker.genealogy.com/users/h/a/r/Allen-Lee-Harp/GENE11-0006.html

am assuming that this summary is no more or less accurate an account than those presented by the newspapers above.

The Bald Knobbers

"It was a dark and stormy night...."[391]

.... on March 1, 1892, when John Wesley Bright, insanely jealous of his lovely wife Matilda Gideon being a little too friendly with their neighbor, Mr. Jones, shot her in the back and left her dead outside their Taney County cabin. His daughter, oldest of their four small children, ran for help to the neighbors, and soon a posse was after Bright. The children went to stay with their aunt Nancy Minerva Gideon and her husband, Isaiah Stewart.

Bright was soon captured and jailed on murder charges, and held in the Forsyth jail. Forsyth, home to a large faction of the "Bald Knobbers" vigilantes of the post-civil war Ozarks, didn't take too kindly to one of their own women being treated in such a rude fashion. Why, Matilda's uncle, J.J. Gideon, had been a star defensive attorney for the Bald Knobbers in one of their many trials for hanging no-count ruffians like Bright. So, the cards were stacked somewhat against the hapless Mr. Bright as he sat awaiting trial in the flimsy Taney lockup.

On March 12, after the first day of hearings, a tension could be felt in Taney. Men stood on street corners, talking in hushed tones. The local saloon was doing a brisk business. After several hours of drinking, a group of men appeared in front of the jail and began pounding on the locked door with a sledgehammer. Bright, alone inside the jail, must have been feeling a little concerned about then.

Sheriff Cook and Deputy Williams watched from across the street. Rumor has it that Cook was himself a Bald Knobber, and he did nothing to stop the mob. Finally, Deputy Williams decided to put an end to the uprising. Pushing through the crowd, he blocked the door of the jail and ordered the men to go home.

In the heat of the moment, two shots rang out from the crowd, and Deputy Williams fell dead on the ground. Now, Bright was getting *real* nervous. Two men crossed the street to the town well, and cut the rope from the bucket. It was soon tied around Bright's neck as he was dragged from the cell. He was hoisted onto a horse behind another rider and the mob headed for the big oak tree in the cemetery. They threw the rope over a sturdy branch, and soon John Wesley Bright paid the price for shooting

---

[391] Although this phrase resulted in San Jose State's famous annual "Bulwer-Lytton Fiction Contest" for composing an opening to the "worst of all possible novels," it seems that Edward George Bulwer-Lytton, noted author of such works as "The Last Days of Pompeii," had already become popular in Missouri. Lytton's estate was used in 1989 by Tim Burton as "stately Wayne Manor" in the movie "Batman," thus confirming his star status.

Matilda Gideon in the back.

Sheriff Cook, wanting to make an example of Bright, threw his body on the steps to the Taney Courthouse and left it there, the rope still around his neck, for days. Wild hogs dined on the murderer's corpse.

While the local citizenry was largely pleased with Bright's demise, the murder of Deputy Williams left the good people of Forsyth a tad uneasy. The Governor of Missouri offered a reward for the capture of the lynch mob.

Arrested for taking part in the murders were cousins of Matilda Gideon: Abraham Lincoln "Link" Weatherman, Samuel W. Weatherman, Martin Weatherman, Luther Keithley, and James Stewart, along with about a dozen other men. George Friend, at the center of the controversy, turned state's evidence and agreed to testify against the others. Many were prominent citizens of Forsyth, including Link Weatherman, Justice of the Peace.

In a bizarre incident, as the prisoners were transported to a trial hearing in an open wagon, they were all unshackled and given loaded guns to protect themselves in case of an attack by Bright's relatives. No attack occurred, and none of the prisoners attempted an escape. Were they perhaps confident of an acquittal?

Sheriff Cook selected the jurors for the trial, most of whom were Bald Knobbers. At this point, the prosecuting attorney dropped the charges against George Friend, since he had promised to testify against the others. Friend immediately refused to testify, so the prosecutor dropped all charges against the others.

John Wesley Bright had signed over all his property to his brother-in-law, Isaiah Stewart, who in turn agreed to post his bail money ... which, of course, Bright never got a chance to use. (Cousin James Stewart was part of the Lynch Mob.) Stewart transferred the property to the names of the four young orphaned children of Matilda Gideon and John Wesley Bright. Stewart and Nancy Minerva Gideon raised the four children.

This was the final incident in the long history of the Bald Knobbers, and was decisive in ending the midnight rides of the infamous vigilantes of the Ozarks.

All of the newspapers referencing the story of the Bright murders can be found at the Missouri Historical Society, located in the basement of the main library on the campus of the University of Missouri in Columbia, Missouri.

www.ingramcontent.com/pod-product-compliance
Lightning Source LLC
Chambersburg PA
CBHW071705160426
43195CB00012B/1578